Making a Killing

HMOs and the Threat to Your Health

Jamie Court
Francis Smith

Common Courage Press   Monroe, ME

Library of Congress Cataloging-in-Publication Data

Court, Jamie, 1967-
    Making a killing : HMOs and the threat to your health / Jamie Court,
Francis Smith.
        p.   cm.
    Includes bibliographical references and index.
    ISBN 1-56751-169-4 (cloth). -- ISBN 1-56751-168-6 (pbk.)
    1. Managed care plans (Medical care)--United States. 2. Health care
rationing--United States. 3. Medical care--United States--Cost control.
4. Medical care--Utilization review--United States. 5. Health services
accessibility--United States. 6. Consumer education. I. Smith, Francis,
1949- . II. Title.
RA413.5.U5C68 1999
362.1'04258--dc21   99-37783
                                                                                CIP

Common Courage Press
PO Box 702
Monroe, ME 04951

207-525-0900; fax: 207-525-3068
orders-info@commoncouragepress.com

www.commoncouragepress.com

First Printing

Contents

	Acknowledgments	iv
	Foreword *by Ralph Nader*	v
	Introduction	1
1.	The End of Health Care Who Plays God in a System Bent on Profit	6
2.	A Deadly Fraud Behind the Caring Image of HMOs and Managed Care Companies	40
3.	The Death of Community Health Care and Hospitals	70
4.	The Financial Sting—Paying More for Less	99
5.	Getting Away with Murder Why You Can't Sue Your HMO	120
6.	The Battle to Make Health Care Work	153
	Appendix One HMO Patient Self-Defense Kit	178
	Appendix Two State Regulators	189
	Appendix Three Consumer Resources	197
	Notes	201
	Index	222
	About the Authors	231
	Stay Involved	232

Acknowledgments

The authors wish to acknowledge the invaluable guidance and support of Sharon Arkin, Ralph Nader, John Richard, Harvey Rosenfield, and Pam Solo. Andrew Pontious, Cynthia Dennis and Doug Heller tirelessly compiled research. Mike Bidart, Chuck Idelson, Mark Hiepler, Rose Ann DeMoro, Linda Peeno, Bill Shernoff, and the California Nurses Association have our gratitude for seeking new solutions and remedies for patients with too few options today. Our special thanks to all the patients and their families who have shared their stories with us to stop the suffering of others. As always, Steven Olsen and his struggle continue to inspire us. This book was completed with the generous support of the Institute for a Civil Society, but the authors' views are their own.

Foreword

A retired New York City surgeon, often described by his peers as a doctor's doctor for his skill, dedication and fealty to placing patients first, wrote me recently with a list of principles that he believed necessary for a universal health care system. These principles included being economically available and geographically accessible to everyone, with a free choice of physician and the preservation of the one-to-one patient/physician relationship. Physicians would be on a fixed salary, adequate and commensurate to the locale and expertise of the individual physician. Hospitals would be stratified, as to the complexity of procedures (primary, secondary, tertiary), compensated on a service experience for a particular year, and subjected to regional quality control. Along with standards to ensure accountability and fiscal sustainability, he insisted that the system must be administered on a non-profit basis.

Profits-before-patients is easily translated into corporate-dominated medicine. Greed and focus on stocks, stock options and quarterly earnings rapidly degrade everything they touch. Professionalism of physicians and nurses is undermined by the juggernaut of commercialism *uber alles*. The critical relations of care and compassion between server and patient are replaced by categorical protocols imposed by corporate bureaucrats commanded by monetized minds at the top of the corporate hierarchy. The exercise of judgment, discretion and mercy at the server/patient level is relentlessly eroded by the forces of Mammon—the giant HMOs, their masterminding corporate law firms and their political allies who safeguard their immunities and privileges in the face of growing public and professional outrage.

This was not the way it was supposed to turn out in the minds of the pioneers of prepaid medicine. Commencing with Dr. Michael Shadid's mobilization of poor farmers around Elk City, Oklahoma, in the 1920s[1] to form the first cooperatively owned hospital in America and then into the Puget

Sound and Kaiser Permanente health care plans, the ideal was quality health care with attention to preventative services within an affordable system of prepayment. Organized medicine, led by the American Medical Association (AMA) and its fee-for-service medicine, fought these plans and successfully opposed Harry Truman's universal health care proposal to Congress in the early '50s.

In the '60s, Medicare and Medicaid took the steam out of the reform movements among the elderly and poor, while preserving much of what the AMA wanted to keep. In the '70s, the federal government began encouraging the formation of Health Maintenance Organizations (HMOs) whose non-profit status and prevention orientation were believed to be well suited to curbing the excesses of the fee-for-service system with its incentives to sell too much to patients. As costs annually far exceeded the general inflation rate and health care absorbed ever greater percentages of the GNP, the alternative of "managed care" emerged as a way to control costs. A dominant format also emerged—the giant, for-profit HMOs and their entrepreneurial billionaire bosses securing large clusters of customers and seeking more and more mergers. A series of perverse economic incentives were insinuated from top to bottom so as to seriously compromise the independent clinical judgments of physicians and other health professionals and often turn the pocketbook allegiance of the health care servers against the interests of their patients, as with gag rules, bonuses for not referring and the like. The HMO and its deepening swamp of commercialism over service, of profiteering over professionalism, of denial or rationing of care where such care is critically needed, of depersonalization of intensely personal kinds of relationships, are all occurring and spreading without sufficient disclosure, accountability and structural responsibility before the damage to life and health is done.

The organized flow of corporate power moves in all directions. From the contractual agreements with physician networks and hospitals to the drive to limit the judicial rights of patient-victims to the Niagara of campaign contributions to politicians at the state and federal level to the rush of manipulative television propaganda campaigns, the power of the HMOs and their alliances continues to grow. Impervious to disclosures and scandals, even when widely reported as with egregious medical malpractice or the Columbia/HCA scandals or the routine billings fraud and abuse, more than the facts need to be part of the public debate and activity. Palliatives won't do. The injustices and misallocation of patient, taxpayer and employer dollars invites structural changes and the elevation of patients, public health and the safety of the environment, workplace and marketplace to positions of supremacy in law, organization and public expectations.

The underfunded Canadian universal health care system is probably the best in the world, despite attempts by companies and corporate ideologues in North America to undermine and weaken it. For around 10% of the GNP, Canada provides health care for everyone from cradle to nursing home. Its administrative expenses are about eleven cents out of each dollar compared with double that in the United States, which this year may spend 14% of its GDP on health care, with millions of men, women and children without coverage.

The foregoing is by way of welcoming Jamie Court and Frank Smith and their wide scope and detailed treatment of the contemporary HMO situation. They searched and researched evidence, from inside the industry, the public records, the court judgments, and the documentation of personal tragedies flowing from HMO priorities, and found patterns, not just episodes or examples. It is the system—that breeds the greed, fraud and frenzy—which swoops the savings from rationing and curtailment of needed care upward along the managerial ladders where the rewards grow larger and larger until they mock the very adjective "obscene." Venerable institutions and traditions in need of improvement are instead shut down and destroyed before the onrushing corporate Moloch.

This book moves from a description of corporations making medical decisions, the ensuing harm, the predictable frauds, the shunting aside of community servers, toward both institutional reforms and suggestions for self-help by patients and their families. The authors know well that while information is the currency of democracy, it will take a stronger democracy to achieve the desired changes. This means a critical mass of citizens who are aroused and determined to forge a health care system as if patients and health care mattered. As the only Western nation without universal health care for its citizens, the United States is long overdue. This highly motivating book tells a gripping story of excessive power without restraint that comes down hard on powerless and defenseless people. Who speaks for them and those who follow them? It could be you, the readers.

Ralph Nader
Washington, D.C.
July 1999

Introduction

It was not supposed to be this way. In 1992, at 41, David Goodrich had hit his stride as a deputy district attorney. But by the spring of 1995, he lay hooked to a ventilator, dying of stomach cancer. He worried about leaving Teresa, his wife, who worked as a schoolteacher, with $750,000 in medical bills. The bills were for treatment which, had it been administered in a timely manner, might have prolonged his life. All this occurred despite David's health insurance from one of the biggest companies in America. It was a worry he would take to his grave.

Flash forward to January of 1999. A jury in San Bernardino, California sent the nation's largest managed care company, Aetna, a $120-million message: Human life should not be sacrificed for money. The largest verdict ever against an HMO went to Teresa Goodrich, after the couple's two-and-a-half-year ordeal trying to compel Aetna to approve cancer treatment recommended by her husband's doctors. When it was clear David Goodrich could wait no longer, his doctors administered care without corporate approval. It was too late.

The jury put Aetna on notice that it cannot ignore its own doctors' recommendations and must act more quickly when a patient's life hangs in the balance. In one instance, it took Aetna four months to approve bone marrow transplantation and high-dose chemotherapy; by then, it was too late to benefit Goodrich. Company and industry standards establish a twenty-four- to forty-eight-hour turnaround time on such requests.

Did Aetna get the message? According to the *Hartford Courant*, Aetna CEO Richard Huber, responding to the verdict, said, "This is a travesty of justice. You had a skillful ambulance-chasing lawyer, a politically motivated judge and a weeping widow."

With remorseless defiance of civil dictates, Aetna and its defense lawyers, who made Teresa Goodrich weep on the stand, faulted David Goodrich for

David and Teresa Goodrich

breaking the HMO's rules by taking treatment without approval. The verdict was a repudiation of a common HMO tactic of refusing to authorize
treatment in a timely manner and then blaming the patient for doing what
he or she must do to stay alive.

Aetna's indifference toward covering David Goodrich's treatment also
had a price for taxpayers. $500,000 of the care was paid for by the school dis-
trict where Teresa Goodrich works as a kindergarten teacher.

Aetna CEO Huber said of the Goodrich verdict, "That's no way to get
justice and certainly no way to manage a trillion-dollar industry."

Later, a *Los Angeles Times* columnist reported, Huber "expanded his complaints, telling me that juries are customarily not intelligent enough to consider complicated contractual issues and that this one in particular was too

ill-informed, as a result of the judge's evidentiary rulings, to render a sound verdict."

Ultimately, Huber was forced by the public outcry to apologize to Teresa Goodrich. "I want to assure you that I did not intend for the comment to minimize in any way the devastation you feel at the loss of a loved one," Huber wrote.

While she appreciated the note, Teresa Goodrich said, "he did not apologize for what Aetna did to my husband, and that is really what I would like to have an apology for."

Aetna's callousness is matched by its size. Thousands of doctors across the country have defected from Aetna because reimbursements do not allow them to provide quality care. The problem is slated to get worse; as the industry leviathan, Aetna will insure one of every eleven insured Americans after its pending merger with Prudential. In some markets, where Aetna/Prudential will cover more than half of the patients who have insurance through HMOs, like in Bergen County, New Jersey, physicians will have few other options.

If Aetna was alone in its practices, penalties such as the $120 million verdict might deter rogue companies, even one as big as Aetna/Prudential. But during the last decade, an alphabet soup of managed care companies— including health maintenance organizations (HMOs), preferred provider organizations (PPOs), and other for-profit managed care organizations (MCOs)—have wrestled control of the American health care system away from doctors, nurses, and patients. Their promise is a seductive one, to tame medical inflation while providing a variety of preventive health care benefits. Consider a few of the slogans:

- Your health care options just got better...Raising the quality of health care in America. Aetna U.S. Healthcare;
- Vote for U.S. Healthcare and Elect The Coverage You Deserve;
- Few things in life are perfect. We're one of them! Kaiser Permanente

But as David and Teresa Goodrich and thousands of other Americans have found out, these companies have misled the public, swindled those paying the premiums, and grievously and fatally harmed patients in the process. In an effort to avoid accountability and maintain profits, some have tampered with justice. This has taken a toll, reflected in the statistics from recent surveys:

- 65% of Americans fear that when they are sick their managed care company will be more interested in saving money than in providing the best medical care.[1]
- 48% of all Americans report that they or someone they know has had problems with their HMO including difficulty getting permission to see a specialist, difficulty getting a plan to pay an emergency-room bill, and being unable to file an appeal to an independent agency for a denied claim.[2]
- HMO patients are 59% more likely to have problems getting treatment.[3]
- HMO patients over 65 are 93% more likely to have worse outcomes than fee-for-service patients.[4]

American medicine has been taken over by the mores of the corporate marketplace. The doctor-patient relationship and its concomitant social values of trust and confidentiality has been eroded by the search for profits. This development threatens not only the health of our citizens but also the foundations of our democracy and civil society.

A decade after HMOs began to dominate Americans' health coverage options, the verdict on for-profit corporate health care is in: unsound and unsafe at all costs.

If our health care system endangers patients, its $1 trillion per year cost reveals colossal waste. The United States spends more per capita on health care and covers fewer people than any other nation in the world. Where does the money go? Twenty to 30% goes to corporate overhead and profits.

Not content with hefty profits, other companies go further. Columbia/HCA, the nation's largest for-profit hospital chain, is one example. Columbia is alleged to have both bilked the government for care it never gave and cut hospital staffing back so far that patients were at risk. In short, do anything to make a buck. Former Columbia/HCA Vice President Marc Gardner blew the whistle, saying, "I committed felonies every day." The documented malfeasance is so wide-spread that, as of this writing in June of 1999, Columbia is expected, as a result of federal charges, to pay one of the largest fines in history.

Reforming our health care system will come too late for David Goodrich and thousands of others. It is not too late for the rest of us. Civil society can restore the fundamental balance of power in medicine that has shifted from the patient, doctor and nurse to the for-profit corporation. But it will depend upon understanding the issues, and organizing for a health care system that has medical and civic ethics at its core. It will require concerted community and political action. It will mean ending the isolation of individuals confronting for-profit medical bureaucracies. This book outlines the problems of the current medical regime and offers steps for returning the concerns of the patient to the primary position in health care decisions.

Do HMOs commit medical negligence and fraud? The first two chapters explore these questions. The third exposes the pillaging of our community hospitals and community-held assets by the corporate managed care empires. The fourth chapter answers whether HMOs are truly cost-effective and reveals the costs imposed upon the system by HMO medicine's short-sightedness and greed. In Chapter Five, we pull back the curtain on the ways HMOs are immune from liability for their wrongdoing and how this shield has allowed HMOs and insurers to deny and delay medically necessary treatment with impunity. The last chapter presents a series of legislative solutions to the crisis in HMO medicine, such as prohibiting HMOs from being owned and operated as for-profit, investor-run entities. Until those reforms are adopted, the appendix offers patients a self-defense kit to demand and receive care.

Was Aetna's treatment of David Goodrich typical of how American HMOs deal with patients in need of life-saving care? Did the jury in the Goodrich case speak for other Americans? The verdict is yours to write.

Jamie Court
Francis Smith
Santa Monica, California
June, 1999

CHAPTER 1

The End of Health Care

Who Plays God in a System Bent on Profit?

"In the spring of 1987, as a physician, I caused the death of a man," testified Dr. Linda Peeno, to Congress. "Although this was known to many people," she continued, "I have not been taken before any court of law or called to account for this in any professional or public forum. In fact, just the opposite occurred: I was 'rewarded' for this. It bought me an improved reputation in my job, and contributed to my advancement afterwards. Not only did I demonstrate I could indeed do what was expected of me, I exemplified the 'good' company doctor: I saved a half million dollars."[1]

"The decision about the California patient [in need of a heart transplant] was made from the 23rd floor of a marble building in Louisville, Kentucky," added Peeno, herself a Louisville resident, a medical reviewer for Humana and medical director at Blue Cross/Blue Shield Health Plans. Peeno had no license to practice medicine in California, but to her employer, this was irrelevant. "The patient was a piece of computer paper, less than half full. The 'clinical goal' was to figure out a way to avoid payment. The 'diagnosis' was to 'DENY.' Once I stamped 'DENY' across his authorization form, his life's end was as certain as if I had pulled the plug on a ventilator."[2]

Peeno summed up her work in a chilling message: "Whether it was non-profit or for-profit, whether it was a health plan or hospital, I had a common task: *using my medical expertise for the financial benefit of the organization, often at great harm and potentially death to some patients.*"[3]

Welcome to "utilization review" (or U.R. as it is called) a system whereby the bureaucratic review of HMOs second-guesses the calls of practicing

Dr. Linda Peeno

physicians while the health of seriously-ill patients dwindles against an ever-expiring clock.

Peeno is a hero for her honesty in bringing industry practices to light.

Fortunately, other doctors are swinging into action too. Signed by 2,300 Massachusetts physicians, this "Call To Action" appeared in the December 3, 1997 issue of the *Journal of the American Medical Association.*

> *"The time we are allowed to spend with the sick shrinks under the pressure to increase throughput, as though we were dealing with industrial commodities rather than human beings...Doctors and nurses are being prodded by threats and bribes to abdicate allegiance to patients, and to shun the sickest, who may be unprofitable. Some of us risk being fired or 'delisted' for giving, or even discussing, expensive services, and many are offered bonuses for minimizing care."*

A Stockton, California gynecologist recently made an even stronger statement. He quit his practice over these concerns.

In a letter to all his 2,651 patients, Dr. Daniel Fisher wrote: "As of 7/1/98 I am quitting the practice of medicine. The system of HMOs, managed care, restricted hospitals and denial of needed medications has become so corrupt, so rotten, that I cannot stomach it any longer."

"My dad told me I had to like the guy I saw in the mirror when I was shaving," the 61 year-old physician said. "And I was getting where I didn't like that guy any more…[The system is controlled by] for-profit HMOs with dividend-hungry shareholders and high-salaried administrators…The prime concern became profit. And they make that profit by exacting the highest possible premium from employers and paying out as small a benefit as possible to patients."

Fisher recounted how he requested a hysterectomy for a woman whose menstrual pain was so severe she was unable to live normally for one-third of the month, but Fisher was denied by a staff nurse who relied on a book of HMO criteria. "I had fifteen years of postgraduate training, but my medical judgment counts for nothing," Dr. Fisher said. He also felt the pressure from HMO economic profiles that track doctors' prescribing patterns and pressure doctors to write less prescriptions to cut costs. "I was beginning to feel the pressure and change my prescription habits from the best medicine I knew to the one that would look best on my profile; and I was hating myself for it."[4]

Incompetent physicians were once the principal perpetrators of medical negligence by violating the standard of care or treatment. But today, managed care corporations are the new threat to quality health care. The malpractice is both blatant and fiscally shrewd.

While HMO bureaucrats overrule the best medical judgment of professionals on the scene, managed care companies have also recently designed a more insidious system that can pit doctors against their patients. Where once doctors were paid based on the treatment they dispensed, under this scheme physicians are paid a fixed budget for every patient under their charge, regardless of how much treatment is warranted. The less doctors do for patients, the more of that budget they get to keep. Ultimately, this calculated profit formula will decimate medical ethics, leaving the patient without an advocate in a foreign medical wilderness.

The main question we must ask about both the role of bureaucrats and the capitation system of paying doctors is, are HMOs responsible for their patients? Despite their advertising, which claims they are dedicated to the best medicine, HMOs consistently argue that they are not responsible, that they are simply the down-sizers. In fact, they argue that those making the backroom decisions that override the doctors are not practicing medicine.

As Dr. Peeno's stunning testimony at the beginning of this chapter shows, they do not want to be responsible for the consequences of their downsizing.

The Rise of the Bean Counters over the Physicians: "Quantity, Not Quality"

Doctors and nurses would hardly downsize themselves and their patients' care voluntarily. HMO bureaucrats now control much of the medical system from top to bottom. They replicate the ethic of bureaucrats at Ford and General Motors. Rather than disclose or fix safety defects in the Pinto and Corvair, they turned the safety experts' warnings about the loss of human life into budgetary line items, the cost of doing business.

The HMO bureaucrats may have MBA, MD, PhD or some combination next to their names—but their role dictated by management becomes that of accountants. For example, the Director of Utilization Management Cheryl Tannigawa, of Long Beach-based Harriman Jones Medical Group and later of PacifiCare, was clear to a California ophthalmologist when she was trying to curb the number of cataracts operations he performed. In a memo, she put it bluntly. "I have thought about our discussion yesterday and I would like to make one issue clear," wrote Tannigawa. "My intent was not to find fault with your professional integrity. I feel that you are an excellent surgeon and physician. My focus is on *quantity* and not *quality*. I apologize if you felt that I was questioning your skills."[5] [emphasis in original] As with Peeno, this focus is rewarded: Tannigawa later went on to become a medical director at PacifiCare. The ophthalmologist, criticized for performing more cataract surgeries than other doctors, had a population of patients who were older. In subsequent patient satisfaction surveys conducted by the medical group, the ophthalmologist's ratings were among the highest.

Today, Tannigawa claims her written remarks have been "misconstrued" and that, "Cataract surgery is the most common surgery performed in the United States. I'd like to believe all of those were warranted but history and past research suggest otherwise."

HMOs hire "medical directors" like Tannigawa to approve or deny physician decisions not only about operations like cataracts but also on such life and death issues as cancer care. These directors, while MDs, typically do not examine the patient and often are not specialists in the treating doctor's area of expertise. Many times they are not based in the same state, and not licensed to practice medicine in that state. But they are often stock-sharing employees with a stake in keeping medical costs to a minimum. The fact that they do not examine patients when making decisions which can have a devastating impact on the patient, actually works to the companies' advantage: no examination generally means they cannot be held liable for medical negligence resulting from their decisions.

Recognizing the problem, numerous state medical boards have launched efforts to regulate medical directors who override other doctors' decisions without an examination. The California Medical Board recently passed a resolution that says the "making of a decision regarding the medical necessity...of any treatment constitutes the practice of medicine," and anyone making such a decision without a medical license is violating California law. Board spokesperson Candis Cohen said, "This resolution is another way the board is expressing its commitment to the sanctity of the physician-patient relationship."[6] Despite documented abuses, there have been no traceable cases where a medical director has actually been sanctioned.

Overriding the Doctor-Patient Relationship

While the California Medical Board has taken a stand against the unauthorized practice of medicine, utilization review is still widespread. It can be deadly when bureaucrats disregard the recommendations of expert physicians.

Judith Packevicz would have had her cancer treated sooner if not for this process. The New York woman suffered from a rare form of metastatic cancer of the liver and, through 1998, was delayed and denied potentially life-saving treatment by her HMO. According to the family's lawsuit, her HMO—Mohawk Valley Medical Plan (MVP)—refused to pay for a liver transplant recommended by her oncologist with the support of all her treating physicians, causing the woman to live out a death sentence. Without the transplant, she faced certain death. Her quality of life, according to the lawsuit filed May 27, 1998 in Federal Court, Northern District of New York, was "indescribably miserable both physically and mentally." Her son, Thomas Dwyer was "ready, willing and able" to donate part of his liver to save his mother's life. Fourteen friends of the family also volunteered to donate a part of their livers. According to the family, the treatment was available close at hand at Mt. Sinai Hospital in New York City, but at a six figure cost. But on the grounds that it "does not meet the medical community standard of care for this diagnosis," the HMO's medical director said no, without a physical examination. On this life and death decision, there was no explanation of why the procedure failed to meet the standard.[7]

The mother of four children, Mrs. Packevicz was the stepmother of three and a grandmother of nine. A well-known figure in Saratoga Springs, she was an active and successful singer in a Sweet Adeline quartet until her illness forced her to stop. Packevicz's physicians predicted a very high probability of survival with significantly improved quality of life if the transplant was performed in a timely manner, and therefore recommended it. That was not enough. Mrs. Packevicz was forced to sue the HMO and, only then, did the company relent.[8] Packevicz died during the transplant procedure because, according to her family, she had become so weak from the delay that her veins were paper thin.

For its part, MVP claims Packevicz's death was solely the result of complications from surgery, not any delay caused by its denials. MVP also says that it sent Mrs. Packevicz's file to two external review organizations (see Chapter Six regarding review companies) who, though not examining her, said the procedure was not warranted.

According to the HMO, the Packevicz lawsuit did not spark its sudden about-face in approving the transplant, but that the company simply lacked sufficient information from Mt. Sinai. This claim rings hollow given the fact that before MVP's denial, the company received a letter from Packevicz's oncologist, Dr. Brian Izzo. Izzo stated: "Judy lives perpetually on the edge of hepatic failure…14 individuals have stepped forward to volunteer the left lobe of their liver for transplant…Judy saw Dr. Max Sung, a medical oncologist at the Mt. Sinai Medical Center regarding a second opinion for what type of treatment should be offered next…He feels strongly that liver transplant is recommended at this juncture and that the procedure should be done sooner rather than later…Regarding the issue of out-of-plan coverage, I don't believe there is another medical center available that could or would attempt this particular procedure, thus making the choice of Mt. Sinai unarbitrary." MVP did not mention any lack of information or any treatment alternatives in its letters denying the procedure. The bureaucracy defied Packevicz's doctors and put the burden on the family to fight back.

Renee Berman, a resident of West Los Angeles, is another example of how HMOs deploy this cost-cutting tactic at the expense of human life. Five doctors examined her after a cancerous tumor appeared on her liver. All five recommended immediate surgery. But a sixth doctor, who never examined Mrs. Berman but did know of the other recommendations, denied her operation. This physician was the head of the utilization review committee.

Renee's husband, Peter, blames this doctor and the HMO system for Renee's death in the summer of 1997. He believes that their HMO, Health Net, could have stopped his wife's cancer with the procedure but refused to do so in order to save money.

No system, profit or nonprofit, private or government funded, can afford to spend large sums of money on an infinite number of experimental treatments. According to the Berman family's legal complaint, however, Renee's "treatment options were neither experimental nor investigational and were even covered under the Health Net plan which provided benefits to her. Those treatment options, however, were not within the expertise or skill of the Health Net medical providers and required Health Net, under its plan, to permit Renee Berman to obtain the treatment necessary to treat her medical condition 'out-of-network'."[9] Renee Berman stayed alive because she sought those treatments against Health Net's advice. But, according to Peter, delays in getting her the surgical procedure she needed ultimately cost her her life.

If these were isolated cases, cases where borderline judgment was involved, cases grouped in one hospital, or even one HMO, these anecdotes, painful though they are, could be excused as aberrations. But they are not. The most frequently cited cases demonstrating the pernicious behavior of medical directors come from Health Net, now called Foundation Health Systems after a 1997 merger. Health Net became a national example for the worst of managed care. While company officials testified the problems had been corrected, Renee Berman's ordeal post-dated the more high-profile nightmares that sprung from the same practice of medicine without a physical exam.

Christine deMeurers, a mother of two, was one of a string of women denied life-saving bone marrow transplants by the HMO's medical directors, even though practicing physicians recommended them and the transplant was listed as a covered benefit. In fact, once she received her bone marrow transplant—delayed because she had to wrangle with the HMO and then paid for by university doctors themselves—her cancer went into remission. She received treatment on September 23, 1993 and had almost two years with her family, dying on March 10, 1995, including at least four completely disease-free months. Her family will never know the impact of the delay and anxiety caused by being forced into the streets to fundraise in a campaign for her life. Her children told her husband that they often went to bed with this on their mind.

In the deMeurers's case, the arbitration panel that heard the facts issued a stinging $1 million rebuke of Health Net and condemned the interference in the doctor-patient relationship by Health Net medical directors as "extreme and outrageous behavior exceeding all bounds usually tolerated in a civilized society."

Did Health Net get the message of this infamous case—the subject of a *Time* magazine cover story? Responding to deMeurers's death and the arbitration judgment, Dr. Sam Ho, then a Health Net Medical Director and now a PacifiCare Medical Director, put it this way: "I'm sorry the panel didn't see that Health Net was doing what was best for the patient, which was to deny the treatment as investigational, and which in the end was proven the right decision."[10] Meaning, because she died, Health Net was redeemed for its lack of payment.

The case was not an isolated incident.

This managed care philosophy is not just aimed at consumers; cost-cutting can be focused on one's own employees. Janice Bosworth was a top performing employee for Health Net, but Health Net initially refused to pay for her cancer treatment. Bosworth's oncologist recommended a bone marrow transplant with high-dose chemotherapy. However, a Health Net medical director called City of Hope Medical Center, where Bosworth was being examined in preparation for the transplant, and explained that Health Net would not pay for the treatment. The medical director, according to Bosworth's husband Steve, also stated that the City of Hope physician should not say anything about the protocol, but instead should say that nothing could be done and send the Bosworths home. According to Steve Bosworth, Health Net went so far as to threaten City of Hope with cancellation of their contract with Health Net if the medical center performed the transplant. City of Hope's contract was cancelled, but has since been reinstated.

Ultimately, Janice Bosworth received the transplant from City of Hope free of charge. The Bosworths threatened to sue the HMO, forcing Health Net to pay for the procedure. Janice Bosworth's boss at Health Net also intervened on behalf of the company employee. Janice lived with her son and husband for another two years.

But Steve Bosworth believes the story might have had a happier ending if Janice had received a mammogram five months earlier, at her routine examination. It could have caught her breast cancer early enough and the chances are that she would be alive today. Why was none performed? Unknown to Janice at the time, according to Steve, the doctor at Health Net received a financial incentive to prevent his wife from receiving a mammogram.

Bosworth says, "I blame my wife's death 20% on cancer, and 80% on managed care."

Health Net's practices are legendary. The woman whose case first shined the spotlight on the company was Temecula, California resident Nelene Fox. Her brother, Mark Hiepler, then a young lawyer, tried the case.

In December of 1993, a California jury found that Nelene was denied a bone marrow transplant, despite being a prime candidate for the procedure. The jury, outraged that Health Net employees themselves received bone marrow transplants, awarded $89.1 million to Fox's family for Health Net's conduct. Later, Health Net paid a much smaller out-of-court settlement, because of the family's desire for closure. Ironically, a critical witness in the case was Janice Bosworth, who claimed, "They hadn't learned anything by going through it with me."[11]

As the Bermans' case concerning denial of surgery shows, the conduct goes far beyond bone marrow transplants. The delays that the families believe took the mothers from the Bermans, Foxes, deMeurers and Bosworths have a common thread—bureaucracy dictating to medical doctors who have based a recommendation on a physical examination. A physical exam must be done by those making the medical decisions. This is a necessary element of any responsible medical decision-making process. Because HMOs consistently undermine practicing physicians, the powerful HMO industry lobby has vociferously resisted any legislation preventing an HMO medical director from denying a seriously-ill patient treatment unless a qualified doctor has physically examined the patient.

HMO bureaucrats who never examine patients should not overrule qualified doctors and make life and death decisions. HMOs claim this never happens. But if this were so, HMOs would not object to reforms like California Assembly Bill 794 in 1997 and Assembly Bill 332 in 1998, which both passed the California legislature and were vetoed, at the behest of the industry, by Governor Pete Wilson. The bills simply required that if a doctor recommended treatment for a very ill patient, an HMO could not deny it without providing an equally qualified physician who performs a physical exam.

Unfortunately, it is not just at large HMOs like Health Net where doctors' treatment decisions are being overridden by corporate honchos.

Blasting "what can only be viewed as 'unmanaged care'" in July of 1997, for instance, an arbitrator required a small Pomona, California-based HMO to pay $1.1 million, including punitive damages, to a Medicare patient who suffered from kidney failure. The HMO's medical director prevented the 69 year-old woman, Joyce Ramey, from receiving a renal biopsy, which was recommended by her doctor.

The arbitrator, retired Appeals Court Judge John Trotter, found that Inter Valley Health Plan breached the covenant of good faith and fair dealing because the HMO's corporate medical director denied doctor-recommended treatment and "whatever chance plaintiff may have had for her condition to be diagnosed and treated at an earlier stage was lost by defendants' conduct."

"The actions of the defendants are not capable of any rational explanation," Judge Trotter stated in his decision. "The refusal of authorizations, the delays, the lack of timely notice to plaintiff are unconscionable…The facts present a compelling picture of the problems and pitfalls of what has come to be called 'managed care'."[12]

Judges across the nation have echoed this condemnation for similar practices (when patients have been lucky enough to get before judges). Regulators have also taken HMOs to task for bureaucratizing medicine, even though most states have weak regulatory structures.

Clerks Override Doctors

It's one thing to have a doctor in a corporate office in another state vetoing the decisions of a patient's doctor. But some of these bureaucrats are little more than clerks with no medical license. The interference of such clerks in the doctor/patient relationship is tantamount to the practice of medicine without a license, and legislation sponsored by state medical boards to confront the problem is proliferating across the nation.

At some plans, these so-called "utilization reviewers" are clerks and/or nurses empowered to override treating doctors' decisions in emergency cases. In turn, many doctors have dubbed these over-the-phone authorizers as "1-800 nurses from hell."

Kaiser, for instance, was recently warned by government regulators because investigators found that, "Clinical Financial Review nurses have the authority to overrule physician decisions." This astonishing process led the regulator's audit to conclude that medical decisions at Kaiser could not be "independent of fiscal and administrative considerations." Kaiser money was dictating what medicine could be practiced by emergency doctors.[13] Emergency room physicians, working in hospitals outside the Kaiser network, would treat Kaiser patients who could not get to a Kaiser approved hospital in time. The physicians would call up Kaiser phone clerks seeking the right to provide treatment. But clinical financial review nurses on the other end of the line could and often would deny the physician's requests. How endemic is this problem? The California auditors found that Kaiser, using this process, denied 25% of all emergency room treatment claims for its members outside of the HMO's network. The state required the company to "substantiate" that this was "reasonable."[14]

The problem wasn't just in California. In Georgia, a jury awarded $45 million to a 6 month-old boy who was forced to have all his arms and legs amputated because Kaiser's emergency phone line representative, a nurse, sent the family to a hospital forty-two miles from their home where Kaiser received a discount, rather than to closer hospitals where Kaiser did not. James Adams had a 104-degree fever and was limp when his mother called the HMO hot line. By the time he arrived at the hospital, he had gone into cardiac arrest. James was revived, but the blood flow to his extremities had stopped and amputation was necessary because gangrene had set in. Even after the verdict, Kaiser medical director Richard Rodriquez contended that the delay made no difference and, "Our issue is quality. Quality pediatric care was most available at [the hospital with discounted rates for Kaiser] Scottish Rite."[15]

Mrs. Adams responded, "No one can tell you that a child going into cardiac arrest did not make matters worse."

In 1998, Texas regulators fined Kaiser $1 million for complaints investigated by the state attorney general which involved delays and denials of payment for emergency room care and Kaiser's failure to deal with quality of care issues.[16]

How does Kaiser's retrenchment in paying for out-of-network services play out for patients? Unlike cancer treatment and transplant operations where there may be enough time to fight with the HMO for approval, these emergency situations cannot be remedied through an appeal. The difference between life and death can come down to how fast care is given.

On May 6, 1993, Dawnelle Barris called the paramedics because her 19 month old daughter, Mychelle Williams, had gone into respiratory distress and had a 106.6-degree fever. In the next crucial hours, Dawnelle came up against a system where cost-cutting and "managed" care created delayed responses and fatal miscommunication. The paramedics transported Mychelle to the local hospital trauma center, and hospital staff called Kaiser for permission to treat her beyond basic breathing treatments. Nearly four hours of delay followed.

A Kaiser administrative doctor, who had never seen Mychelle, advised the local hospital not to do any treatments beyond breathing therapy, and to have Dawnelle transport her severely ill daughter in her own car to the Kaiser hospital. Dawnelle, frightened by her daughter's condition, refused to simply put her daughter in her car. She struggled desperately with the Kaiser representatives over the telephone, trying to order an ambulance. But Kaiser wouldn't budge. When Dawnelle returned to her daughter's bedside, the girl was having seizures, and Dawnelle had to search for a doctor to treat her. It took this increase in the severity of Mychelle's condition to convince Kaiser to authorize an ambulance, but the HMO still declined to authorize initial blood work and antibiotics. By the time Mychelle finally reached the Kaiser hospital across town, it was too late. She went into full cardiac arrest, and died. An autopsy later revealed that had she been given routine anti-biotics in the County emergency room, she would be alive today. Kaiser lost this case before a jury too.[17]

"My baby daughter was in the trauma center and Kaiser wouldn't authorize the treatment she needed," said Dawnelle. "I kept trying to talk to my HMO doctor but they couldn't locate him. They wouldn't let her be treated and she died. No one should suffer the way that my family and I suffered. I don't feel safe with HMOs anymore."

Kaiser, of course, is not alone in creating bureaucratic systems that are unresponsive to the urgent medical indications of patients.

In October 1998, Humana faced a $13.1 million verdict in Louisville, Kentucky in the case of Karen Johnson, a young wife and mother of two children who had cancer of the cervix and whose gynecologist recommended a hysterectomy.[18] Without it, she would have to undergo repeated surgical procedures, which would leave her at a significant risk that the cancer would become invasive. But Johnson was denied approval.

"The evidence presented to the jury in this case revealed a systematic scheme to deny one out of four requested hysterectomies that would save Humana between $13 million and $25 million over a three year period," said Dr. Peeno, an expert witness in the case against Humana. "The jury heard that Humana paid $1.7 million over the same period of time to a California company to review what Humana considered costly medical procedures. The physicians who worked for the California company never reviewed the patients' medical charts, never examined the patients, nor did they know the patients' medical history prior to denying the hysterectomies, and other medical procedures."

Humana's own reviewers had incentives too. "The jury also heard evidence that Humana paid its in-house medical reviewers a $5,000 bonus for limiting hospital admissions and another $5,000 bonus for shortening hospital stays," said Peeno.

Humana has appealed the verdict, saying that it stands by its denial of Johnson's hysterectomy because three board-certified gynecologists had recommended against it.[19]

Stonewalled to Death?

Sometimes medical negligence amounts to preventing patients from seeing the right doctor, the one who could save their life. In the case of Glenn Nealy that physician was his cardiologist. If not for the rule of the bureaucrats, Nealy would likely be alive today, according to a court case filed by his family.

According to the family's lawsuit, in March 1992, Glenn Nealy, 35 years old and the father of two young boys, was notified by his employer that there would be a change in his health care coverage and that he could elect coverage under one of three plans. Glenn chose an HMO after receiving assurances from its agents that the plan would enable him to continue treatment of his unstable angina and would allow him to see his cardiologist. The doctor was treating Glenn with a complete drug regimen including nitrates, calcium blockers, and beta blockers.

On April 2, 1992, at the direction of the managed care company, U.S. Healthcare, Glenn went to the office of a participating primary care physician for the purpose of obtaining a "referral" for follow-up treatment by his cardiologist. However, the U.S. Healthcare doctor refused to see Glenn until he had a valid company card. On April 3, Glenn returned to the primary care doctor's office with a copy of his enrollment form, which the company advised would be accepted by its primary-care provider. But again the primary-care doctor refused to see Glenn. Between April 2 and April 21, Glenn contacted representatives of U.S. Healthcare to obtain a valid card, but he was issued two incorrect and invalid cards. These kinds of bureaucratic mishaps can happen in any organization. The question is, at what point do they cross the line into deliberate delay and at what cost?

On April 9, 1992, the primary care doctor finally met with Glenn and drew blood, but did not make a referral to the cardiologist, even though he acknowledged the seriousness of the condition. The doctor renewed Glenn's angina medications, but Glenn was unable to fill the prescriptions because U.S. Healthcare provided incorrect and invalid information to Glenn's pharmacy. Between April 9 and May 18, Glenn repeatedly tried to get the

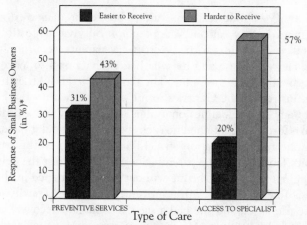

According to Small Business Owners, Have HMOs Made it Easier or Harder to Access Care?

■ Easier to Receive   ■ Harder to Receive

*The survey results in the chart are based on the responses of 401 out of 800 heads of companies and organizations with fewer than 100 full-time employees between March 18 and May 9, 1998. Preventive services describe services such as immunizations, health screenings, and physical exams.

Source: Kaiser Family Foundation/American Small Business Alliance Education Fund Survey, June 17, 1998.

insurer to authorize follow-up care by his cardiologist. On April 29, U.S. Healthcare, allegedly in violation of its previous assurances, formally denied in writing Glenn's request for follow-up visits with his cardiologist, because it had "a participating provider in the area." On May 15, after being repeatedly denied authorization to see his cardiologist, Glenn obtained a referral from his new doctor to see a cardiologist "participating" with the managed care company on May 19. It was one day too late. On May 18, Glenn died from a massive heart attack, leaving behind his wife Susan, and his two sons.[20]

Delay and stonewalling, unfortunately, are at the heart of our managed care system. The cold calculations of this system are unbefitting both our nation and a modern medical system fully capable of curing.

There may be no instance where HMOs and managed care companies play as fast and loose with patients' health as finding the right doctor in a timely manner.

"Take Two Aspirin, Go Home and Die"
versus the Army of the Faithful

In January 1993, nine year old Carley Christie was diagnosed with a rare and malignant kidney cancer, Wilms tumor. Survival is possible, if swift action is taken. In dealing with the crisis, her parents were running against the clock. Harry Christie and his wife had twelve hours to make the right choice to save their daughter's life. The terms of the HMO they had joined, TakeCare, instructed the Christies to use a surgeon within the HMO. But the federal advisory guidelines on Wilms insisted they use a pediatric specialist. TakeCare's list contained no such specialist, nor did it have a surgeon who had done a single operation on a child with a tumor of this type.

The question faced by the parents: Should they entrust the delicate, life-threatening operation to someone without prior experience in the field, or should they find an expert with a proven track record? Luckily for Carley, they chose the latter, and she had a successful surgery, recovery, and subsequent cure. "You only get one chance at removing a tumor correctly to insure the highest probability of survival," said Harry Christie of Woodside California. "What we discovered about our HMO and our rights in the aftermath of Carley's operation produced an infuriating and frightening struggle against our HMO," whose response could not have come at a more inappropriate time. "The HMO called us while our daughter was still in intensive care and informed us that they refused to pay any of the hospital bill." So much for "taking care" of Carley.

"The HMO decision was medically indefensible," said Harry, "but we learned that when we signed the HMO application in California, we gave up our seventh amendment right to trial by jury or any other legal remedies and had agreed to binding arbitration. Binding arbitration is part of the HMO grievance process in California—and one that favors the HMO."

Carley is well today, but had Harry listened to TakeCare and not found the most qualified surgeon himself, she might well have died. If Bill Beaver had listened to his HMO, Kaiser, he would unquestionably have had far fewer years with his family. "When I needed hope, my HMO gave me denial," says the Pollock Pines, California resident.

One morning in 1993 Beaver was running and began to have problems with one of his legs. He went to Kaiser to have it checked out, but was told it was nothing serious. Still, his leg problems persisted. He began to have trouble walking and could no longer run. Five months later, Kaiser conclud-

Bill Beaver

ed that Beaver must have had a stroke on the morning when he first noticed his leg problem.

"In my mind though, I just didn't fit the profile of a stroke victim," said Beaver. "My problems with my legs and nerves worsened over the next two years and my HMO wasn't able to develop any remedy."

After more extensive testing, doctors finally discovered that Bill's problems were due to a deadly brain tumor that had been misdiagnosed two years earlier.

"I had difficulty understanding this new diagnosis and why it had taken so long to come to light," Beaver recalled. "They told me the tumor was inoperable and predicted that I would live two years at best. They told me normally they would perform a biopsy of the tumor to confirm the diagnosis and order treatment, but in my case the procedure was much too risky and would most likely leave me paralyzed, comatose or dead, and regardless of the findings there were no known treatments that could prove beneficial."

What did Kaiser do for Beaver? "Essentially they were saying take two aspirin, go home, and die," Beaver recounts. "What was taken from me that day was hope. In a very few minutes I was cast from the herd, of no more use to the well being and future of my peers. I felt like a sickly gazelle left as prey outside the protective circle because it is not economically feasible to do otherwise."

Beaver could not believe there was not anything that could be done. Having spent many years teaching positive outcomes from negative circumstances, he could not give up. Bill and his wife drafted a list of family and friends to find some answers, "our army of faithful I called them."

One afternoon Bill received a telephone call from his sister-in-law. While sitting in a waiting room, she read an article about a young man who had the same condition and was treated successfully at John Hopkins Hospital. "The article went on to reveal the compassion and competence exhibited by John Hopkins and how they have earned the distinction of being the leader in health care and wellness," said Beaver. "I used all of my savings and began traveling to this prestigious teaching hospital. They contradicted the opinion of my HMO doctors by performing a biopsy and recommending radiation therapy for treatment, and then the doctors at John Hopkins convinced my HMO to administer the radiation treatment.

"Four years have passed since I was given a death sentence from my HMO and I am grateful for the fortunes during this time," said Beaver in May 1999, just before his death. "While I am not well, I do not know what the situation would be if I had had the best possible care from the onset. I do know that my HMO still refuses to pay for my life-saving treatment at John Hopkins."

For Charla Cooper, it was not her life, but her fertility that was jeopardized by HMO delays. Charla Cooper was alone and in the dark as her health care options expired. Kaiser did not provide $70,000 in out-of-network specialist care she required for a cancerous cervical condition and ovarian complications. HMOs like Kaiser do not like to provide such out-of-network care, because it is more costly, even when no specialists exist in the HMO's network. Cooper recalls, "Kaiser did not return my phone calls, scheduled procedures three months after they were needed and returned test results up to two months after the tests were performed." While Cooper's chances of becoming a mother faded every day, it was to Kaiser's benefit to stall. She has still not been able to conceive, although Kaiser, only after bad publicity and the threat of a lawsuit, relented and approved fertility treatment at a university medical center outside of the HMO's network. "I was treated with total lack of concern by Kaiser," said Charla. "While I am still hopeful that, God willing, I can be a mother, I think were it not for Kaiser I would be today. If I become a mother it will be in spite of Kaiser, not because of them."

Beaver and Cooper both had to accept the risks of their own treatment. Such a breach of the doctor-patient ethic is all too common. What HMOs do not tell you is that more and more of the risk is being passed on to patients—who, because they are sick, are often least able to accept it.

What are HMOs paid premiums for if not to accept risk? What are doctors trained to do if not treat illnesses? What are cures for if not to be used? What is the denial of those cures if not medical negligence?

Fifty-three year old grammar school nurse Betty Hale had been continuously covered by Blue Shield health plan programs for over thirty years, according to a legal complaint she filed against the company. But when she found she had breast cancer, she was denied benefits for treatment with high-dose chemotherapy ("HDCT") and autologous bone marrow transplant ("ABMT"), according to court documents.[21] Knowing this was her only chance for cure, Betty, like other breast cancer survivors, was forced to make public appeals to raise the money for treatment—taking on the risk to pay for her own treatment.

In a counseling session, Betty was advised to get her "ducks in a row." That is just what she did. Betty made small wooden ducks, decorated them with ribbons and pearls and sold them for $1.00 each. Students, faculty and friends held fashion shows and other fundraisers aimed at helping Betty reach the goal of $50,000 needed by the hospital to start treatment. The outpouring of donations soon reached $30,000 and, because of the urgency of her condition, the hospital agreed to provide treatment despite the shortfall. Betty Hale is alive and cancer-free today, but, after the operation, still owed the hospital $184,000. The health plan denied Betty's claim on the grounds that "HDCT" and "ABMT" were experimental and investigational, according to the family's complaint. Thirty years of paid up premiums were not enough customer loyalty to justify such an operation.

Ultimately, Hale entered into a confidential settlement with Blue Shield, under which the company denied liability.

"A decent country doesn't let the survival of mothers depend on money raised at car washes," stated a local newspaper editorial, reacting to a similar story of a cancer victim forced to hold car washes to fundraise for cancer treatment, and faxed so frequently among patient advocates that its masthead is now unidentifiable.

In our medical system today, decency and the longstanding medical dictate of "do no harm" have been sacrificed to greed. A haphazard collection of policies and decisions by bureaucrats did not create this horrifying picture. The system has been designed to control medical costs and show financial gains. It takes risks with patients' lives, plays the margins, removes power and discretion from the physicians and their patients. Who are the designers?

The Accountants' Design Takes Over

The daily micro-management of care for HMOs, hospitals and managed care companies across the nation is designed and maintained by the Seattle-based accounting firm of Milliman & Robertson. This is the actuarial company that sets the health care standards for the nation.[22]

Milliman & Robertson's business is to engineer health care rationing protocols which standardize and downsize medical procedures, such as births, mastectomies and cataracts. The company issues generic guidelines which tell health plans which services to authorize and which to deny. Such "cookbook medicine" has become the new rule in authorization of medical care.

Milliman & Robertson's protocols have stated that patients:

- cannot stay overnight for a mastectomy;
- cannot stay more than one day for a vaginal delivery;
- cannot have cataracts removed in more than one eye unless they are young and need both eyes to work;
- cannot see a neurologist for new onset seizures; or stay more than three days in a hospital for a stroke—even if a patient can't walk.[23]

These penny-pinching protocols have become virtually the law of the land—determining discharge times for stroke victims, hospital admission guidelines for heart attack patients, and neonatal intensive care unit stays for preterm newborns. Milliman's recipe is too often used to overrule medical providers' best judgment and has poisoned the doctor-patient relationship.

Civil society has battled back against some of the more shocking profitability recipes. The conservative, Republican-controlled Congress in 1996 finally prohibited premature discharge of newborns following birth, so called "drive-thru" deliveries. Still, Milliman & Robertson keeps pushing back—recently promoting the out-patient mastectomy, despite the counseling needs of women who undergo the procedure.

Now, the bean counters have taken aim at children. A new 400-page Milliman & Robertson book of guidelines downsizes the average 5.3 days children are hospitalized each year for various problems. The guidelines dictate that children with bone infections should have a two-day hospital stay; kids with asthma attacks so intense that they need bedside oxygen should be discharged after two days; tykes with heart-valve infections rate only a three-day stay.[24]

Have we really come so far as to accept these type of guidelines to usurp the practice of medicine across America?

Milliman & Robertson sold more than 20,000 copies of its guidelines through the end of 1997, affecting the treatment of 50 million Americans. The company's West Coast offices have expanded to 120 health care experts from just four in 1991, and its partners charge upwards of $450 per hour for their services.[25] In 1995, Milliman had $150 million in revenue.[26]

Hard-pressed to justify the use of such benchmarks in their denials of treatment, HMOs claim that the guidelines are simply advisory. How does a Milliman & Robertson protocol really play out?

Dr. John Vogt is a Kaiser executive who gave an infamous speech about putting the bottom line first and drafting cost-cutting guidelines over whiskies, a speech posted on the Milliman website until it resulted in a successful lawsuit against the HMO (See Chapter 2). Vogt put it this way about the Texas goals: "We needed to get from 300 [hospital days per 1,000 patients] to 180 days in less than two years...we're basically on-line to getting to 180 days by 1996. We also have to cut our costs by 30%, not only within hospitals, but within the rest of the cost structure...So, as you well know, *any time you have to balance the budget, how do you do it? You cut utilization. Drop referral rate, drop your hospital utilization. The budget balances...Do you know what 'CEM' is? It's a career-ending move. A CEM would have occurred had we said, 'No, you can't do it'*[emphasis added]."[27]

Was it just executives or physicians affected? Again, Vogt clarifies how Milliman & Robertson trained doctors to limit treatment: "*we really need to hit not just the chiefs, not only the managers, but you had to hit the frontline, because those are the ones who are really doing the work.* They came in (Milliman & Robertson did) to train our chiefs and our UM [utilization management] people. And then they came back again and they trained our frontline people [emphasis added]."

What does all the accountants' fidgeting with numbers mean for the life and health of a real patient?

Consider Lake Elsinore, California resident Barbara Roberts. The 61 year-old mother died from an untreated, massive pulmonary embolism after waiting six and one half hours in Kaiser's emergency room for treatment she never received.

"She would have lived had I taken her to a County emergency room or a Veteran's hospital, rather than to the HMO to which she paid premiums," said Linda Ross, Barbara's daughter.

"In November 1991, the HMO misdiagnosed and failed to treat blood clots that formed in my mother's leg after she suffered a minor fracture—ultimately forming the fatal pulmonary embolism," said Ross. "A Kaiser doctor declined to conduct tests recommended by an independent orthopedist, even though my mother exhibited physical signs of blood clots. When this doctor and another HMO doctor finally saw my mother in the emergency room the night she died, after my mother waited four and one half hours, they failed to give her an expensive blood thinner that could have saved her life. Had the thinner been administered in a timely manner, my mother would have had approximately a 97% rate of survival. My mother was refused admission as well as the life-saving drug she needed."

Milliman & Robertson guidelines help to determine whether patients like Barbara Roberts are admitted to the hospital and how they are treated at every step along the way.

Did Kaiser protocols affect whether or not Barbara Roberts was admitted?

Ross, who won a unanimous arbitration judgment against Kaiser, may never know, but she does suspect. "When my mother and I arrived at the HMO's emergency room, a nurse told us, 'I'll put her in line to see a doctor,'" said Ross. "The nurse left without doing any kind of exam or evaluation and without starting any kind of monitoring of my mother. We began to wait. I had no idea that we would wait for the rest of my mother's life.

"Even though the doctor could have begun treating my mother with blood-thinning agents, he chose not to. This doctor later admitted that he knew this was a life-threatening condition, that it was common practice to administer preventative treatment for blood clots given the indications of previous trauma and that he had done so with other patients in the past. There was nothing to stop him from taking this cautious action, except, perhaps money."

The death of caution is an idea patients should not stand for and more and more good doctors cannot stomach, but it is a pivotal reality of the managed care system.

Dr. Thomas W. Self

Pitting Doctors Against Each Other:
Finances on the Front Lines

San Diego pediatric specialist Thomas Self has emerged as one of the heroes in the landscape of for-profit managed care. A San Diego jury found in April 1998 that Self was unreasonably fired by a medical corporation for allegedly spending too much time with his patients and ordering too many tests.[28] The company, afraid of a larger punitive damage award, quickly settled the case.

The San Diego jury concluded that Self was retaliated against for simply practicing good medicine. His case was one of the first where a physician successfully beat a medical corporation that black-balled him simply for standing up for his patients. The verdict heralds physicians today who refuse to sacrifice their patients and stand up to for-profit managed care corporations interloping in the doctor-patient relationship.

But while an HMO-inspired, cost-cutting mentality victimized Self, it was not an HMO that harassed and fired him. It was other doctors at the seventy-five-doctor Children's Associated Medical Group, where Self worked. If Dr. Self is the hero in his case, the villain is Dr. Irving Kaufman, head of the Group. The jury awarded $650,000 against Kaufman personally for trying to whip Self into line with today's managed care values by saying that Self, a Yale-trained pediatric gastroenterologist, ordered too many tests, was dysfunctional, and lacked clinical confidence.

What could create this sort of climate, where physicians turn on one another? Healers, like Dr. Self, are too often faced with the Hobson's choice of being drummed out of the business or becoming money managers in a setting driven by profits. The edicts of capitation force doctors into an inevitable conflict between financial gain and additional treatment. In such a setup, doctors are blackballed and harassed not just by HMO bureaucrats, but by other doctors—the heads of medical groups, who are the new "managers" of care.

How have things gotten so out of control? Capitation is at the root of this question, and at the core of managed care. Where once traditional fee-for-service medicine paid doctors and hospitals a fee for every service they provided, the current health care system of capitation pays a fixed budget for every patient under a provider's care, regardless of how much treatment is needed. The doctor or hospital which receives the HMO payment pockets whatever they do not spend on patients. This system of lump sum payments—or per head, "capitated" rates, paid for every "covered life"—is a structurally built-in financial incentive to withhold care. The fewer services the doctor or hospital or HMO provides, the more money they make.

Capitation at the physician level insidiously aligns the doctor with the corporation and against the patient. A test which makes good medical sense, an exhibition of caution, is suddenly a financial liability to the doctor or his medical group. In the new HMO-induced system, the driving principle has become "less is more." This is far different from the Hippocratic oath of doing no harm. Physicians like Self who stand up for their patients and try to do more, a.k.a. practice quality medicine, face retaliation. Those who succumb set an unsettling standard for other physicians.

Dr. Linda Peeno, the former HMO medical director who turned whistle-blower, recently explained to the United States House of Representatives Commerce Committee the financial pressures imposed on physicians by HMOs:

> If a plan designs its physician contracts and payment strategies effectively, they can essentially make each physician a 'medical director' of the plan—i.e. someone who holds the plan's interest pre-eminent over the needs of the

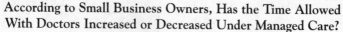

According to Small Business Owners, Has the Time Allowed With Doctors Increased or Decreased Under Managed Care?

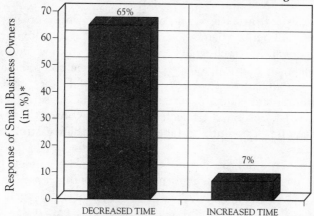

Question asked: "During the past few years, do you think managed care plans have increased or decreased the amount of time doctors spend with their patients?"
*The survey results in the chart are based on the responses of 401 of 800 heads of companies with fewer than 100 full-time employees.
Source: Kaiser Family Foundation/American Small Business Alliance Education Fund Survey, June 17, 1998.

patient before him or her. This can be done negatively (e.g. penalty clauses), positively (e.g. bonuses), or through some combination of both (e.g. with-holds). As a result of this, we are approaching something akin to "economic totalitarianism" in which physicians are willing agents of health plans in exchange for a patient base and continued revenue. Few can afford the dis-tinction of being a difficult player. Even worse, no savvy physician can afford the label: "unsuited for managed care." Managed care's stronghold in many communities ensures that even necessary care is being denied, not just by medical directors protecting the plan, but now by the practicing physicians themselves who have many reasons themselves to protect the plan over the patient. Economics reigns over ethics.[29]

The number of American doctors with capitation contracts has nearly doubled between 1994 and 1997. Other physicians who did not receive their payments on a capitated basis are being forced to rely on capitation. In 1997, one-third of the 483,000 physicians in the United States had capita-tion contracts, according to the American Medical Association. A govern-ment-financed study recently found that patients rated doctors paid on a capitated basis lower than non-capitated physicians. The 2,748 Massachusetts state employees surveyed found capitated doctors exhibited

less concern and familiarity with patient problems and did not provide adequate answers to questions, according to researchers at the Boston-based
New England Medical Center.[30]

It is the system, not the venality of doctors, which creates these
results. If we paid our mechanics a fixed budget for every automobile, $6
per month per car, how well would they run? Mechanics would focus on
quantity, not quality, and this is precisely the system corporations have
chosen to maintain our health—a system that forces doctors to see twenty-five patients before lunch, perform fewer tests, prescribe cheaper
drugs. In fact, Dr. Self says he rejected a capitated contract that offered
pennies per child per month to take care of all their gastrointestinal
needs.

Does capitation mean the doctors get our premiums? No—some primary
care doctors, for instance, are literally paid $6 per month per patient for the
gammet of that patient's primary health needs; meanwhile, premiums are
hundreds of dollars per month.[31] Premium dollars are paid to HMOs and
managed care insurers who keep, right off the top, 20–30% for their own
profit, overhead and marketing campaigns. (By way of contrast, the "overhead" for government-administered Medicare is two cents of every dollar.[32])
HMOs then pay a lump sum, capitated payment to medical groups, who can
keep another 20–30% for their overhead and profit.

Another expense from the same premium dollar is "stop loss" insurance—
paid as premiums by medical groups, sometimes back to the same HMO that
pays them the capitated rate—in order to indemnify the medical group
against catastrophic care like AIDS treatment. By the time the average
patient sees a part of the premium dollar to treat him, it has been nearly
downsized out of value.

Dr. Self frowned on capitated rates for the majority of his years as a physician, but Children's Associated Medical Group accepted them from HMOs.
Self, like many other physicians today, became entangled in managed care's
primary operating system despite his wishes. The resisters are too often
forced into capitation.

"Most physicians do not want to get into these arrangements," said Dr.
Martin Edelstine, president of the New York-based North Shore Physicians
Association. "The insurance companies tell us, 'This is what the future is.'
We figure you've got to prepare for this eventuality."[33]

Why are more physicians not speaking out? Following the Self verdict, a
physician writing to Consumers For Quality Care spelled it out in chilling
terms: "What astounds me is that we are not seeing more of these items and

issues in the press. Many physicians are afraid to speak out and thus they abrogate their responsibility regarding being an advocate for the patient. The best description of what is going on is the so-called Stockholm Syndrome. This occurred with many of the intellectuals and bureaucrats in Germany in WWII...Afraid to speak out, many simply went along with the flow. So it is with many of my colleagues."[34]

Even some of the managed care industry's biggest boosters admit that full-risk capitation for small medical groups—five physicians or less—should be banned. Sole practitioners could be bankrupted by a string of particularly ill patients. An HMO industry-dominated California task force led by Kaiser consultant Alain Enthoven recommended just this in order to keep the rest of the HMOs' large medical group franchises off of the hot seat.

At the larger medical groups, physicians obviously face the same pressures concerning their patients' interests. To keep within the budget, and armed with HMO-prepared data about utilization, doctors at the top of such medical groups pressure practicing physicians like Self to curb expensive referrals, tests, procedures, and to see more patients. Doctors who prescribe too many drugs or perform too many procedures risk their jobs, even if they are practicing the best medicine.

Medical groups routinely "profile" doctors for their use of high-cost drugs and procedures in order to curb costs. The financial logic of capitation makes medical group doctors function like the HMOs they once despised.

Orange County, California-based Greater Newport Physicians, for instance, used charts prepared by the California HMO PacifiCare to profile the amount each doctor in the medical group spent on prescriptions and rank the physicians from the thriftiest to the costliest. The comparative profile helped determine bonuses paid by the medical group. "Pharmacy utilization and performance will be part of the 1997 physician rating formula for potential surplus distribution," the medical group's medical director stated in a cover memo. Even though some doctors have older patients who need more expensive and regular prescriptions, the physicians were compared in the written profile without regard for the distinctiveness of their patient populations—based only on dollars. The medical group denies the profiles alone determine physician compensation.[35]

But the *Orange County Register* reported, "The group also says if doctors don't think differently, they will feel it in their wallets. Doctors who routinely run up high drug bills that they can't justify might find themselves out of Greater Newport. 'It's not only probable, it's very likely,' said [Dr.

Donald] Drake [the medical director who wrote the memo]. 'There will be consequences.' "[36]

Alta Bates Medical Group in the San Francisco Bay Area similarly prepared an economic profile of a doctor stating that the physician's drug utilization practices cost him a "total potential profit/loss per month" of $965.18 and cost the medical group "potential losses for the month" of $295,651.98. The profile also recommends downgrading from effective remedies to cheaper, less effective ones—such as switching from a non-sedating antihistamine for allergies to an over-the-counter sedating product.[37]

Health Net profiles its physicians too. One Health Net profile tracks use of high-cost drugs such as the anti-psychotic drug Prozac and recommends cheaper alternatives, telling the doctor that his utilization is above the Health Net target.[38]

HMOs argue that it is not just cost, but quality, that dictates such targets. But physicians like Dr. Self are increasingly criticized for practicing good medicine, not rewarded for it. In one memo presented in Self's case, an administrator wrote the chair of Self's utilization review committee to criticize Self for recommending tests for a child with gastric esophageal reflux. The memo criticized Self for wanting to rule out potentially serious problems and because the mother "was then told that because of her insurance, that he could not order these tests...It distresses me that [Self] still doesn't understand how managed care works." While HMOs and medical groups support armies of quantitative utilization reviewers, they do not have "quality control specialists."

But is a doctor really more likely to be less cautious and deny treatment simply because his group is capitated? The case of Simi Valley, California resident Joyce Ching illuminates this issue. Ching died of colon cancer at the age of 34, leaving her three year-old son and husband, David, behind. Her husband said she had complained of constant and excruciating pain, as well as rectal bleeding, to her HMO's primary care physician on three visits. But the physician, the "gate keeper" at MetLife, refused to send Joyce Ching to a specialist for x-rays or tests, despite the Chings' repeated requests for specialist care. That gatekeeper physician was paid a monthly "capitated" fee for providing medical care to Joyce Ching. Any referral he made came out of his own pocket.

In a Simi Valley lawsuit, David Ching claimed that financial incentives prevented Joyce's primary care provider from referring her to a specialist, who could have detected her cancer and treated her. David Ching had to demand care for his wife from the physician, who finally ordered a $261 barium enema x-ray exam and sent her to a gastroenterologist—but not until her colon cancer had advanced too far. In November 1995, the Ching family won in a court. A jury awarded $3 million for negligence, which was reduced by a two decade-old California cap on damages to $700,000. The judge, however, did not let the jury consider the charge that the physician's financial incentives caused the tragedy.

Still, Mark Hiepler, the Chings' attorney and brother of cancer victim Nelene Fox, said, after the verdict, "This sends a clear message that when you mix incentives and money with medicine it equals death."[39]

Following the death of Joyce, Mr. Ching put it this way. "I said to myself, 'Here's God, whatever problem she has, the doctor will take care of it'...There's that kind of fear they put in you with an HMO that you can't go anywhere unless your doctor tells you to. He's the law. He's God. He tells you where to go, what to do and when to do it."[40]

The narrow margin for critically ill patients often depends on whether or not they receive a timely test, or go outside of their HMO network for a second opinion. But patients do not know instinctively to be skeptical of their HMO doctors' advice. Patients do not understand capitation. Consumers will be less likely to do so in a context where they are bombarded with HMO advertising that spews out assurances on these very issues.

The Blame Game

Another technique of cost control arises when patients are injured because their doctor did not do the right thing. Increasingly, HMOs place the blame on patients for not advocating hard enough for themselves. This is the tell-tale omen of a system built on profit, not service.

For eighteen months Cypress, California resident Mary Schriever repeatedly asked her PacifiCare physician for a referral to a specialist for her 16 year-old son Bill because he talked about committing suicide, burned and carved his arms, was failing in school and had various run-ins with the police. PacifiCare covers "crisis intervention," but Schriever was told by PacifiCare that "my plan didn't cover mental health."

"To this day, I am unable to determine what my HMO deems to be a crisis," Schriever says. "The doctor told me that my HMO would only approve a referral in the event of a suicide attempt. Assuming at least some suicide attempts are successful, this probably does tend to save my HMO money. He stated that he had as a patient a teenage girl who was raped and requested a mental health referral and the HMO would not approve care for her, so they would not approve care for my son."

Like most PacifiCare doctors, Schriever's was paid on a capitated basis.

The physician also refused her request to put her son on Prozac, and instead prescribed a cheaper alternative, Luvox, which was on the list of PacifiCare's approved drugs. Bill told his mother it had no effect.

"We were left on our own with nowhere to turn and my son's condition deteriorated rapidly," recounts Mary Schriever. "In one of his final incidents, he became very agitated and he called the police. My son told me he was going to have them come over and shoot him. He made a lot of statements about having the police kill him. When the police finally took control of the situation and took him into custody, they were very adamant about Bill needing mental help. Bill and I agreed, but told them that I had been unsuccessful in getting him any through my HMO."

Bill Schriever was jailed and, during this process, a doctor prescribed Prozac for him. He was seen by a court-ordered psychiatrist. When Mary visited Bill at the detention center, she felt he was doing better, possibly because of the Prozac. Tragically, another inmate stabbed Bill, and he died many hours later without receiving medical care.

"I saw him the day before he died for two hours and he looked good. He was joking and asking about the dog. I personally don't think my son would have ended up dead if he could have had the proper medication and counseling much sooner in the process."

After a local newspaper revealed Bill's story, PacifiCare called Schriever back.

"They said my son's case dropped through the cracks and I should've been pushier," Schriever remembers. "How many times do they think you can get a 16 year-old boy to see the doctor, asking for a mental health referral? I don't know that they could've saved him. I don't know about the path not taken. But I certainly can say they didn't try."

PacifiCare spokesperson Ben Singer commented, "It's a classic example of what can go wrong when there's a lack of communication between the member, the plan and the physician. The doctor was dead wrong."[41] Later, he added, "I just wish we had all done a better job communicating with one another."

Is it really Mary Schriever's job to be pushier? Do we want a health care system where the doctors are silenced, financially turned against the patients, then blamed when something goes wrong, because they played by the HMO's rules? Is this the HMOs' fault? Is it the doctors'? In either case, it is the patients who pay the price and managed care corporations who set up and profit by the system.

The Death of Caution and Passing Of Risk: Hippocrates versus the Oath of the HMO

Fee-for-service medicine was not cheap and was prone to over-utilization because there was nothing to discourage doctors and hospitals from prescribing extraneous tests and procedures. Insurance companies are also prone to price gouging or over-charging for their product. Every dollar they take in as a premium is invested at a very generous rate of return, so insurers want to charge as much as possible.

What have we lost in moving to a system of managed care and HMOs? The nation's foremost medical malpractice scholar, Dr. Troyen Brennan of Harvard, spelled out to Congress what it all boils down to: "At the hospital level, the major risk factor associated with negligent injury is the total amount of resources expended in the care of patients."[42] In other words, in the hospital, less medical dollars means more danger.

In other venues the same is almost always true—for cancer patients, those with infectious diseases, chronically ill patients consigned to a skilled nursing facility. Unless an incompetent physician proceeds with an unnecessary operation, quality, as noted earlier, is often a function of dollars directed toward your care. That is why those who are sick do not do well in HMOs and managed care plans. The statistics comparing HMOs to traditional fee-for-service medicine tell the story:

- HMO patients are 59% more likely to have difficulty getting treatment.[43]

- HMO patients over 65 are 93% more likely to have some decline in physical health than fee-for-service patients.[44]

- 48% of Americans report that they or someone they know have experienced problems with their HMO including difficulty getting permission to see a specialist, problems getting a plan to pay an emergency room bill, and being unable to file an appeal to an independent agency for a denied claim.[45]

Insurance once was a business in which insurers assumed risk in exchange for a premium. Through the capitated rate, however, risks are passed back to the doctors and, because the capitated rate is frequently too low to be finan-

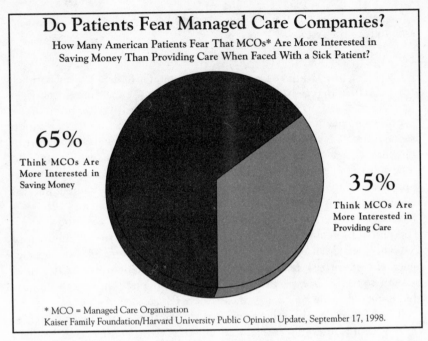

Do Patients Fear Managed Care Companies?

How Many American Patients Fear That MCOs* Are More Interested in
Saving Money Than Providing Care When Faced With a Sick Patient?

65%
Think MCOs Are
More Interested in
Saving Money

35%
Think MCOs Are
More Interested in
Providing Care

* MCO = Managed Care Organization
Kaiser Family Foundation/Harvard University Public Opinion Update, September 17, 1998.

cially viable for the medical groups, ultimately the risk is passed to the
unaware patients.

Always anxious to scapegoat the legal system for their own price-gouging,
traditional insurance companies blamed "defensive medicine"—the use of
medical tests and procedures allegedly for the purpose of protecting doctors
and hospitals against malpractice suits. "Defensive medicine," however, was,
in large part, careful, protective medicine, "ordered to minimize the risks of
being wrong when the medical consequences of being wrong are severe," as
a 1994 Congressional Office of Technological Assessment (OTA) report
concluded.[46]

Prophetically, the OTA warned of managed care's "new incentives to do
less rather than more," and that to "remove incentives to practice defensive-
ly…could also remove a deterrent to providing too little care at the very
time such mechanisms are most needed." In fact, those old safeguards have
now evaporated just when they are most needed.

Managed care's prime directive that "less is more"—the fewer dollars
spent on health care, the more the doctor and the company make, the more
job security they have, the more the company's stock is worth—is a threat to

good health. Patients expect and deserve as much treatment as is warranted, regardless of cost. This is why they pay for health insurance.

Unfortunately, medical malpractice is now often caused by the gap between a patient's reasonable expectation of high quality health care and an HMO's financial dictates. A missed referral, postponed test or untimely response to a patient's hospital call button can be the margin between health and injury, life and death. In medical terms, less is rarely more. Wellness and preventive medicine does not mean ignoring danger signs. Patients understand this, but efforts are made to keep these relationships obscure.

In every state in the nation, physicians are bound by an oath to practice proper medicine. HMOs take no such oath and are bound by no such laws, which is why, too often, they commit medical negligence—violate the standard of care—with impunity.

Why aren't more physicians speaking out if there is an epidemic of HMO-driven medical malpractice? Gag orders, confidentiality clauses that prevent doctors and nurses from disclosing information about their treatment decisions and pay to patients, are the final insult of managed care— binding and tongue-tying doctors and nurses.

Companies have gone to great lengths to demand loyalty from caregivers at the expense of patients.

Sharp is one of California's largest hospital chains and a partner of Columbia/HCA, the nation's largest for-profit hospital chain. Nurses and other medical personnel in Sharp HealthCare were told to place the best interests of the corporation ahead of those of patients, according to the Sharp Employee Handbook.

In a section titled, "Conflict of Interest," the handbook instructs: "All employees have the responsibility to place the interest of Sharp HealthCare above their own and those of...a patient."[47]

"Provisions like this compromise the most fundamental relationship in the health care process—the trust between a patient and their nurse or doctor," said Kit Costello, RN, President of the California Nurses Association (CNA), which publicly released the handbook with Consumers For Quality Care.

The nurse, who turned over the Sharp clause to the CNA but wished to remain anonymous for fear of violating the clause, said, "It's clear that we can be terminated for any reason. The message is we have to perform to their budgetary expectation, not the expectation of patients and their families. Our managers give lip service to patient care and quality. Never once do we hear about safety. We always feel we are trying to give nursing care with one hand tied behind our back and not giving the care we were educated to give. I am being stopped from what I am trained to do."

"Nurses must be free to raise concerns about a patient's readiness to be transferred from intensive care or sent home from the hospital without fear of losing their livelihood if these decisions cost the hospital or HMO more money," said Costello. She also noted, "The nurse who gave a copy of this handbook to the CNA had it rolled up inside a newspaper and was afraid to talk about it."

Sharp spokesperson Stephanie Casenza responded in the *San Jose Mercury News* that, "The problem is the way this was written into the employee handbook. It will definitely be changed when we update the handbook. The intent is to tell employees to put Sharp's mission first and that mission is quality patient care."[48]

How restricted are HMO doctors from informing patients of their medical condition and best treatment options—even if the HMO does not pay for them—or how the HMO system works? Health Net's agreement with doctors provides a clear answer. "Neither PMG [physician management group] nor HEALTH NET shall disclose the reimbursement or payment provisions of this Agreement." This provision prevents the public from knowing that physicians are given financial incentives to deny or delay care. The contract also reminds physicians to whom they ultimately answer (not the patient, but the corporation): "If Group determines that Provider's utilization of Outside Providers is excessive then Group may terminate this Agreement...effective ten days." Of course, the agreement itself is "confidential...not to be disseminated..."[49]

Medical corporations also do all they can to restrict public scrutiny of health care environments where standards of care may be deteriorating. Patient advocates say they are silenced by contractual provisions such as that written in the Oakland, California-based Alta Bates Medical Center Employee Handbook. It reads, "Do not give any information to newspaper, TV or radio reporters or press photographers in person, writing, or by phone."[50] Under this clause, nurses were disciplined for talking to the press about a controversial child-birth technique, according to the California Nurses Association. Alta Bates claims the clause simply protects patients' privacy.

U.S. Healthcare's anti-disparagement clause in its physician contracts is sweeping. "Physician shall agree not to take any action or make any communication which undermines or could undermine the confidence of enrollees, potential enrollees, their employers, their unions, or the public in U.S.

Healthcare or the quality of U.S. Healthcare coverage," according to a physician agreement with the HMO, which merged in 1996 with Aetna to become the nation's largest managed care company.[51] Such a disparagement clause prevents a physician from alerting a patient or the public to any unsafe medical practices. The HMO oath also states, "Physicians shall keep the Proprietary Information [payment rates, utilization review procedures, etc.] and this Agreement strictly confidential."

Foundation Health's contract follows suit: "Provider shall keep strictly confidential all compensation agreements set forth in this Agreement and its addenda."[52]

What kind of "compensation agreements" would so concern the public? Consider the one from MetLife, "Surplus Sharing. In the event that there is a surplus in the Hospital Fund...fifty percent (50%) of the surplus shall be paid by METLIFE to IPA [Independent Practice Association, of doctors]. Deficit Sharing. In the event there is a deficit in the Hospital Fund...fifty percent (50%) of the deficit shall be payable to METLIFE by IPA from the surplus in the IPA Withhold Fund...up to an amount equal to five percent (5%) of the hospital fund."[53] In other words, the HMO and doctor split monies not spent on the patient.

Doctors and nurses are certainly aware of the system's impact on patient care. In a July 1999 survey of over 1000 doctors and 700 nurses by the Kaiser Family Foundation, the medical profession spoke clearly:

- 87% of the doctors said their patients had experienced some denial of coverage for a needed health service during the past two years including (79%) a drug they wanted to prescribe; (69%) a hospital stay; (52%) a referral to a specialist.

- Almost half of the nurses reported that they had seen a decision by a health plan result in a serious decline in a patient's health.

- 95% of the doctors said managed care had increased paper work, while 72% said it decreased the quality of care for people who are sick.

Medical ethics themselves are being downsized. In the environment HMOs have created, medical carelessness is more acceptable than financial expense.

Are HMOs up-front about this? Do the promises made by HMOs measure up to reality? Are HMOs committing fraud?

CHAPTER 2

A Deadly Fraud

Behind the Caring Image of HMOs and Managed Care Companies

Heather Aitken chose the nation's largest HMO, Kaiser Permanente, as her HMO based on the company's holy triad message of "trust, caring, understanding." Of Kaiser, she said, "I trusted this facility to take care of my children," a sentiment at the forefront of any parent's concerns. "As a mother and a human being, I thought I was doing the right thing."

On July 18, 1995, Aitken took Chad, her five-and-one-half month-old son in for a checkup in Woodland Hills, California. According to Heather, her Kaiser pediatrician "became hostile with me and accused me of having used their facilities for six months without insurance."

"I was confused by this accusation because I had just had the baby five months ago, and another one of my children had a minor operation, and no one had mentioned our insurance coverage before to us," Aitken says. "Although we had been members for over five years, the doctor told us that we had been coming in under fraudulent circumstances and refused to see my son. This accusation was the result of a clerical mix up on our insurance coverage dates through my husband's ex-employer."

Heather says that because the Kaiser doctor thought Chad was not covered, he refused to address breathing problems Chad experienced after his first round of vaccinations. But Chad was given more vaccine shots, according to Heather, because the law required them and Medicaid paid for them.

Unfortunately, the July 18th vaccine caused more severe respiratory problems for Chad.

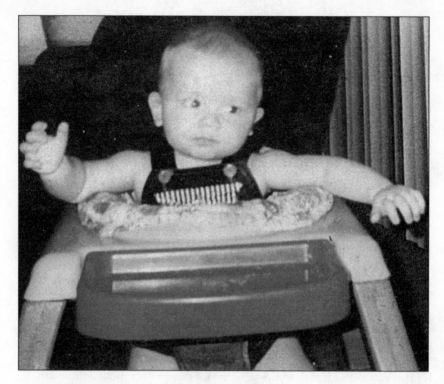

Chad Douglas Aitken

"I called my HMO and requested they see Chad again," said Heather. "The urgent care nurse told me they could not because Chad's chart had been red-flagged. She could not discuss Chad's case. She told me not to come in."

Heather says that Kaiser knew that all her children had a history of severe breathing problems. After Chad's reaction to his first shots, in fact, a Kaiser doctor prescribed antibiotics. This time, Chad went untreated.

"Refusing treatment after an invasive procedure like drug injections is not only unethical, it is unconscionable," said Aitken. "If doctors administer treatment, they are supposed to follow through with the job, not leave it half way. Chad's breathing problem was directly related to his adverse reaction to the vaccine shots. But without my HMO seeing and treating Chad for this reaction, what could have been prevented, became fatal."

By August 8, 1995, Chad was dead. "The microscopic report clearly indicated that the cause of death was due to Chad's reaction to the vaccine shots," said Aitken. "My life without my son has been devastating and I wouldn't want to see another parent go through the same nightmare as we have been put through."

Why did a little child, a citizen of the wealthiest nation on earth with doctors and medical technology that are the envy of the world, die over a dispute about whether he was entitled to care? The answer lies in the larger picture of how the U.S. provides health care.

As the nation's biggest HMO, Kaiser is an important barometer for the pressures and climate changes in the medical marketplace. A non-profit, Kaiser was once the gold standard for HMO care. But the company's recent history tells a sad story about a mission gone awry. A dramatic shift occurred during the 1990s as Kaiser was suddenly forced to compete for "customers" with for-profit insurers. Kaiser's 1995–1997 business plan in Southern California slashed the medical budget by $800 million even as the company increased its membership. The plan included adoption of such reckless care-cutting practices as outpatient mastectomies and replacing skilled nurses with less skilled workers. The business plan forthrightly stated the goal behind the cuts: attaining "an overall 3% median single party rate advantage over its major HMO competitors...and a 6% advantage when quoting new groups"—in other words it intended to undercut its for-profit competitors' prices.[1] Kaiser finally recognized that it competes in a nearly completely for-profit market, an economic landscape where those who rake in the most dollars in contracts for care while spending the least to get those dollars win. In an effort to stay on top, Kaiser downsized services and cut costs—joining its for-profit competitors in the race to the bottom in health care quality.

Competition for new members had become so intense that by 1998 Kaiser had increased its membership by 20% but posted a $200 million loss because it so undercut its competitors' prices. It won those customers by selling its services below the actual cost of delivering those medical services—a practice that can be called predatory pricing. In a traditional business, if the service is cut to the bone customers can in theory go elsewhere to pay for better services. But, in the managed care setting, while it is the patient who gets the care, it is the employer who often pays most of the membership costs. Employers can save money by using an HMO that controls benefit costs; the consequences of poor care are borne by the patient, not the employer.

Ironically, once the customers were in the door, Kaiser announced double-digit premium increases in March of 1998.[2] The fact that Kaiser gained so much ground on its competitors even as it cut its medical-care budget dramatically demonstrates that competition in the managed care market is based on controlling cost, not providing quality care to win over patients.

By the mid-1990s, Kaiser's rapid medical downsizing took a toll on patients' safety and care. Responding to a pattern of problems with emergency medical care, Texas regulators in April 1997 required Kaiser to implement specific steps to assure high quality health care and levied a fine on the HMO of $1 million.[3] On the federal level, regulators ordered Kaiser to correct life-threatening safety problems at California hospitals or lose federal Medicare and Medi-Cal funding. The safety issues included the handling of patients in the emergency room and transporting them without proper stabilization.[4] In August 1996, California regulators found "systemic" problems at Kaiser. Among the auditors' findings: medical decisions at Kaiser, in apparent violation of state law, did not appear to be "independent of fiscal and administrative considerations."[5] This was compounded by high-profile wrongful death cases, embarrassing disclosures about premature discharges of patients at its facilities and chiding by the conservative California Supreme Court about its tactics of delaying justice for a dying patient.

Even Kaiser's own physicians sounded off in the internal Kaiser newsletter titled *Hope*. "The root causes of these costly and humiliating developments—perhaps unprecedented in our great organization—are not clear. That the events occurred independently in two states made the publicity even more incriminating."[6]

Kaiser moved swiftly to address these issues, spending astronomical sums of money to increase not the quality of its medical care but its *advertising*. In an internal Kaiser video created to inform staff about its advertising effort, Joellyn Savage, Director of Member and Marketing Communications couldn't have framed the problem more clearly. "There were many challenges we faced, one of which was our reputation, and the only way to address the challenges in the reputation area was to develop a very aggressive advertising campaign to change the perceptions of the general public," she said.[7] In 1995, Kaiser increased its advertising and marketing budget to $60.3 million—a 641% jump from 1992. In 1996, the advertising budget grew still more, to $61.8 million.[8]

In a health care system focused on health, not profit, these dollars would have been used for patient care, a point not lost on Kaiser's physicians. Angered that money was being sucked from their patients to be spent on advertising, they noted in their internal newsletter that "Despite the budget cuts absorbed by our patients, hospitals and staff, our overall expense structure has not significantly improved and may, in fact, be slightly worse."

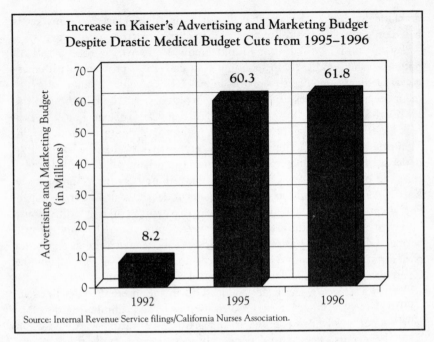

Increase in Kaiser's Advertising and Marketing Budget Despite Drastic Medical Budget Cuts from 1995–1996

Source: Internal Revenue Service filings/California Nurses Association.

Furthermore, "Practicing physicians struggling to preserve quality care under the duress of budget cuts may worry about whether it is wise or even necessary to continue shifting resources 'to invest heavily in more IT [information] technology and advertising' in a time when patient care is under increasing financial strain."[9]

While physicians were frustrated, Kaiser televised the opposite message, placing the image of satisfied doctors at the core of its advertising and marketing campaign. In the late 1990s, Kaiser dumped tremendous resources into what they called "The Personalized Care" campaign. Billboards and television advertising featured smiling doctors in intimate settings with their patients professing the satisfaction of being able to take care of their patients correctly.

Sparing no expense, Kaiser created a video tape about the remaking of the Kaiser image—aimed at its own employees. "We've known all along that the most important reputational message is in fact quality of personalized care and now we are finally able to use that," Kaiser's Savage intoned. "Although there are a great number of people who are involved in the delivery of health care as a team, the relationship that is most important to our

"Practicing medicine from the patient's point of view." We "focus on your care." These Kaiser Permanente slogans, taken from a TV clip, stress "the opportunity to practice medicine without being second-guessed by an insurance company." Unmentioned in the ads was a survey rating Kaiser physician morale that reflected a grim reality. On a scale of zero to ten, with ten being the highest, physicians rated their morale at two.

target audience is the physician. Therefore we are providing primary focus on the physician in this campaign again."

But while Kaiser's advertising agency marketed the HMO's reputation for satisfied doctors delivering "personalized care," Kaiser physicians continued questioning its reputation and commitment to physician-driven care. Were most Kaiser physicians really satisfied about their opportunities to deliver the type of personalized care that Kaiser portrayed in its ads? A 1997 internal Kaiser physician satisfaction survey, cited in the HOPE newsletter, rated the average physician morale "2" on a scale of "10" ("10" = "excellent," "0" = "absent"). More than one-third of the respondents expressed a "0" confidence level in the Kaiser administration. Comments from the survey include: "I feel we have a totalitarian system" and that Kaiser should "Treat physicians as partners, not employees."[10] What does it mean for a patient to be confronted with a doctor who has zero morale about the resources available to him?

Of the low confidence levels among physicians, the newsletter authors say:

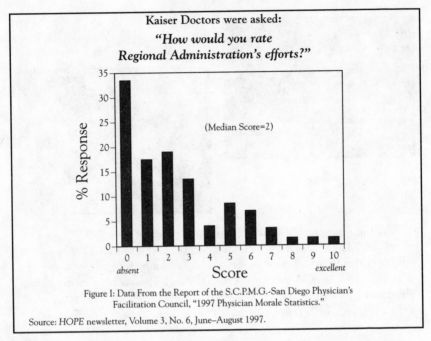

Kaiser Doctors were asked:
*"How would you rate
Regional Administration's efforts?"*

(Median Score=2)

% Response

Score

absent / excellent

Figure I: Data From the Report of the S.C.P.M.G.-San Diego Physician's
Facilitation Council, "1997 Physician Morale Statistics."

Source: *HOPE* newsletter, Volume 3, No. 6, June–August 1997.

In other comparable surveys (imagine such results in a M.A.P.S. or T.O.P.P.S. survey), scores so closely approximating zero (perhaps indistinguishable from zero if confidence intervals are taken into account) might have provoked widespread alarm, global reassessment, and the prompt imposition of stern disincentive measures.

As the newsletter article notes, the Permanente Medical Group Board's response to the survey, like Kaiser's response to its deteriorating reputation, was swift:

...within months of this survey, partners saw the Board glibly vote its appointed members—the subjects of this data—an up to 20% increase in bonus compensation...Board enactment of these bonuses was seen by many partners as an open disregard of majority partnership sentiment. Many partners could not help but privately wonder, 'Whose interest is the Board pursuing?'

The physicians were not alone. Kaiser nurses, also portrayed in the advertising, expressed outrage that Kaiser deployed so many resources to improving its image at the expense of its care. In 1995, Kaiser paid out $96.1 million to its top four consultants alone: $41.1 million to Deloite & Touche, consulting, accounting; $24.8 million to Kresser, Stein, Robaire for advertising services; $16.2 million McKinsey & Co, strategic planning; and $14 million to Anderson Consulting for consulting. The California Nurses Association, which represents mostly Kaiser nurses, pointed out that the same $96 million could pay the *total* health care costs for San Diego County for about two-and-a-half years and could provide another 73,600 hospital days for California mothers and their newborn infants.[11]

The gap between Kaiser's image and reality underscored that patients were not receiving the personalized care from physicians that Kaiser promised.

"Through focus group testing, we have learned that personalized care translates to the general consumer in terms of relief of anxiety and respect," Denise Daversa, Kaiser's Director of Advertising and Meetings Services told Kaiser employees on the company's internal video. "And from that we have pulled out three key words which the three executions of Phase Two Reputation Campaign will focus on. Those words are trust, caring and understanding."[12]

Was Kaiser, even on reduced resources, living up to its slogan? Here are some of Kaiser's pitches to the public, made in advertisements featuring visually beautiful images of the most intimate doctor-patient relationships:

> "There are times when a little caring goes farther than a long way. When a little time makes all the difference. Those are times when you can count on physicians with Kaiser Permanente. Physicians know this is one of the most important relationships you will ever have. Our team of medical professionals are on hand working together to deliver personal care. Because they know the art of medicine is really the art of caring."

Turning to the reality behind the advertising, a Kaiser Los Angeles facility received national attention in 1995 for prematurely discharging newborns and their mothers as early as eight hours after delivery, which led to federal legislation in 1996 banning the practice.[13] Medical experts recommend forty-eight hours as a minimum discharge time. Proper breast-feeding, for instance, is often a casualty of premature discharge. During post-partum, nurses typically can educate mothers, particularly new ones, about breast-feeding, and other aspects of child care. New mothers often do not realize how frequently their newborns need to eat or that they may need to be awakened in order to be fed. As a result, newborns discharged early are at heightened risk of suffering from malnutrition and dehydration. According to research by the American College of Obstetricians and Gynecologists, jaundice is a particularly serious health risk for newborns discharged before forty-eight hours, a malady that is not typically detected until the child's second day of life.

Just how often do these problems occur when infants and mothers are discharged early? Dr. Judith Frank, chief of neonatology at Dartmouth Medical School, found that newborns discharged at less than two days of life are 50% more likely to be readmitted to the hospital and 70% more likely to return to the emergency room.[14]

One infamous Kaiser memo announced the *eight hour discharge policy*. Entitled "Positive Thoughts Regarding the Eight Hour Discharge," it listed reasons for staff to offer patients in order to get them to accept the premature discharge time, such as "hospital food is not tasty" and "unlimited visitors at home."[15]

These were hardly isolated incidents of an ad campaign gone awry.

Kaiser Print Ad: "We don't have insurance administrators telling your physician how to treat you. And there are no financial pressures to prevent your physician from giving you the medical care you need."[16]

Kaiser Reality: Drastic reductions in critical patient services were disclosed in the confidential "Kaiser Permanente Southern California Region Business Plan 1995–1997." The document shows arbitrary business goals dictate to medical practitioners at Kaiser. The plan's goals include:

- dramatically reducing (by more than 30%) the number of patients hospitalized through such dangerous measures as "shifting surgical cases from inpatient to outpatient (i.e. gall bladders, mastectomy/lumpectomy, appendectomy)";

- rationing prescriptions of high-cost drugs;

- "aligning physician bonus pay and leadership compensation to target achievement," i.e. the quotas for rationed care—doctors who reduced their hospital admissions were paid financial bonuses[17];

- "implementing care paths for chest pain and stroke [i.e. early discharges or early removal from Intensive Care Units]...";

- "reducing staff in surgical and primary care specialties...";

- "alternatives for SNF [Skilled Nursing Facility] admissions and lengths of stay," i.e. shunting patients into nursing homes or their own homes at critical stages in their care.

Kaiser claims: "You can count on physicians with Kaiser Permanente. Physicians know this is one of the most important relationships you will ever have. Our team of medical professionals all on hand working together to deliver personal care." Commercials in 1998 presented urgent medical situations followed by the question, 'What if?' to drive home the fact that Kaiser doesn't require its doctors to seek approval from outside administrators for medical procedures or referrals. One spot shows a woman in labor while the narrator says, "What if there are complications?" The commercial ends, "Kaiser Permanente. In the hands of doctors."

Kaiser reality: One of the most scandalous deprivations of patient care at Kaiser, given the advertising claims, is that mothers giving birth are not always allowed to see a doctor—instead, a nurse mid-wife performs the delivery. There is nothing inherently inferior about midwifery but in problem births competent doctors are required. High-risk births have slipped through the system without doctors in attendance and newborns have been injured because no capable physician was on hand to deliver them. Kaiser has refused to respond to questions about the pervasiveness of the practice and its casualties.

One example is Colin McCafferey. "Unfortunately, during each of my wife's pregnancies, there were complications," recalls Colin's father, Kevin McCaffery, a Kaiser member and resident of Woodland Hills, California. "When my wife Pattie became pregnant the third time, our HMO doctor, during her initial visit, immediately classified Pattie as 'high risk' and assigned himself to her case. That was the last time we ever saw him. Each subsequent attempt to arrange a visit with the doctor was met with resistance by the HMO's staff. Our repeated pleas went unheeded, and only a mid-wife was assigned to her case. This is standard practice at Kaiser. No doctors, just mid-wives."

During one of Patty's last examinations, just a few days prior to delivery, the sonogram revealed that the baby would be large, close to nine pounds. Pattie was concerned. Kaiser's staff assured the McCaffereys that everything would be okay. They were wrong.

"Colin was big," Kevin recalls. "During the latter stages of delivery, after the baby's head was out, all hell broke loose. The mid-wife began yelling for the doctor. Nurses ran in and out, and one actually jumped up on my wife and began pushing down hard trying to get the baby out. I was terrified.

"The baby was pulled out and placed on a table. The baby looked beautiful to me. I couldn't figure out what was wrong. Then I noticed the nurse working on his arms. In their attempts to get the baby out quickly, which I later discovered were completely unnecessary, Colin's shoulder had caught on my wife's pelvic bone and been severely stretched. They said it would heal. I wondered where the doctor was. It turns out no doctor had been covering the floor during my wife's delivery." Kevin remembers when the doctor on-call finally came in—it was obvious that he was reading his wife's chart for the first time.

Colin's injury never healed. "They call it Erb's Palsy," said Kevin. "He will never have full use of his arm or hand. He will never be able to raise his hand over his head, catch a ball with two hands, hold a bat, or play any of the other games boys play."

Kevin later learned that there was no urgency to remove Colin. A doctor would have known this. On top of this, delivery techniques were available to handle the baby's quick removal. But they were not used because the midwife had either not been trained or simply had panicked.

"All in all, it was a nightmare that didn't have to happen," Kevin says now. "And Colin must now suffer for it for the rest of his life."

But that is not even the worst part of Kevin's ordeal. "Six months after Colin's birth, our HMO asked me to attend a clinic with Colin," Kevin recounted. "They wanted to evaluate him to see if some new procedure might be applicable to him. As I waited in the waiting room at the hospital, I began to well up. When I looked about the room I saw over fifty babies, all under the age of two, clinging to their parents. None of them were smiling. They all had Erb's Palsy. One little girl around one year had such a sad look to her. Her arms, both of them, just dangled lifelessly by her side. I got up, picked up Colin, hugged him tight, and walked out."

Fifty young children in one regional facility with a preventable malady like Erb's Palsy is a sight that modern medicine should not tolerate.

The McCaffereys, of course, were not featured as patients in Kaiser's commercials. The doctors were real Kaiser doctors, but the patients were actors. How fictional were the portrayals? Pediatrician Carol Woods was featured in one commercial: "When I saw what happened with exam rooms they created, to allow the sound to come in the walls were removed, there were fifty people around one little set, I saw that it couldn't be done in my exam room."[18]

"It was interesting how perfect every little detail had to be," said Milton Sakamoto, a Family Practice physician from another television commercial.

Dr. Alfredo Aparicio, a Urology specialist, noted that in one Kaiser ad, "I actually got the pleasure of working with an actress who was 80 years-old, her first name was May, she had been an MGM starlet, she had been in John Wayne's first movie, she had been acting since the thirties...her experience was just incredible...and she was trying to convey all these feelings of relief as I was giving her all the news she was in good health."[19]

Pediatrician Woods was featured in one heart-warming advertisement signing a little girl's cast with a drawing of a heart. "This little girl I just worked with had just completed a movie with Danny Devito," recounted Woods. "I thought she would come in and we would sign one cast. Instead, there were seven or eight casts made. We did this reenactment seven or eight times. I think more than the actual signing of the cast what was important in this commercial was to see the rapport the pediatrician had with the patient and that it wasn't just checking the circulation and the fingers but it was, Tell me about how this happened on the playground, and Tell me about summer camp."[20]

On the employee training video, Kaiser Advertising Director Denise Daversa made it clear what they were after with these commercials: "We have learned that personalized care translates to the general consumer in terms of relief of anxiety and respect."[21]

Americans are barraged by advertising all day long. But do consumers get lulled into complacency about their health care when they cannot afford to be?

Has Kaiser crossed the line from merely misleading advertising? Or did it just fail to comprehend the chasm between an image purchased at over $60 million annually and reality? Maybe the designers of Kaiser's ads didn't know of Chad Aitken or Colin McCafferey. Additional evidence indicates that Kaiser should have known its advertising was misleading at a minimum.

First, in addition to the internal Kaiser-produced video tape, "Kaiser Permanente On The Air Finally...The Personalized Care Campaign," Kaiser also produced a video that made crystal clear the reality for patients. Entitled "Straight Talk From Members," it contains interviews with frustrated patients who fume about the lack of personal care at Kaiser and the bureaucratic nightmares they endured. The same people who produced the commercials appear to have interviewed these patients. Remarks from real Kaiser patients, captured by Kaiser video makers, paint a portrait dramatically opposed to those broadcast through the HMO commercials.

One interview puts the lie to the slogan of personalized, physician-driven care.

"I came in today for an appointment today...I received a card in the mail...I came today...The receptionist...said class? She said this was not a prenatal class date. That I had to go through a prenatal class until I could see a doctor. My concern is that I am going into eight months of pregnancy.

I was here a few weeks ago because I had a severe asthma attack where I had cracked some ribs and I started to go into labor. Doctor ___ called me at home to set up an appointment to see him. The nurse told me I could not just see him, that I had to go through prenatal classes...I have a history of high-risk pregnancies. My concern is I have been having cramps a lot, that I am going to go into labor and deliver this baby before I even get in to see the physician...This is not the first time I have talked to the nurses. Their attitude is very abrasive. They will not let me see any physician no matter what until I have these classes. This is my third pregnancy. I think I know what I am doing. I really, really would like to see a physician because my asthma is flaring up...but with ___ it is getting worse.."

What about the advertised image of caring?

"I had to wait six months to get my own doctor. Then I saw my doctor just once. Then she was on maternity leave. Then when I got to see her again she was so overbooked with patients she didn't have the time to really listen to what I had to say. I even told her I had a pain in my side. She told me that if I did not have that pain all the time, not to worry about it. But I'm worried about it. It comes and goes and it does hurt."

Understanding?

"Any time you come in they act like it is a machine. This is the way they do things and they don't vary from that routine. Not one iota, no matter what. You just fit in however, or they don't provide services. I have had several nightmare experiences here when I have been unable to get care."

Trust?

Trust is one quality Kaiser seeks to attach to its reputation. "It's fifty years of attracting physicians from top medical schools and giving them the opportunity to practice medicine without being second guessed by an insurance company," says one commercial. This sentiment is echoed in another advertisement: "They are the kind of people you will find at Kaiser Permanente. Physicians who have chosen to work here where they can focus on your care rather than on the cares of running a business. Where they can practice medicine without someone else calling the shots."

A second piece of damning evidence suggests that Kaiser knew well the disparity between image and reality. Illuminated by an Austin, Texas lawsuit, a transcription of a December 1995 speech refutes Kaiser's claim on trust. It reveals the lack of autonomy physicians have and the mentality of corporate cost-cutting at Kaiser. In the speech, a Kaiser executive boasted to other HMO managers how Kaiser executives always put the bottom line first. A plan to cut hospital costs by 30% was drafted when he and a colleague were drinking heavily during a delayed flight from San Jose to Dallas that stopped in Los Angeles. Kaiser's Resources Management Director in Texas, Dr. John Vogt, celebrated how whiskey was a wonderful tool for honing the bottom line:

> "I am a light chardonnay drinker. But the stuff that you're going to see in terms of the 1995 plan was generated in June on a Friday afternoon when Jim and I, I think—I don't know how many Wild Turkeys on the Rocks I had, and he's Irish...so, he had Irish Whiskey, and we're flying over L.A. trying to land...a two hour, fifty-minute flight is now going to be seven-and-a-half or eight hours and we're going to get in at 1 o'clock in the morning."[22]

During his speech, Vogt boasted about the HMO's true, cynical inner workings:

- "The first thing that ever comes out of a Kaiser CEO now is what's the bottom line. I'm trained to do that now almost automatically."

- "How many of you who are in utilization management are beaten on all the time when your CEOs walk in and say PANIC...hospital utilization went through the roof last week...The initial approach that we used in early 1994 is what we affectionately call 'tap dancing.'...when we are still unsatisfactory in terms of getting down to our goal, he came and tap danced and he was one of those panicky people...anytime it went up he came and tap danced on me. I had to go and get some shoulder pads."

- "Our urgent care doctors, you know, were having patients come in and see them and they would look at them and say, 'You need to be in the hospital.' And the adult physician on call would come in and say, 'You don't need to be in the hospital.' The member says, 'Whoa, I am not feeling well. I think I'd rather pay attention to the UCC doctor.' We basically said to the UCC doctors, 'If you value your job, you won't say anything about hospitalization.' All you say is, 'I think you need further evaluation and Dr. Schmoe is going to come in and talk to you.'"

- "Early neonatal discharge program [of pre-term newborns]...They can go home at 1800 grams. So, what we'll be doing in 1996 is implementing an earlier discharge of these pre-term infants."

Physicians felt the implementation of such tactics on the ground—and didn't like it. A January 1996 e-mailed letter from fifty-six Kaiser Permanente doctors called for the ouster of the executive director of the Northern California Permanente Medical Group over "drastic" cost-cutting and "sweeping changes...that negatively affect patients and staff." The physicians claimed medical rationing sacrificed the "caregiver-patient relationship," cut front-line medical staff while doubling the number of high-paid administrators, and took medical decision-making power out of the hands of doctors.[23] Do they care about image versus reality?

The discontent expressed by physicians in the e-mailed memo about the depersonalization of care at Kaiser could not be isolated and had to be known by the corporate designers of Kaiser's commercials.

According to the physicians' letter:

> "Changes have become mandated, and the results of pilot programs are ignored in making sweeping changes (e.g. call centers) that negatively affect the patients and the staff. How will we finally know when a critical level of reduced quality has been reached, and will it then be too late?
>
> "Losses of large numbers of front-line personnel such as dedicated advice nurses, nurses, medical assistants…[while] we have doubled the number of administrative [sic] exempt employees at the highest pay scales…
>
> "Physicians are facing increasing scrutiny of every decision we make, yet administrators are not held to the same expectations for accountability…We need an executive director who views the caregiver-patient relationship as the most valuable asset we offer.
>
> "We have been told that to become the best program that exists, we must build the best computer system available—somehow these systems will make up for the numbers of persons no longer available to provide human contact."

Is this the Kaiser system portrayed in its advertising?

Heather Aitken expressed it this way: "We feel the takeover of the medical profession by HMO administrators is a threat to the health and safety of everyone—young and old."

Of course, Kaiser is not the only HMO with deceptive advertising. Because Kaiser houses its hospital and physicians under one roof, it is easier to trace the internal problems. The fact that the nation's last big non-profit HMO has engaged in such duplicity says a great deal about the widespread misrepresentations by for-profit heath care companies.

Advertising is not the only arena which diverges from reality, and Kaiser is not the only organization engaged in selling image over reality.

Kiddie Scams/Easy Marks

Keya Johnson and her family received their health care from various clinics and doctors. Eligible for public medical assistance, Johnson and her family had previously paid for their health care with a sticker from plastic Medi-Cal cards—one for each service provided the family. If they did not like the care, they could simply go to another doctor who took the stickers. During her pregnancy, an HMO salesman showed up at her door making promises. By enrolling her in an HMO, the public assistance money that pays her health care would go to the HMO. "I was told I would get better care," said Johnson. "I would have one doctor...that I would no longer have to pay for medicine...that if I needed [transportation] to the doctor, it would be provided."

The solicitor's promises fell apart as soon as Johnson signed up for CIGNA Health Care of California, an HMO. CIGNA would "manage" all of the Johnsons' treatment within its own network of doctors, hospitals and clinics.

Under CIGNA's management of her care, Keya Johnson was never assigned the physician she said she was promised. Instead, a physician's assistant, who received less training than a nurse practitioner, became her primary caregiver. During her extraordinarily difficult pregnancy, Johnson gained eighty pounds and the fetus weighed more than twelve pounds. Despite these clear danger signs, no doctor was assigned to her high-risk case. During the grueling and painful delivery, Johnson's son was stuck in the birth canal for thirteen minutes and emerged, according to medical records, "blue and limp...without any pulse or respiratory effort." No doctor was provided and no Caesarean section performed.[24]

Keya's son, Adrian Broughton, had to be resuscitated. His left arm was paralyzed.

Johnson contends not only that the brain damage her son Adrian suffered was the result of CIGNA's cost-cutting, but that she was defrauded—promised high quality health care by an HMO solicitor and forced to endure a preventable, medical horror story. Increasingly, consumers are promised high quality health care, lulled into a false sense of security, and end up injured.

CIGNA points out that it no longer enrolls Medicaid recipients in California. The company claims that Adrian Broughton's case is simply a medical negligence claim and that "when the matter is finally adjudicated and a decision rendered, the finding will be in favor of the health plan." If Johnson's allegations are true, it is fraud—which is why the California Court of Appeal said Johnson could pursue her deceptive business practices claim outside of an arbitration agreement which normally prevents patients from suing. CIGNA would have breached its part of the contract by not living up to its promises. (As of this writing in June 1999, CIGNA has appealed to the California Supreme Court, which accepted review of the case.)

The for-profit corporations managing our care have broken their contract with all of us—by promising accessible care and then forcing too many of us to fight for every service when we are sick and least able to fend for ourselves.

But how can you condemn an entire system based on one or two or one thousand or twenty thousand patients' bad experiences with managed care? CIGNA, in this example, claims that Keya Johnson's experience is anecdotal and aberrational. But the assumptions and conditions which thread the nightmare experiences of managed care casualties are always consistent— the company intentionally promises the moon in order to maximize its profits. The system is based on a lie that is perpetuated daily by HMO advertising, marketing and public representations—that patients come first and profits do not even enter into the equation.

How can one door-to-door salesman be held up as the paragon of a problem? Unfortunately, the CIGNA solicitor that approached Keya Johnson was no rogue operator. He is part of a core of HMO-backed hustlers preying upon low-income residents for the lucrative trade in "covered lives," as patients are called at HMOs. Both the company and its agent profit when another "head" is signed up because the HMO is paid a lump sum by the government for each "head" regardless of how much care it provides. With this so called "capitated" rate, the less medical care the HMO provides, the more it profits. When it comes time to live up to its promises, too often patients like Adrian Broughton pay the price. The price raises disturbing moral questions: Should financial profiteering ever cause preventable injuries? Should human health ever be priced out of existence, if there is a preventable and financially feasible way to preserve it?

In the door-to-door solicitation game—a microcosm of the industry's pitch to us all for its continued survival—CIGNA is only one offender. Foundation Health's deceptive door-to-door marketing campaign to Medi-Cal recipients has been a well-documented scourge on low-income communities. More than one hundred San Francisco Medi-Cal patients told the City's Department of Public Health that they were lied to or deceived by Foundation agents about the health care they would receive if they joined the plan, then denied access to that care once enrolled. The scandal grew so bad it prompted San Francisco's Department of Public Health to call for an end to Foundation's door-to-door marketing campaign.[25]

Just as Adrian Broughton suffered for CIGNA's profit, kids like Albert and Michael Rochin would pay for Foundation's. According to the Rochin family's lawsuit, Foundation Health's door-to-door solicitor met Albert and Michael's mother, Monica, at her stoop. He was sent into Monica's neighborhood because a large number of non-English speaking Medi-Cal recipients resided there. Monica declined to convert her family's Medi-Cal to the managed care plan because Michael and Albert had very special medical needs. She told the HMO salesman that her children had asthma and Michael was on a special milk and under the care of a specialist since his birth.

Monica's nightmare began when she tried to re-order the special milk for Michael. She was denied the milk and informed that her family was no longer covered by Medi-Cal, but by Foundation Health. The pharmacy told Monica that Foundation would not pay for Michael's special milk as Medi-Cal had in the past. According to the family's lawsuit, this abrupt shift happened, Monica learned later, because the salesman had forged her signature on a Foundation enrollment form.

Because six month-old Michael was unable to obtain his special milk, he became very ill with breathing problems, diarrhea, and a severe rash. Michael's Medi-Cal physician was unable to treat him because of the unauthorized enrollment. Worse, because of Michael's heart condition, Foundation Health's physician allegedly refused to treat Michael without records from his previous treating physician.

Albert, Monica's two year-old, suffered from chronic asthma, and required regular breathing treatments and medication. Without treatment, Albert became ill with a very high temperature and for the first time suffered a seizure. Foundation assured Monica they would disenroll her, but it would take some time to get her back on Medi-Cal. According to the family, Foundation ignored the Medi-Cal procedures that allowed it to expedite the processing of the disenrollment request and that would have restored the family's Medi-Cal status within two to three days. Instead, Foundation delayed processing Monica's urgent disenrollment request for over three months. Foundation's "excuse" was that it needed to investigate Monica's forgery claim. According to her lawsuit, which resulted in a settlement, Monica believed that Albert's seizure activity was the direct result of the lack of adequate medical care caused by Foundation's unauthorized enrollment of her family and its delay in restoring the family's Medi-Cal enrollment status.[26]

Reports of patients duped and pressured by Foundation's fast-talking sales people were so pervasive that public interest organizations filed a lawsuit against Foundation for "deceptive and abusive marketing practices."[27] There were also serious problems in Florida for the company.[28]

In their treatment of our children, Foundation, CIGNA and other HMOs have failed the test.

The modus operandi is clear: treat patients like easy marks—say anything, do anything, to get patients "in." Once they are in, don't deliver. Once patients are "in," as Monica Rochin's story shows, it is often difficult to get "out."

Plastered on billboards, on television, in magazines, at bus stops is a company logo next to what is usually a wholesome picture of a smiling American family with a healthy child in their arms. The values at the heart of the managed care system are not the family values portrayed in HMO advertising. Too frequently, the lives of children and their parents are handled with callous indifference. Too often, a goal of for-profit managed care is merely profit. Both social and private promises are broken.

Killing Them with Fine Print

Riverside, California resident Sara Israel rolls her eyes when she sees Health Net's billboards and advertising promoting the HMO's commitment to keep families healthy and well—part of a big advertising push to promote the HMO as a "family wellness" provider. "They were not there for me," says Israel, a kindergarten teacher. "I just felt it was a lot of PR. There was no backing to the promises."

Israel was denied benefits for the birth of her son in April 1994 because she was sixty-nine miles from her HMO's doctors group—even though she delivered at a Health Net facility.

According to the fine print in Health Net's policy, women were prevented from traveling more than thirty miles from their HMO's doctors group once they are eight months or more pregnant. The fine print was not in the "pregnancy" section of the coverage contract, but in the "emergency" section. In fact, Israel did not know of the provision until after the birth when Health Net denied payment of her $5,000 hospital bill. Perhaps assuaged by Health Net's feel-good advertising, Israel says, even then, "I was sure the HMO would come through for me. I felt that I had delivered at a facility that took Health Net and I had contacted my home clinic within forty-eight hours and, as soon as I got this letter denying this payment of bills I made a call to customer relations. She assured me that they would pay. It was an emergency. I could not make it back to the regular hospital."

But, Israel says, "Even though I appealed it and had gone through all their steps, Health Net still denied the bills twice. I spent my entire summer trying to get it cleared. I got bills. I had to tell the hospital they would get paid. I continued to get my bills. Day after day I would be making calls. I would tell the story over again. I put it in a letter. It was just the same letter of denial again and again. It was just a very cold letter. After all I had tried to do to take care of it, it was the same letter back to me. I knew I was being treated unjustly."

When Sara went to see an attorney, she found out that she could not take Health Net to court to recover the cost of the bills because her Health Net contract forced her into binding arbitration.

"I hadn't paid attention to that fine print either," said Israel. "You don't know these things until you are in the middle of these things. They say arbitration is quick, but it took a long time. It took from February of 1995 to December 1996 until a decision was made. It was long and drawn out. I was given the impression the process would be quick."

While Israel ultimately forced the HMO to pay her bills, she asked the arbitrator for damages to cover her time, energy and the HMO's bad faith. She waited a year before losing her claims. Ultimately, Israel's fight changed Health Net's policy—but the company, like other HMOs, is constantly searching for "exclusions" to its contacts. They know that delay will not cost them much, so they stonewall.

This is the heart of the indictment against HMOs and managed care companies. They publicly profess that they value caring and delivering treatment, but the universal tendency—the core rule of their business—is to delay and deny at a great cost to the patient and a substantial savings for themselves.

Should we have to fight with HMOs and managed care companies for care they promised, marketed and contracted for? Are HMOs lying outright to us about their intentions and practices? How do they get away with it?

Most patients simply do not use their HMOs. Companies can produce patient satisfaction surveys showing popular contentment, because they poll their patients who are healthy—those who rarely use the HMO—not the sick and chronically ill patients who actually need treatment. HMOs must be judged by how well they treat the ill. These most vulnerable patients are the ones who know all too well the managed care mantra of deny and delay—the stonewalling of services that the companies know they *should* provide, but do not until they are pushed. The companies know many people will give up and even the tenacious consumer, who receives benefits, will do so only after the HMO's money has more time in the capital markets.

The "Not A Covered Benefit" Ruse

Another artful means of lowering costs is to deny that care is covered under a plan, resulting in an increasing bone of contention between patients with chronic illnesses and HMOs.

Entire illnesses now fall outside of coverage categories. Autism, for instance, is medically known to be a biologically-based brain disorder. Because HMOs cannot restrict coverage of illness resulting from biological disease, many HMOs classify autism as a mental illness—so that it falls under a coverage exception—according to activists at the autism associations.

Any pervasive developmental brain disorder that is neurological in nature constitutes a "biologically based brain disorder" according to the medical experts. California Insurance Code Section 10123.15 spells out that insurance companies must cover biologically-based brain disorders and developmental disorders like autism. HMOs, however, are not regulated by the California Insurance Department. To avoid paying for treatment, they have reclassified autism as a mental illness, essentially rewriting the rules of medical science. Many insurers, until they are challenged by an autism association, also do this.

Autism is not the only condition where HMOs have cut back on coverage through reclassification. HMOs have tried to claim that breast reconstruction is outside policy limits, characterizing it as a cosmetic surgery, even *after* a mastectomy for breast cancer. Operations for birth defects, such as a baby born with one ear or a cleft palate, are also being denied under the cosmetic surgery exclusion. "It used to be that if you were born with something deforming, or were in an accident and had bad scars, the surgery performed to fix the problem was considered reconstructive surgery," said Dr. Henry Kawamoto, a surgeon at UCLA. "Now, insurers of many kinds are calling it cosmetic surgery and refusing to pay for it."[29]

HMOs, which promise families full-service protection in their advertising, also drastically limit coverage for conditions such as anorexia, bulimia and other eating disorders. While anorexia frequently requires years to treat effectively, as well as months of hospitalization, HMOs often have a $10,000 cap on treatment. Other HMOs apply a $30,000 lifetime cap, which translates to fewer than thirty days of inpatient care. For the five million women and young girls who suffer annually from an eating disorder, HMO medicine's message is one that is never advertised. "If you've got diabetes, no problem. If you've got anorexia—big problem," said Dr. Hans Steiner, co-director of the Eating Disorders Program at Lucile Packard Children's Health Services at Stanford University. Steiner has noticed "astonishing" changes in how anorexia patients fared in recent years with HMO medicine's growth.[30] National Public Radio reported that in the mid-1980s the average hospitalization for an eating disorder patient was between two and seven months, but managed care companies only cover hospital stays that "range from ten days over the patients' lifetimes to ten to thirty days per year."[31]

For years, HMOs covered impotence, *until* there was a cure. Kaiser and other HMOs announced in June of 1998 that they would not cover Viagra, even though their contracts with consumers included coverage for impotence. The State of California had to force Kaiser to cover the drug.[32] While there is certainly recreational use of the drug, it is a temporary cure for impotence.

HMOs accept risk when they contract for coverage, they should not be able to dump risk when treatments are developed to cure a disease.

Promises, Promises...

Foundation Health's problems are disturbingly similar to its competitor, Kaiser. Its marketing is similarly alluring: "When you need us, we'll be there. The things in life that count the most are things that can't be counted. A smile, a hug, a healthy mind and body. Employers and families depend on Foundation Health to be there when it counts. Foundation Health. When you need us, we'll be there."[33] Yet its record is a disaster:

- Widespread marketing abuses, such as those that put Albert and Michael Rochin in peril.

- The *Sacramento Bee* reports Foundation's relationship with its physicians "has been strained at best, outright hostile at worst—an erosion begun over a decade ago by complaints of 'low pay, slow pay and no pay.'"[34]

- When a patient needs Foundation doctors to level with them, they cannot. Foundation's agreement with physicians requires the doctors "keep strictly confidential all compensation agreements," so that patients do not know the financial pressures to deny health care.[35]

In financial communities, Foundation is known as a moneymaker at the expense of medical ethics. As a Dow Jones Wire Service commentator noted, "When it comes to pressuring doctors, dentists and hospitals to cut their bills, few outfits measure up to Foundation Health." The commentator, Bill Alpert, continued, "How has Foundation maintained its profit margins while competitors faltered? By keeping a firm hand on medical costs, for one thing. So firm, in fact, that some doctor groups lose money working for Foundation, and must borrow large chunks of money from the HMO to survive."[36]

Listen to the soothing words of PacifiCare, based in Cypress, California, in advertising in the *Los Angeles Times*:

"If experience has taught us anything over the years, it's that *no one should have to settle for less*. Well, when it comes to health care, things aren't any different...Secure Horizons offered by PacifiCare. [And in a separate 1999 ad] Secure Horizons offers: Unlimited Annual Pharmacy Benefit • Unlimited Generic Medications • Unlimited Brand Name Medications [emphasis added]"[37]

But PacifiCare's approved drug list exchanges effective high-cost, antipsychotic drugs such as the schizophrenia drugs Risperdal and Prozac, with less effective, but cheaper, alternatives. PacifiCare's formulary replaces Risperdal, which is recommended by the American Psychiatric Association and the National Alliance for the Mentally Ill, with Haldol, a cheap, older generation drug with severe side effects that include uncontrollable shaking and restlessness. While a thirty-day supply of Risperdal costs about $240, the same supply of Haldol is $2.50.[38]

Or take another managed care company, Aetna, whose "Informed Health" advertisements claim:

"THE MORE YOU KNOW THE BETTER YOU FEEL. When you have health questions, you want answers. You want to know about all of your options. You want info, info, and a little more info. Okay. Introducing Informed Health from Aetna Health Plans."[39]

In 1996 Aetna merged with U.S. Healthcare, whose agreement with physicians included the following gag clauses:

"Physician shall keep the Proprietary Information [payment rates, utilization review procedures, etc.] and this Agreement strictly confidential."

"Physician shall agree not to take any action or make any communication which undermines or could undermine the confidence of enrollees, potential enrollees, their employers, their unions, or the public in U.S. Healthcare or the quality of U.S. Healthcare coverage."

Such disparagement clauses prevent a physician from alerting patients and the public to unsafe medical practices.

Did such gag clauses continue in force after the merger? The American Medical Association (AMA) noted in a February 1998 letter to Aetna CEO Richard Huber the "presence of a 'gag clause.' While you state that 'Aetna U.S. Healthcare opposes gag clauses and our contracts contain anti-gag clauses,' this is flatly contradicted by the language of the contract. Provision 1.2 prohibits the physician from 'imply(ing) to Members that their care or access to care will be inferior due to the source of payment.' It is disingenuous to deny that this clause functions as a 'gag clause.' As we have already indicated, this clause could easily be interpreted to bar a physician from informing a patient that the treatment that he/she recommends is not covered by the plan even though the physician believes that it is medically necessary. The AMA is aware of other plans that have threatened to terminate physicians for precisely this type of communication, and there is nothing in the Aetna contract to assure against this occurring."[40]

In December 1998, the Texas Attorney General named six HMOs in a lawsuit charging them with rewarding physicians for withholding care. Four of the six HMOs are owned by Aetna. The Attorney General also charged, according to *The Dallas Morning News*, that Aetna "penalizes doctors who speak frankly with patients about the insurer's coverage."[41]

Ultimately, in October 1998, after a public outcry, Aetna U.S. Healthcare announced that it was altering its contracts to "emphasize our opposition to gag clauses" and other "protections for our members."

On January 18, 1999 the AMA confirmed that the new contracts were riddled with other problems including, "mandat[ing] the 'least costly' treatment alternative" so that the contractual definition of medically necessary services is "the least costly of alternative supplies or levels of service." In February 1999, the AMA also complained about Aetna's right under its contract to unilaterally amend all terms of its contracts with physicians without any requirement to notify physicians. According to the AMA, this allows the HMO to "impose barriers to care in order to ratchet down medical expenses, especially if it is under financial pressure to meet shareholder expectations."[42]

In this historical light, consider Aetna's other advertising and marketing claims.

A print advertisement in the *Columbus Dispatch* on April 3, 1996 represents: "We will encourage strong patient/physician relationships in which all health care information—including treatment options—is freely shared."

Aetna U.S. Healthcare's certificate of coverage promises "Participating Physicians maintain the physician-patient relationship with Members and are solely responsible to Members for all Member Services."

Aetna's advertisement in the *Wall Street Journal* on October 29, 1997 says, "First of all, the paramount focus of health care must be quality. It should be the only reason we're in this business—to help raise the quality of care."

Aetna's advertisements to Medicare recipients claim: "The way it works is that they [the government] give us 95% of what they would normally pay out on Medicare and, in exchange, we provide the coverage. The condition is that we have to provide at least as much coverage they do. The reality is that we are able to provide quite a lot more. We do it by reducing administration costs, which are a huge part of today's health care costs, and using the savings to increase the benefits we offer."[43]

In reality, Medicare administration for fee-for-service patients has a 2% overhead cost.[44] Aetna's overhead cost—administration, marketing, profit, executive compensation—accounts for roughly 20% of the premium dollar paid to the HMO. In 1995, Aetna spent only 81.4% of its revenue on medical care, and in 1994 only 77.4% on medical services.[45]

California-based Inter Valley Health Plan advertises in its billboards:

> "They treat you like a person, not a number. They go the extra mile to help. We not only care for you, we care about you. We get excellent doctors and hospitals."[46]

In July 1997, an arbitrator ruled against Inter Valley in the case of a Medicare patient with kidney cancer who was denied care by the HMO. This was the judge's characterization of the HMO's behavior: "The actions of the defendants are not capable of any rational explanation. The refusal of authorizations, the delays, the lack of timely notice to plaintiff are unconscionable...The facts present a compelling picture of the problems and pitfalls of what has come to be called 'managed care'."[47]

Unfortunately, those who HMOs aggressively market to, then fail most frequently, are the most vulnerable among us. Worse, it is not just those whose money is tight that are the targets of this pernicious salesmanship, but any group of people for whom the government pays a portion of health costs—including older people.

Senior Scam

Seniors are among the most lucrative "lives" that an HMO can cover. In urban areas, HMOs are paid approximately $500 per month for every patient in their plan regardless of whether or not medical services are provided to them. The companies go to incredible lengths to market to the healthier seniors, making bold promises, sending out so-called "senior ambassadors" who themselves are senior citizens paid to sell HMO programs like Amway sells soap. But when it comes time to deliver on that care, seniors are often given short shrift.

Angered by what he perceived to be deceptive advertising, New York City Public Advocate Mark Green referred a half dozen HMO ads in 1995 to the New York State Attorney General and the New York City Department of Consumer Affairs, saying that "For some HMOs, the letters stand for 'Hyping Medicine to the Old'."[48] Among the ads, Elderplan Inc. claimed it has "The $0 Premium Health Plan," when the elderly are actually charged a monthly premium of $46.10. Another ad from Oxford Health directed at seniors claimed "Oxford Health Plans is No.1"—but the plan referred to in the ad is not open to the elderly.

An earlier investigation by New York state Health Department investigators, posing as enrollees, exposed a new sort of fraud—they had problems getting appointments with doctors at thirteen of eighteen HMOs.[49]

This "bait and switch," where prospective enrollees are promised new health care benefits that fail to materialize is increasingly common. HMOs, for instance, attract Medicare recipients with promises of free eyeglasses, prescription drugs, dental care and other items that traditional Medicare will not pay for. But once seniors join the HMO, the inducements they were marketed dry up.

In 1998, premium increases or benefits cutbacks were announced by Medicare HMOs in California, Maryland, New Jersey, Pennsylvania, New York and other states. Only three months after Coalinga, California resident Mike Megarian, 81, signed up for California Blue Cross to "save ourselves some money and get the benefits," Blue Cross ended his free drugs, eye glasses and dental care benefits, and required a $65 monthly premium. "We let our good policy go and signed up with this," Megarian said. "We didn't think that after three months they were going to start raising prices."[50] Megarian's complaint is an increasingly serious one. Once patients sign up for HMOs and terminate secure Medigap policies designed to cover what Medicare will not, it is cost-prohibitive to buy a new Medigap policy when their HMOs go back on their word. Once seniors that have paid into these policies for years abandon them, the Medigap insurers are all too happy to keep the premiums and dump the aging patient.

Federal investigators at the General Accounting Office (GAO) reported in April 1999 that HMOs routinely give false and inaccurate descriptions of costs and benefits to Medicare recipients.[51] The GAO reviewed documents from sixteen HMOs and concluded that there were "significant errors and omissions." For instance, some HMO materials said that women needed a referral from a doctor to receive a mammogram, but federal rules do not allow this. Another GAO report on the same day found Medicare HMOs often do not tell patients that they can appeal HMO denials of services.

HMOs not only mislead consumers and break promises, but, because these companies can keep for themselves every dollar they take in that is not spent on the patient, they also shun the sick in favor of soliciting the well. HMO senior ambassadors give their pitches at shuffleboard centers, bridge clubs, golf club houses—places frequented by healthy seniors, not the chronically ill. HMOs and insurance companies have been caught red-handed in this process of "cherry-picking" seniors whose health costs are likely to be lowest. This shifts a heavy burden onto the fee-for-service system that must cope with a disproportionate number of sicker patients.

In 1997 the GAO spelled out the costs of cherry-picking to the taxpayer when it concluded that the Medicare program paid HMOs $1 billion more than it should have because HMOs enroll people who are healthier than the typical Medicare recipient.[52] Later that same year, the GAO found that "new HMO enrollees tended to be the least costly." Whatever the burden on the taxpayer, the fate of the sick was worse. The GAO stated that "the rates of early disenrollment from HMOs to FFS [fee for service] were substantially higher among those with chronic conditions,"[53] meaning the sick were forced out. Moreover, the GAO found that as enrollment grows, the problems increase.

Just how bad is this tendency for the sick to be disenrolled? One out of every five Medicare HMOs had disenrollment rates above 20% in 1996. Most of the enrollees left because of problems receiving medical treatment.[54] In stark contrast to the images presented in advertising and marketing, the ill elderly are running into so many obstacles that they are literally being forced out of HMOs.

In late 1998, Medicare HMOs began dropping out of counties where they felt their reimbursements were not high enough or their costs too high. While urban seniors were attractive to enroll at about $500 per month per head, caring for those with health care problems can be expensive. When HMOs could cherry pick the best risks among the older Americans, the companies set enrollment records. When the cherry picking was no longer so simple or tolerated, the HMOs suddenly pulled out, dumping their elderly patients, particularly in rural areas. As mentioned earlier, while the patients can get Medicare, any earlier Medigap policies which they left behind when they enrolled at the HMO are available only at a prohibitive price.

As of October 1998, three dozen private health plans that participate in Medicare said they would not renew their contracts in 1999.[55] HMOs withdrew from more than 300 counties in at least twenty-two states. The pull-outs directly impacted more than 400,000 Americans—one out of every fifteen beneficiaries enrolled in HMOs.[56] In 1999, of the 39 million Medicare beneficiaries who are elderly or disabled, 18%, or 7 million, were covered by an HMO.[57]

Fifty thousand Medicare beneficiaries were left without an HMO option for health care, according to President Clinton, who condemned the exodus of HMOs from the Medicare market.

"We expanded the number and type of health plans available to Medicare beneficiaries, so that older Americans, like other Americans, would have more choices in their Medicare," said Clinton in October of 1998. "I think it ought to be said, in defense of this decision and the enrollment of many seniors in managed care plans, that one of the principal reasons that so many seniors wanted it is that there were managed care plans who thought for the reimbursement then available they could provide not only the required services under Medicare, but also a prescription drug benefit.

"Well, today there are 6-1/2 million Medicare beneficiaries in HMOs. As we all know, in recent weeks the HMO industry announced that unless all Medicare HMOs could raise premiums and reduce benefits—all—some health plans would drop their Medicare patients by the end of the year. We told them, 'No deal.' That's what we should have done. We were not going to allow Medicare to be held hostage to unreasonable demands. So, several HMOs decided to drop their patients. These decisions have brought uncertainty, fear and disruption into the lives of tens of thousands of older Americans.

"Now these HMOs say they are looking after the bottom line...We were asked just to give all HMOs permission to raise rates whether they need to or not without regard to how much money they were making or not, and I think that was wrong,"[58] Clinton concluded.

In 1999, the HMOs' demands increased. On July 2, 1999, the *New York Times* reported Medicare HMOs will raise premiums or reduce benefits for most of their senior enrollees, and at least 250,000 Medicare patients will be dumped by their HMOs because the companies will no longer provide service in their area unless the HMOs are paid more.

HMOs have, indeed, turned into fair-weather friends to taxpayers and Medicare recipients. False promises are not atypical for this industry.

Hundreds of millions of dollars spent annually on advertising paints a far more secure and pleasing portrait of our health care system than truly exists. How can they get away with it? While the answers will be explored in more detail in later chapters, it is clear that managed care companies and HMOs are pursuing profit with a vengeance.

Double Jeopardy: What is "Medically Necessary"?

In advertising, HMOs emphasize blanket protection and security. Yet before courts and legislatures, HMOs argue that they are not full-fledged insurers and they have limited responsibility for the provision of medically-necessary care within their coverage areas. To patients in need of treatment, HMOs say that "medically necessary" does not mean what the doctor, or traditional insurance, orders.

Ten year-old twins in Covina, California show just how narrowly the term "medically necessary" can be defined. Since birth, Steven and Bradley Sarver have had rare sleeping disorders similar to "crib death" called sleep apnea (cessation of breathing) and bradycardia (slowing of the heart rate). They are in constant danger of dying in their sleep as their heart beats slow like clocks winding down and their breathing stops. Since the condition affects the body only during sleep, and Steven and Bradley could die or suffer permanent brain damage as a result of just one of these events, the boys need professional home-nursing care, as well as sophisticated medical monitoring equipment. The home-nursing care prevented the boys from being hospitalized full-time and has enabled them to attend regular school and participate in most normal activities of children their age. But Blue Shield, a managed care company that offered the Sarvers a preferred provider option (PPO) plan, denied critical in-home nighttime nursing care, deeming it "not medically necessary." The same treatment was previously covered as "medically necessary" by their traditional indemnity insurer.

The entire cost of the boys' home-nursing care and treatment until October of 1993 was covered by their father's traditional group health insurance plan through the City of Beverly Hills. The problems arose when the Police Department changed to Blue Shield. The boy's medical condition did not change—only their insurance company was "arranging" for their care, rather than indemnifying them against illness, a critical shift in service under "managed care."

Steven and Bradley's treating physician, a preferred provider who was approved by the new managed care company, insisted that the boys' care was medically necessary, and ordered that the boys have professional home nursing care. However, the company continued to deny coverage for the boys' treatment until a lawsuit was filed. In March of 1994, the Sarvers won a preliminary injunction forcing the health plan to pay for the twins' care until their trial was complete, and the company ultimately settled the case.[59]

Blue Shield's shield didn't cover Linda Sarver's children any more than Health Net's net caught Sara Israel during her pregnancy, Foundation supported Monica Rochin's twins, or CIGNA lived up to its word for Adrian Broughton.

If how well children and seniors are treated is a critical indication of any system's worth, then many managed care companies are failing our nation.

How secure, then, are patients in Secure Horizons? How healthy are Health Net's enrollees? Do Prucare patients really have a piece of the rock? Is Humana humane? Nowhere is managed care's pernicious downsizing more a threat to patients or communities than in hospitals across the nation, where seriously ill patients are supposed to be cared for. It is this transformed landscape of hospitalization that we examine next.

CHAPTER THREE

The Death of Community Health Care And Hospitals

Two year-old Steven Olsen had one of those routine accidents that can happen to any child. He fell on a rotted tree branch while playing in the woods. A doctor had to remove a twig that went in his mouth and punctured his cheek and sinus. But a few days later, Steven grew feverish and lethargic. Twice, his parents, Kathy and Scott Olsen brought him to the urgent care doctor. Kathy told the medical staff, "Something is very wrong with Steven." But twice the urgent care staff told her not to worry. By then, Steven was rubbing his forehead, barely awake. On the third visit, Steven was finally admitted to the HMO-approved hospital, where Mrs. Olsen asked the medical staff, "Please do a CT scan."

A few years ago, under traditional, fee-for-service medicine, Steven would have gotten that scan. But Steven got his health care under the family's "managed care" HMO plan, as do 90% of those Californians fortunate enough to have insurance. The doctors and hospitals which contract with the HMOs know that every penny they spend on patients like Steven comes out of their own pockets, subtracted from the monthly per-patient fee paid them by the tightfisted HMOs.

So Steven's doctors told his parents a scan was unnecessary, ignoring his mother's concerns, and saving all of $800 the test would have cost. Three days later, the boy fell into a coma. The cause was a brain abscess. Expert physicians testified that had Steven received the scan when requested, he

Steven Olsen

would be perfectly healthy today. The abscess could have been easily detected by a scan and then successfully treated.[1]

Today, Steven has cerebral palsy, is blind and subject to seizures if he does not receive his medicine in a timely way. Steven and his parents face a lifetime of expensive tests and treatments. Steven Olsen is a symbol for the death of caution under HMO medicine.[2]

Hospitals were once the centers—literally cradles—of communities, centers of medical excellence where the injured were rushed to be mended and the emergency room was always open. The community hospital was the refuge for the patient in crisis. It was the last bastion of an ever vigilant society: always open, always ready to aid, the best of civil society and America's Good Samaritan spirit.

Hospitals defined communities, centered them, anchored them. Babies were born there and grandparents died there. Communities fundraised for their local hospital. Religious orders helped finance them. Today, for-profit outside corporations—not community or medical ethics—often control the hospital. The contrast is stark.

The most visible manifestation is the so-called "drive-thru" delivery, where mothers and their newborns were put out of the hospital as early as eight hours after birth, even though serious health risks are associated with such a premature discharge and experts recommend a forty-eight-hour stay. The death of caution at all levels of hospital treatment is the biggest consequence of for-profit corporations controlling hospitals across the country. As Steven Olsen and many others show, the dramatic downsizing has catastrophic results for human life, growth and health.

Avoiding negligent injuries like those arising from failure to treat Steven Olsen's brain abscess is no mystery. During the debate surrounding President Clinton's proposed universal health care system, an author of the landmark *Harvard Medical Malpractice Study*, Dr. Troyen Brennan of the Harvard School of Public Health, put it to Congress this way: "At the hospital level, the major risk factor associated with negligent injury is the total amount of resources expended in the care of patients…As the Administration attempts to attain control of costs, it must ensure that resources are distributed evenly. Otherwise patients hospitalized at relatively poor hospitals will be at much greater risk for negligent injury."[3]

Dr. Brennan was discussing potential dangers of a system run by government bureaucrats. Yet these very dangers have been realized in the corporate bureaucracy of managed care. Since profits motivate every decision, our nation has a system of medicine that is far less compassionate and every bit as bureaucratic as any governmental system could be.

Hospital beds are vanishing, facilities are closing, services are shrinking. HMOs are a major cause, as hospitals are transformed under the crunch of medical downsizing.

Dr. James Robinson surveyed the problem for the *Journal of the American Medical Association*. He found that, "between 1983 and 1993 hospital expenditures grew 44% less rapidly in markets with high HMO penetration than in markets with low HMO penetration. Of this, 28% was due to reductions in the volume and mix of services [less coverage], 6% was due to reductions in bed capacity [less beds], and 10% was due to changes in the intensity of the services provided [less surgeries, MRIs, etc]."[4] In other words, HMO medicine means less hospital services or, at least, less specialized care.

Dr. Robinson writes, "rates of admission and lengths of stay have plummeted. Hospitals are merging, reducing bed capacity, and, in some instances, closing altogether. These economic dynamics are leading to a fundamental change in the organization of health care."

Is such a "reorganization" really bad?

The industry argues there are too many services and hospitals beds. Nurses, doctors and consumer advocates will tell you that the problem is rather that for-profit companies are taking unnecessary and unreasonable chances with patients' lives.

Patients themselves report serious problems. Consider the findings of a survey of 24,000 patients recently discharged from 120 hospitals nationwide:

- Nearly one-third of the patients indicated they were discharged from the hospitals before they were ready;
- 30% reported they were not alerted upon discharge to danger signals to watch for; and
- 37% said they had no idea when they could resume normal activities.[5]

The Picker Institute, a non-profit Boston-based research group that conducted the poll and subsequent focus groups, found that hospitals are a "nightmare to navigate" for many patients who "see an increasing trend toward care that is cold and impersonal." More than one-third of patients reported having too little control over their care, while about the same said they had "problems getting answers to important questions." Nearly one-third reported problems with continuity and transition of care.[6]

William Speck, president of New York's Columbia-Presbyterian Medical Center said of the conclusions, "The whole system has become depersonalized. A lot of the decisions have not been made in the best interest of the patients, but on financial imperatives—and that is a shame."[7]

It's important to ask, just how big is this problem? Early discharge and poor service may be inconvenient, but what is the actual impact on the public's overall health? Each year there are 80,000 deaths and 300,000 injuries in hospitals alone due to medical negligence, according to the most recent estimates of Harvard researchers.[8] While these results are not specific to managed care, they certainly show that in the hospital environment, more, not less caution, is warranted. This prescription is antithetical to the corporate goals of ever-increasing profits.

Amputations to Go?

What happens to all the patients not hospitalized?

In medical language, it is explained, thus: "Decreases in inpatients utilization were offset in part by a 75% increase in outpatients visits and a 168% increase in outpatient surgical procedures," Dr. Robinson reports.[9]

Hence the origins of the outpatient mastectomy—a dehumanizing process by which women with breast cancer who undergo a mastectomy are released from the hospital the same day, often with no counseling. This "drive-thru mastectomy," amputate and go, is a serious problem for the average breast cancer patient, who is 63 years-old. When she comes out of anesthesia, this woman must deal with pain and trauma to both her body and psyche. In 1997, fourteen states banned the outpatient mastectomy. In 1998, two others followed suit.[10] National Women's Health Network executive director Cindy Pearson asked of the practice, "What part of a man's body would they amputate in the same-day surgery?"[11]

In Napa California, an 88 year-old woman was rushed out of the hospital after a mastectomy, according to a report from the California Nurses Association.

"The surgery was a radical mastectomy performed on January 27, 1996 around 11:30 a.m.," said the woman. "When I came out of the anaesthetic, the social worker came to talk to me. She told me that I would be released from the hospital around 5 p.m. that same day and that I had to be sure someone would be there to take me home. I refused to leave."

Others came and spoke to her about the need to leave by 5 p.m.

"I still refused," she said. "I was nauseated and needed care. I was also due to come back to the hospital anyway at 9 a.m. the next day to see my doctor. I was 88 years and 11 months of age. I had no one at home to help me. I had to explain that my husband was legally blind and had to utilize hearing aids in both ears. I had to take care of him and now they were expecting me to care for us both immediately after I had major surgery. After much discussion I was 'allowed' to stay a total of twenty-three hours which meant until 9 a.m. the next day. They basically got me out of their hospital as fast as they could."

Her ordeal didn't end when she got home. The woman was allowed only three home-care visits by a nurse.

"I had no one at home to help me with wound care and the emptying of drainage tubes from my surgical site," she noted. "I had to measure and record the amount of drainage. It was all very perplexing to someone without knowledge."

At one point, the wound became infected.

"This necessitated having to go to the emergency room for treatment," the woman continued. "I was sent to an attendant to change my dressings but she told me that she was unable to do so as she 'had not had that experience.' I asked her how long she had been in health care and she said 'I have no experience at all.' This did not inspire any confidence."[12]

Why the emphasis on downsizing when the costs to patients are so high? Dr. Robinson's research shows that capitation is at the heart of hospital downsizing. "In California, medical groups paid on a capitation basis are continuing to push down on hospital utilization, both through fewer admissions and shorter lengths of stay, thereby achieving the lowest rates of hospital use in the nation," Robinson wrote.[13] Patients run the danger of being discharged too soon or never being admitted. In one astounding case that could have been written up in "Ripley's Believe it or Not," a man was turned away from an Oakland HMO emergency room even though he had a knife in his belly![14]

Patients in need of additional hospitalization or rehabilitation in a hospital environment are also shunted by HMOs to a nursing home or skilled nursing facility, where there are fewer or no doctors and less costs. Such tactics are not confined to older people.

Stephanie Ulrich, a 23 year-old graduate student at Southwest Texas State University, was a teaching assistant when, on January 26, 1998, she fainted in front of a freshmen survey class. All she remembers is waking up in the hospital scared to death. A CT scan revealed what, the doctors believed, was a basilar artery aneurysm. But the hospital discharged her because they did not have the expertise to look at the films. So she went home.

"That night I called my aunt in Maryland and she told me to FedEx the films to her, so a neurosurgeon could read them," Stephanie recalls. "By Thursday, three days later, I was on a plane to Washington, D.C."

At the Washington, D.C. hospital, Stephanie's aunt tried to get approval from Stephanie's HMO, but the company denied her plea. Stephanie's aunt called Stephanie's primary care physician in Texas for a referral for an angiogram that would confirm an aneurysm, and for admission to the hospital. He would not issue the referral because he said he was not informed about the hospitalization, even though Stephanie and her aunt had called his office the day she fainted and informed a member of his staff. Because Stephanie was outside the HMO's network, and her primary care doctor would not issue a referral, the HMO would not okay her admission to the hospital or the angiogram.

Luckily, Stephanie had secondary insurance because of her mother's job. This HMO approved the angiogram, which revealed that Stephanie needed immediate brain surgery.

The following day, Friday, January 30, 1998, Stephanie had the surgery, then spent three weeks in intensive care. The doctors at the hospital wanted

Stephanie Ulrich

Stephanie to be transferred to the National Rehabilitation Hospital (NRH) at the end of February. But her mom's HMO would not approve the doctors' request. She had to go at it alone.

"The therapists would help me to relearn how to feed myself, tie my shoes, and even walk," Stephanie said, after receiving the rehabilitation without the HMO's help. "My mother's HMO refused to pay the NRH, because they wanted to send me to a nursing home. They wanted to put me, a 22 year-old, in a nursing home, because they said that I could not be rehabilitated. They said I was not going to get better. Look at me. I am walking and talking now. I could not do that at the hospital in Washington."

Stephanie was discharged from the rehabilitation hospital on April 25. On Monday, April 27, she started a five-day a week, seven hours a day rehabilitation program. She was in that program for ten weeks and is currently doing outpatient therapy twice a week.

"My mother's HMO is still fighting with us over whether to pay the rehabilitation hospital, because they feel I am not rehabilitable," says Stephanie. "Throughout this whole illness, it has been an uphill battle with the insurance companies. I was at the lowest point in my life, and the insurance companies kicked me in the back. They had no right to do what they did to me and I pray this will not happen to anyone else. The last thing anyone should worry about is who is going to pay their hospital bills. They should concentrate on getting better and not on fighting the insurance companies. Without the help of my family and friends, I may be dead."

Stephanie's aunt Judy said in May 1999 that, "if Stephanie had not called us, I think that child would be dead today. If we were not there with the right resources and persistence, she would not be back in graduate school today walking, talking and eating. She even just got her driver's license back."

Edna and Nicole Asquith of San Jose, California have a similar story.

Nicole's 56 year-old grandmother died after being dumped in a "skilled nursing facility" and ignored by her HMO doctors.

"My three-year-old daughter would be spending her days with Grandma, had Grandma's HMO not rushed her to a skilled nursing facility to save a buck," said Edna.

"My mother was unconscious in the intensive care unit for three-and-a-half weeks, at times near death, on and off a ventilator with pneumonia and a liver condition," said Edna. "On the day she 'came to' she was transferred out of ICU and then immediately to 'one of the best skilled nursing facilities (SNFs) in the area.'"

Edna spent the whole day with her mother at the SNF getting her settled, arranging for physical therapy, etc.

"We were so excited she was finally coming home in a couple of weeks," Edna recalls.

But on her first evening, she developed a 104-degree temperature. Edna was on the phone to the doctor, expressing her concern.

"I called an ambulance to take my mom back to the HMO hospital because her fever would not come down and the 'nurses' didn't know what to do," Edna remembers. "The HMO emergency room doctor said my mom would have to go back to the SNF that night because she was suffering from a simple urinary tract infection."

On day two, Edna was called by a "nurse" who stated that her mom had no pulse and she didn't know what to do. The "nurse" said she called 911 and that Edna better rush to the hospital. At the hospital, the paramedic told Edna the "nurse" could not explain in understandable English what was wrong with Edna's mother.

"My mom didn't die that night," Edna said. "She suffered with sepsis for a while, then died at home at the ripe old age of 57. If the sepsis had been treated early, instead of being ignored, she would probably be alive today."

Downsizing Nursing Care

Hospitalized patients, unfortunately, rarely have the help they need to navigate an increasingly less caring environment. Hospitals have become outright dangerous places, where patients must take extraordinary steps to protect themselves.

Suzy Lobb's advice is simple: "Never stay in a hospital alone." Lobb recommends that a friend or family member remain by your side in the hospital, whether the hospital likes it or not.

In a tragic example of the crisis in American hospitals, Lobb's husband, Dwight, died on his forty-seventh birthday.

"He lay unattended, neglected and forgotten at an HMO hospital and quietly bled to death," Lobb says. "In spite of deteriorating vital signs and complaints of severe pain and abdominal spasms, no physician was called in. Nursing cut-backs on the floor, due to corporate cost-cutting, prevented a nurse from even checking on Dwight. At the most critical time, after he complained of excruciating pain, Dwight went unmonitored for over an hour and a half. When he finally was checked, he was dead. In less than five hours after leaving the recovery room from a routine elective surgery, my husband died from internal hemorrhaging."

One of the most troubling aspects for Lobb was that the night before, when she was leaving the hospital, a nurse told her they were short-handed and just couldn't get around to do everything they needed to do.

Suzanne says, "I believed in my heart that he was in the very best place he could be; that he was with the caregivers. And the feeling of betrayal that I have, I will never get over. My husband was denied the most basic of care, and it cost him his life."

Nurses, the best witnesses to hospital downsizing, condemn it.

"We no longer talk about quality care; we talk about minimally safe care," Kit Costello, president of the California Nurses Association, told 60

Minutes. "HMO after HMO has restructured the way in which care is provided to patients in order to cut costs. This involves shortening hospital stays, treating patients on the outside, and shifting more care onto their families."[15]

Nurse staffing levels have been decimated, and the policy is both perilous and pound-foolish. A 1997 study showed that fewer registered nurses translates into both longer hospital stays and more complications such as bedsores and infections.[16]

Registered nurses are a lifeline for the seriously ill patient. As in the case of Dwight Lobb, when a nurse is not available to respond, the consequences can be catastrophic.

"There's the old common-sense adage, 'You don't run with the scissors'," says Barry Adams, a nursing activist from Boston. "When a nurse has ten patients, fifteen patients, it is not conducive to safe nursing practices. When you're…just pouring pills, just one wrong pill can be the end. Do you know how quickly wrongly administered penicillin can kill somebody?"[17]

Chronic understaffing is a threat to public safety. In the drive to penny-pinch and satisfy HMOs' demands, hospitals replace registered nurses with aides who have less training and fewer skills, often undermining the quality of care and endangering patients.

Consider a *Wall Street Journal* "Work Week" account, where the paper of record for HMO investors takes pride in a practice that would send shivers through any hospital patient:

> "DAILY GRIND: Hospitals once called the job 'housekeeping,' but now 'service partners' such as David Ceronsky toil hands-on with patients. On the night shift at the Fresno, Calif., Kaiser Permanente emergency room, he wheels patients to their rooms, feeds them, records what they eat and responds to their calls. Code blue heart attack? Mr. Ceronsky, 37, who earns top pay of $10.11 an hour, drops his mop to perform CPR if he is the closest at hand."[18]

David Ceronsky was part of a Service Employees International Union (SEIU) negotiating team that cut an agreement with Kaiser in Northern California for other so-called "service partners" to respond to patient call lights. The qualifications are simply a high-school diploma or equivalent and experience in housekeeping, food handling, transporting supplies, or decontaminating containers.

As for training, forget nursing or medical school.

"Employees shall be given on-the-job training necessary to meet the minimum qualifications of the posted position," according to Kaiser's letter of agreement with the union.[19] Of course, emergencies are routine in hospitals and employees are now called upon to perform duties beyond the "posted position."

Unfortunately, the fewer nurses are busier and busier.

Judith Shindul-Rothschild, a professor at Boston College's nursing school, says it's as if nurses are leaning over patients on an accelerating conveyor belt and each "speedup brings them closer to the brink of chaos."[20]

What are the consequences for patients?

Too many hospitals can become death traps.

Marilyn Pon, a registered nurse (RN) in Berkeley, CA, says patients have had strokes unreported in a timely fashion, because there were too few qualified people to check on patients regularly. "They lay there for hours before anyone noticed."[21]

Interviews by the Boston College School of Nursing with Massachusetts nurses attributed fifteen patient deaths to inadequate nurse staffing during 1994, while similar surveys in previous years found no such deaths.[22]

Complaints from California RNs to the Board of Registered Nursing regarding unsafe practices for patients swelled to record numbers during 1996.[23] California, which has the greatest percentage of its population in HMOs, not surprisingly, also ranks 49th in the United States in the rate of registered nurses to patients, according to the Census and Commerce Department data.[24]

The frequency of staffing shortages is frightening. In a single month, Lucille Packard Children's Hospital at Stanford was cited forty-two times for inadequate staffing, then the next month thirteen different times for staffing shortages in its Intensive Care Unit for premature babies and other high-risk infants.[25]

California's Sutter Roseville Medical Center was cited by the Department of Health Services for twenty-six separate incidents of unsafe staffing in its Cardiac Intensive Care Unit and Intensive Care Unit during a three month period.[26]

In August 1998, for the third time in two months, Kaiser Permanente was cited by California health officials for the unsafe and illegal use of unlicensed staff on patients during surgery. Following onsite inspections and interviews with staff, the California Department of Health Services (DHS) described incidents of an unlicensed technician engaged in such practices as suturing deep tissue wounds, pounding metallic devices into bone, and cauterizing veins.[27]

In one case, an unlicensed orthopedic assistant placed a retractor directly in a total hip wound. The DHS citation found this "is dangerous since a person other than a surgeon might not know where the nerves are and where to place the retractor. A retractor (an instrument used to hold back tissue) could cause nerve damage if improperly placed, especially during total hip surgery."[28]

John Daly, the DHS official who oversaw the investigation, said that in his ten years as a regulator he had never seen a case such as this, where a technician clearly exceeded his scope of training. "These were clear violations of state regulations and the regulations are there for a reason," he said.[29]

Need Emergency Help While at The Hospital?
Call 911

Accounts of patients who have paid for hospital downsizing are chilling. The California Nurses Association's *Patient Watch* program reported one letter it received from a friend of a 911 emergency care dispatcher who had taken a patient's urgent call. The friend wrote, "She needed immediate help as she was bleeding and couldn't get it to stop. The thing that flabbergasted him was the origin of the call: a patient room at a local hospital. She had tried again and again to summon help with her call bell, but no one would come."[30]

A Northern California resident recounts in another *Patient Watch* letter: "My experience involved several staff members with no clinical background or limited experience with the protocol of chemotherapy...The IV-tubing for the implanted port-a-cath access device became disconnected allowing the drugs and blood to spill onto the bed and floor. It took several minutes for someone to respond, only to inform me there was nothing they could do but contact my nurse. To my dismay, it was several minutes (more) before my nurse responded, but I had already connected the tubing and cleaned the blood from the floor."[31]

Dan Lake, an emergency medical technician from Vacaville, California, came up against the industry's cost-cutting practices when his wife went into premature labor, and later when his infant son Daniel had to stay in the hospital for several months.

In 1991, Dan's wife Cindie was six-months pregnant when she started having severe chest pains and headaches. When she called her HMO doctor, he recommended that she drive herself to the hospital. Dan, a trained emergency medical technician, saw that his wife was in too much pain to drive, and ordered an ambulance. The HMO doctor refused to pay for the ambulance until Dan insistently demanded that the doctor look at Cindie before making a final decision. When the HMO doctor saw Cindie's state, he authorized payment.

Cindie gave birth to their son Daniel at twenty-four weeks. He needed care around the clock.

"If your kid is in the hospital, you might as well bring a suitcase," Dan said.

Lake found the hospital wards so understaffed that registered nurses had to take care of four intensive-care infants at once. Basic care could not be performed under this skeletal staffing.

"We had things happen like being told to pay for a babysitter to watch our son if we wanted to leave," said Lake. He even monitored the baby next to his, whose parents both had to work and could not watch their child full-time. Dan says this situation is common, and he knows several people "who have lost their jobs because the understaffing in hospitals forced them to go take care of their children in the hospital."

"I think because we were so persistent is part of the reason why he's here today," said Lake, about his son Daniel's treatment. "And if we would have left him there, I don't think he would be here today. With us there were times where the poor nurse now—it wasn't her fault, because she was so busy—she'd poke her head in and say, 'Did you take his vitals?' So I was taking my own son's vital signs to give back to them to chart, because she didn't have time."

The tragedies are not just anecdotal.

A 1996 national survey of 7,500 RNs by Boston College School of Nursing Professor Judith Shindul-Rothschild found that 60% noted a reduction in the number of RNs providing direct care, and 40% reported substitution of unlicensed personnel for RNs. The study found disturbing increases in unexpected patient re-admissions, complications, medication errors, wound infections, patient injuries, and patient deaths. More than one-third of RNs said they would not recommend a family member receive care in their facility.[32]

Downsizing shifts more risks onto patients and away from the hospital system designed to assume them.

Numerous studies in the 1980s and early 1990s, a period in which RNs typically comprised at least 80% of nursing staffs, documented a direct correlation between safe RN staffing levels, lower mortality rates and other positive patient outcomes.

An analysis of studies by Patricia Prescott, RN, Ph.D., in the magazine *Nursing Economics*, makes clear the power of Dr. Brennan's argument that resources have a profound role in determining patient outcomes:[33]

- Thirteen studies—including one that looked at 8,593 high risk surgical patients in seventeen hospitals, another at 5,030 patients from thirteen hospitals, and another at 42,773 patients—showed that hospitals with higher RN to patient ratios had fewer deaths.

- Several studies linked greater RN-to-patient ratios to increased patient satisfaction, quality of life after discharge, knowledge and compliance in treatment, and fewer in-hospital complications.

- Virtually all the studies demonstrated decreased costs and safer shorter patient stays associated with safer RN staffing levels.

While nurses face increasing pressure to deliver quality care to more and more patients, hospitals are also turning them from caregivers to paper-pushers. Over the past twenty-five years, the percentage of U.S. medical care workers doing mostly paperwork skyrocketed from 18% to 27% of total health employment while the proportion of nursing and physician personnel fell from 51% to 43%, according to the February 1996 issue of the *Journal of Public Health*.[34]

Gradually—and unfortunately too late for many—a consensus is building about the harm done by staff cutbacks. Rather than allowing themselves or their patients to be downsized, many nurses with high ethical standards are leaving their practices. This has created a devastating ripple effect. An internal memo at Mercy Healthcare Sacramento in July 1998 documented an "ever-increasing number of vacancies" in nurse staff positions that it could not fill. The voluntary departure of hundreds of RNs was the major problem. In exit interviews, many nurses said they were leaving due to staffing that was "unsafe; too much required; not enough staff."[35]

Kaiser Permanente's Northern California nurse recruitment manager told *NurseWeek* in February, 1998 that "the recruitment infrastructure was demolished during downsizing [because of] several years of not providing opportunities to new grads. It's kind of like nature, you can't reproduce during a drought."[36]

Turning HMOs into Health Hazards

When good nurses disappear from the bedside, patients pay the price. A sampling of the human consequence can be seen in the following excerpts of letters received from patients, their families, and Registered Nurses, in response to the California Nurses Association's *Patient Watch* advertisements.

- "My grandfather survived brain surgery but died three months later, from the effects of malnutrition, dehydration and an infected bedsore. All of this could have been prevented if a registered nurse was at his side. He was a dignified elderly gentleman, a loving husband and the strong center of a family…In the hospital he had become just another dollar sign who was being manipulated to meet the greed of hospital revenue."

- "My wife entered ___ hospital recently and received very poor service. Every time she called for a registered nurse, she got a 'nursing assistant' or 'patient care assistant' instead. It took thirty to forty-five minutes to actually see a registered nurse."

- "Our baby died after we were pushed out of the hospital too soon by ___. The coroner's report said our baby died of meningitis or streptococcus B, and would have lived if we had spent just six to ten more hours in the hospital."

- "Our child was born with a cleft palate that was not detected. She was then misdiagnosed as developmentally disabled. While we were in the hospital, we rarely saw an RN. When we went home, the baby was not feeding properly. The hospital where she was born was unresponsive and of no help to us. We finally took her to ___ Hospital in ___, where she was found to be dehydrated and had to be put on an IV."

- In April of 1995, an aide removed an IV tubing from its IV pump. This was done to facilitate the patient's gown removal. The patient received *90mg of morphine in five minutes*, and had to be rushed to the ICU. The patient did not die, but did suffer a major crisis.

- A 27 year-old man from Central California was given a heart transplant, *and was discharged from the hospital after only four days* because his HMO wouldn't pay for additional hospitalization. Nor would the HMO pay for the bandages needed to treat the man's infected surgical wound. The patient died.

- A 4 year-old girl ran a high fever following a five-hour hospital stay for a tonsillectomy (considered an outpatient operation by HMOs). Her mother took the girl to her HMO pediatrician, who didn't take the girl's temperature, didn't examine her throat, and didn't refer the girl back to the surgeon—a routine procedure for post-operative problems. The girl died of a hemorrhage at the surgical site.

"The biggest way to cut costs is cutting staffing," recounts Marc Gardner, former vice president for the nation's largest for-profit hospital chain Columbia/HCA. "One high-level Columbia executive had had responsibility for the western part of the state, which included Las Vegas. She would send down staffing standards to our hospital. I thought it was very unusual for someone that high up in the corporation dictating staffing standards for one of thirty or forty facilities she had responsibility for. Those staffing cuts were extremely questionable. When you cut staffing at hospitals, you do make more money, because you have less expense. But medical errors increase significantly. I sat on the Pharmacy and Therapeutics Committee, which reviewed medication errors. The medication error rate after the implementation of the staffing guidelines jumped through the roof. These included misprescription, nurses in a hurry, give the wrong dose, give the right medication to the wrong patient."[37]

How have centers of healing turned into potential health hazards? In the hospital delivery game, fewer and fewer players are controlling more and more patients' health care—leading to competition on the basis of cost-cutting and care-cutting, not medical innovation.

In the Sacramento, California area, for instance, seven large medical groups have three-fourths of the region's 1,000 primary care doctors. Three hospital systems account for about 80% of the inpatient care. Moreover, patients face increasing problems gaining access and entrance to hospitals because the "gatekeepers" are HMO agents. Because the Sacramento-area doctors are fully capitated, they have cut the hospital use by 40% according to a recent study.[38]

Skimping on care is not the only crisis. The entire physical infrastructure of the nation's hospital system is being eroded. The community hospital and the open emergency room are disappearing just as quickly as the family doctor and the registered nurse from the bedside.

Columbia/HCA:
An Illuminating Model of Greed

The community hospital was often started by religious and civic-minded groups as a charity to serve all comers. Corporations are now taking over. There were 200 corporate takeovers of non-profit hospitals between 1990 and 1996.[39] While religious orders founded hospitals in their quest to aid the needy and build community, for-profit corporations have the bottom-line as their agenda.

What has been lost?

While physicians who worked at the non-profits hardly took the vows of poverty, the orders who founded the institutions did. The hospitals were run in the spirit of taking all comers, mending all wounds. federal law reflected these mores—requiring that emergency rooms not turn away any patient in need of care without stabilizing them, regardless of a patient's ability to pay.

And the community hospital was the place where civil society and the medical community intersected, each moderating and mediating the other, collaborating on an appropriate balance of public and private, the professional and the civil. The boards of community hospitals are typically chaired by non-physicians, often nurses or community leaders. The goal was not profit but service.

Today, the giant for-profit chains that take over community hospitals dismantle beds and services, in some cases close whole facilities, and make huge profits.

With 355 hospitals at its peak, Columbia/HCA is the nation's largest for-profit hospital chain, and the clear leader in downsizing hospital beds. It also currently faces federal indictment on fraud charges. The company recorded $1.9 billion in profit during 1995[40], feasting on the community wealth charitable organizations have built up over decades. Columbia is alleged to have cheated communities out of medical services and, in its fee-for-service business, the taxpayer out of money for medical services never rendered.

John Leifer—a regional senior vice president for Columbia/HCA in 1994 and 1995—helped arrange takeovers. He's now a former employee of the Columbia/HCA system.

"I think that any time a not-for-profit community-based facility sells to a for-profit, the community suffers," the former Columbia executive explains. "I think that the needs of Main Street are incongruous with the needs of Wall Street. The community-based hospital has, as part of its mission, meeting the total health care needs of the community, and it doesn't have an obligation to pay a return on investment to its shareholders, whereas a for-profit has a very different motivation. They have earnings expectations on the part of their investors, and they have earnings expectations on the part of Wall Street analysts."[41]

Columbia became known as the octopus of the hospital world, a take-over king whose growing empire has sparked many local wars.

Attorney General of Michigan, Frank Kelly, is one of the Columbia/HCA resistors. Kelly stopped the Columbia takeover of a Lansing non-profit hospital, and the court agreed with him to scuttle the deal.

"What I'm afraid is going to happen here with these profit hospitals com-ing in is that they're going to take these facilities," said Kelly. "They're going to take all of the profitable businesses, they're going to take all of the cream off of the top, and then they're going to leave the charitable work, and the poverty work, and all of the difficult cases for some other institution, while they make a profit."[42]

The industry's largest trade magazine could not help noticing the trend: "The effort to convert assets created by civic-minded citizens and religious orders to the benefit of corporate owners and shareholders has created a furi-ous industry debate in recent years."[43] The debate, however, needs to be moved to the public, which still expects that when patients are admitted to a hospital they are in the care of nuns, not the custody of corporate bosses.

The rapid consolidation of the industry is squeezing patients further and further. At the hospital level, it comes down to who will be there and how quickly when a patient, like Dwight Lobb, presses his call button.

In 1996 Columbia/HCA bought the then-not-for-profit San Jose Medical Center and Good Samaritan Hospital. At the two San Jose hospitals, Columbia let go of sixty-eight registered nurses, 12% of the nursing staff.[44]

When Lehrer *NewsHour* reporter Jeffrey Kaye talked to a group of nurses at the facility, they said their patients' lives were in jeopardy:

MELINDA MARKOWITZ, *Columbia* Good Samaritan Hospital: We are required to have more patients than we can adequately and safely take care of.

JEFFREY KAYE: Melinda Markowitz has been at *Columbia* Good Samaritan Hospital for nineteen years.

MARKOWITZ: The potential is there for life-threatening situations, yes.

KAYE: Elaine Legg was so worried about staffing conditions in San Jose Medical Center's emergency room that she left her job.

ELAINE LEGG, Registered Nurse: The staffing was unsafe. It was an unsafe setting.

KAYE: Celeste Lange has worked in *Columbia* Good Samaritan's intensive care unit for twenty years.

CELESTE LANGE, *Columbia* Good Samaritan Hospital: You have that kind of living-on-the-edge feeling when you're in there, because, you know, you're kind of—you may or may not be able to manage what comes along. There's no guarantee.

KAYE: Dr. Kamal Modir echoed that feeling of living on the edge. He's been a surgeon at Good Samaritan for twenty-five years.

DR. KAMAL MODIR, *Columbia* Good Samaritan Hospital: Many times we've got close to disasters.[45]

When hospitals close beds, wings, and downsize services, patients pay. Is it by design?

Former Columbia Executive Marc Gardner, now a whistleblower for the government's case against Columbia, explains, "America needs to know there's a dark side to running a hospital, and it hasn't really been talked about. Let me tell you, this is a ruthless, greedy company—period. Employees are the largest operating expense. Cut that to the bone. Cut nursing to the bone. I mean, cut to—as low as your conscience will allow. We cut it so low that my wife and I had a plan. If she ever got sick and required hospitalization, she'd go to the hospital across town."[46]

Gardner, a 35 year-old former vice president at Columbia's Sunrise Hospital in Las Vegas, said candidly about Columbia's attitude regarding cuts in the hospital's neonatal unit, where sick newborns are treated: "Babies don't complain too much. A baby doesn't know if they are getting bad care."[47]

Such decisions allowed Sunrise, a flagship hospital for Columbia, to take in revenues of nearly $1 billion annually.

Enormous earnings are the reward for hospital corporations that downsize care, nurses and beds under HMO medicine. But patients pay the price. And taxpayers and whole communities pay too.

In 1997, FBI agents descended on Columbia offices across the nation with search warrants and seized over three million documents. Numerous whistleblowers had come forward to bolster various federal indictments against the company for widespread fraudulent billing practices of the government's Medicare and Medicaid programs.

Florida is the center of the probe. Four Columbia executives in Florida have been indicted and two other executives outside the state have been fired.[48] Top managers—including Chairman and founder Richard Scott—stepped down quickly after the first raids, and the company went about transforming its image. Scott resigned in 1997 with $10 million in severance and $269 million in stock.

The company claims it is now dedicated to rebuilding and cleaning house of corruption. But the damage done to communities is just emerging from the trail of documents left in the scandal's wake.

Columbia allegedly cheated the taxpayer of billions of dollars by distorting federal expense claims for reimbursement. How did the company cook its books?

According to a New York Times investigation, documents show that some hospitals charged the government for costs that were not reimbursable—such as advertising dollars. The hospitals allegedly set money aside to cover the costs if discovered. If the government noticed a discrepancy, the hospitals would repay the money without a fine or interest penalty. If the inflated numbers were not noticed for two or three years, the money would be considered profit. Other allegations under investigation by the government include "upcoding"—charging for a more expensive treatment than the one rendered.[49]

In addition, the Times reports outside accountants such as KPMG Peat Marwick knew that Columbia was cheating the government, and in some cases helped. KPMG was named in a whistleblower lawsuit that contends the firm helped Columbia hospitals create secret reserves that would be used to provide refunds to the government if Columbia's deception was discovered.[50]

The records at one Arkansas hospital were reportedly stamped, "Confidential. Do not discuss or release to Medicare auditors."

Such "misrepresentation of costs has occurred throughout the for-profit hospital industry," according to the Times. "Hospitals now owned by Columbia reportedly distorted costs when they were owned by several other companies, including Healthtrust, Basic American Medical and the Hospital Corporation of America."[51]

Whistleblowers close to the Columbia case say they expect the federal government to announce the largest fine in history.[52]

The billions of dollars involved in the swindle is just one example of the money pulled out of communities by Columbia and other for-profit hospital chains when they take over community hospitals and close beds.

There is another way that companies like Columbia can cheat the tax-payers. When a chain like Columbia buys a not-for-profit community hospital, it must value the assets it is buying, then establish a foundation to continue the non-profit mission because of the tax-free dollars that went toward building up those assets.

But like the bills Columbia submitted to the government, these assets' true value are often distorted—this time undervalued. For-profit companies have bought up community hospitals at fire-sale prices. Communities have been cheated according to many.

Michigan Attorney General Frank Kelly could never compel Columbia to produce information about the value of the community hospital targeted for acquisition—that is how he got a judge to stop the takeover. When Columbia took over Timken Mercy Medical Center in Canton, Ohio, the board of trustees—composed of local businessmen—were summarily fired because they asked questions similar to Kelly's.

Robert Rownd, a businessman, was chairman of that board. He explains: "We all looked upon the medical center as a community asset. It was put here by the community. It was funded by the community. It has a lot of sweat and toil from the community. We weren't able to get the information that we needed in order to determine whether it was in the best interest of the community…there were a number of trustees who were asking the same questions that I was asking." They were all fired on the same day after asking questions such as how much the hospital was going to be sold for, to whom it would be sold, why everything was kept secret.[53]

Columbia's rap sheet in communities across the nation shows a pattern of thievery—usurping services and value. Mike Wallace of CBS's 60 Minutes reported of the Columbia record in October 1996:

August, Georgia—When Columbia took over August Regional Hospital in late 1993, charity care dropped by about a third the next year, according to state records.

Indianapolis, Indiana—The state health department took the unusual step of fining Columbia's Women's Hospital last summer, after repeatedly finding too few nurses in the neonatal intensive care unit. A doctor had complained that babies' lives were at risk, a charge the hospital denied.

Destin, Florida—That city filed suit in 1994, after Columbia bought, and then closed, Destin's only hospital. They already owned hospitals in neighboring cities. So, when Hurricane Opal struck in 1995, and more than 100 people in Destin needed emergency care, many of them had to be airlifted to other neighboring hospitals.[54]

The plan behind Columbia's acquisitions was clear. Richard Rainwater, co-founder of Columbia/HCA, admitted, "The day has come when somebody has to do in the hospital business what McDonalds has done in the fast-food business and what Wal-Mart has done in the retailing business."[55]

"Do we have an obligation to provide health care for everybody?" former Columbia CEO and co-founder Richard Scott opined. "Where do we draw the line? Is any fast-food restaurant obligated to feed everyone who shows up?"[56]

Under federal law, the answer is hospitals do have an obligation to treat all comers who are seriously ill. Under the ethic of investor-owned hospitaling, the community does not count. When health care is a business, like fast food, communities can be starved.

Whistleblower Marc Gardner has discussed how the hospital giant he worked for turned the uninsured away—in apparent violation of the federal "take-all-comers" law. One homeless man with pneumonia, for instance, was discharged without having any tests and died an hour later on the hospital lawn. Another elderly homeless man was also released without testing. He went down the road to a Catholic hospital, where a brain hemorrhage was found.[57] Such downsizing falls under the same type of justifications for cutbacks in the neonatal intensive care unit: "babies don't complain too much." After all, homeless men don't pay premiums.

While Columbia allegedly skimped on patients, it spent big bucks on advertising. Columbia spent nearly $200 million for advertising in 1995 and 1996—the largest expenditure in hospital-industry history. In 1996, Columbia spent more than $1,567 per bed in advertising, or $106 million total.[58]

But it did not stop there. To corner the market, Columbia sought to kill off all competing community hospitals. One Columbia administrator Jon Trazona reportedly wrote to surgeons in Fort Pierce, Florida, "I pledge to you that Columbia/HCA will utilize all appropriate resources to insure the failure of *any* competing surgery center in our community [emphasis in original]."[59]

CEO Richard Scott himself allegedly told one hospital chief in handwritten comments on his evaluation of a rival hospital, "Don't let St. Mary's attract your patients." According to Marc Gardner, despite federal prohibitions on physician self-referrals, Columbia had physicians buy shares in the hospitals where they worked and paid doctors thousands in monthly fees to bring patients in the door.[60] This cut-throat competition has a debilitating effect on communities and an inflationary impact on patient bills.

First, Columbia appears to have inflated prices and padded its Medicare billing. In one Columbia-owned hospital in Georgia, the average stay for a stroke victim cost $14,582, while a similar public hospital charged $6,735.[61] The *New York Times* reported "Medicare had paid far more for Columbia patients receiving outpatient services than if care had been billed at the state average."[62] So the taxpayers are cheated twice.

Second, the for-profit, not-for-patients ethos affects non-profit and community facilities, which must compete and play by the same rules.

For instance, Northridge Hospital Medical Center in Los Angeles was caught by the state of California refusing to give a woman in labor an epidural—a spinal block used in childbirth—because she would not pay cash up front to the anesthesiologist. The surgeon demanded payment from the husband in the delivery room before he would administer the pain killer. The woman was a Medicaid recipient.[63] The hospital was not alone. Sally K. Richardson, the Medicaid program's national director, said Medicaid patients report they were asked to pay cash for an epidural at a dozen hospitals in Los Angeles, and Florida officials report similar problems.[64] *Los Angeles Times* reporter Sharon Bernstein also uncovered that the County of Los Angeles, in a cost-cutting tactic, required poor women, even in high-risk cases, to undergo vaginal deliveries, rather than perform the more costly caesarian section. As a result, the County paid $24 million between 1992 and 1997 to settle forty-nine claims of mothers and children who died or were injured due to the policy.[65]

Public hospitals that have treated the indigent for years are pitted against franchises of the for-profit hospitals which, in the age of managed care, are even looking for Medicaid patients—while turning away the indigent who do not qualify for federal assistance.

Abraham Verghese tells how pressures from for-profit satellite hospitals have undermined care for the indigent and community hospitals, such as the one he works at, R.E. Thomason General in El Paso, Texas.

> Suddenly, Medicaid patients, who for decades were not so subtly turned away by other providers and sent to Thomason, are now desired by all.
>
> It hardly seems like a fair fight. Sierra and the four other for-profit hospitals in town have all been taken over by either Columbia/HCA Healthcare or Tenet Healthcare, two national for-profit chains. These companies have deep pockets and no public accountability.

Thomason, on the other hand, is the only public hospital for a population of about 600,000. Like many other county hospitals across the country, it is overburdened with care of the poor. The 300 or so hospital beds at Thomason represent only 14% of the total hospital beds in the city. Yet by county mandate the hospital is required to provide medical care not only to Medicaid patients but to the 240,000 or so El Paso residents who have no medical insurance or Medicaid cards. These residents are medically indigent because they do not meet the income requirement to qualify for Medicaid or because they are illegal aliens or because there is simply not enough Medicaid financing for all who qualify.

Thomason managed to care for them, despite the unwieldy bureaucracy that oversees the hospital and in the face of the increasing resentment by homeowners over the rising property taxes that go to support it.

The price tag for indigent care is about $40 million annually. The property tax generates about $30 million. The difference is made up by Medicaid and Medicare patients, who constitute 40% of Thomason patients and who indirectly underwrite the care of the indigent by allowing the hospital to have certain services and specialists in place—like neurosurgeons—that would otherwise be unavailable.

It used to be that Thomason's childbirth unit, the hospital's only consistent moneymaker (most pregnant women are eligible for Medicaid), was so busy that the hallways routinely served as holding areas. But the number of deliveries is dwindling as pregnant women are courted away by the for-profit chains whose elaborate labor and delivery suites look like Scandinavian design showrooms.

If Thomason loses its Medicaid base but continues to serve the indigent, it cannot possibly survive. Predictably, the city commissioners have seriously discussed closing the hospital or selling it.

Of course, it is hard to begrudge Medicaid patients, once the pariah of the for-profits, their new-found popularity. But those without Medicaid will suffer. Their voices are not well heard, and those who speak for them are an old guard of community activists and do-gooders whose plaints sound numbingly familiar.

If Thomason is forced to close and if Medicaid dollars are cast across El Paso, the indigent will likely be passed down from one hospital to another.[66]

The for-profit hospital industry does not dispute that it is closing beds, but says there are simply too many hospital beds.

Of course, this is a self-fulfilling prophecy. When bureaucrats refuse patients who need admittance, hospital beds go unused—but this does not mean that patients are not in need of hospitalization, simply that they are not allowed in or to stay over night.

The industry relies on hospital census data to show that there is so-called overbedding and excess capacity. But the "census" data is rigged and does not reflect the real number of patients actually in beds, just those staying past midnight.

Nurses now refer to the "twenty-three hour" hospital day. Census counts used by hospitals are invariably taken at midnight. They reflect patients who have actually been *admitted* to the hospital for an overnight stay. They do not account for the large numbers of patients who may spend all day in those beds but are not formally admitted as "inpatients."

"Outpatients," who undergo chemotherapy or an angiogram, spend hours in a hospital bed, but are not included in the census, which reflects an empty bed for the day. The California Nurses Association reviewed staffing census charts for an Oakland hospital and compared census counts made during the day shift with the official census count at midnight. Over a nineteen-day period, there was an 11% difference, 378 patients who were in the bed during the day but not included in the official census count. That's an average of twenty patients per day or 7,262 patients for an entire year.[67]

By artificially lowering the patient census count, hospitals also lower the number of nurses who must be on staff to meet regulated "acuity" standards—the number of nurses required for a specific number of patients with an acute condition. Other accounting manipulations in the census include deducting the number of patients in hospital observation units, a "short stay" unit. The patients in their bed at midnight were actually subtracted from the census count.

The industry also has an interest in manipulating census numbers because they artificially demonstrate that hospitals can be closed—reducing overhead costs. But that's little comfort to the trauma patient who has to be transported the extra forty miles to the next town because his community hospital closed. While profits to corporations like Columbia for the dismantling of hospital beds are substantial, the cost of rebuilding those hospital beds, when needed by a community, would be astronomical.

During the winter of 1998, for instance, an influenza epidemic exposed the "empty bed" myth. In California, the hospital industry had progressively downsized its hospital beds, boldly claiming an overbedding crisis. Unfortunately, when patients were stricken with a flu outbreak in the fall of 1998, there was suddenly a tremendous shortfall of hospital beds—with patients forced to wait in emergency rooms, hallways and parking lots. Prompted by the spectacle, the California Emergency Medical Services Authority issued a report in October 1998 that found there was not enough capacity in the state's emergency rooms and hospitals to deal with catastrophes.

During an earthquake or other natural emergency, hospitals are needed. As the hospital downsizing continues, though, community infrastructure will evaporate just when communities need them. The issue of required capacity is simple: do we close firehouses because there is not a fire every week, or do we keep them open so when fire hits, communities can respond appropriately? In the age of corporate medicine, the same civil values that keep a fire station open do not apply to hospitals.

When Desperate for Profits, Imprison Patients—
The Tenet Story

Columbia is not the only corporate culprit in the hospital game. The nation's second largest hospital chain with 123 hospitals—now called Tenet—has a similarly checkered past. In 1994, Tenet, then called National Medical Enterprises (NME), pleaded guilty to federal conspiracy charges for paying kickbacks to doctors from the late 1980s through 1991. The company paid $375 million in fines and penalties, which is the largest health fraud settlement in U.S. history to date, though it could be surpassed by Columbia's pending fine. Now Tenet is hoping to pick up the turf of its former competitor, Columbia—which, in the throes of scandal, is divesting many of its hospitals.[68] Ironically, one of the counts against Columbia is the same for which Tenet was busted by the feds—having inappropriate financial relationships with physicians. According to whistleblowers, Columbia also paid doctors special bonuses in order to have them refer patients to Columbia facilities so that the company could charge whoever was paying the bill.[69] These sorts of abuses are endemic to health chains operating in a for-profit environment (be they not-for-profit or for-profit companies). The tendencies of the for-profit medical corporation—to emphasize profit, market standing, and empire building—are subjugating ethical patient care and community medical values.

Even after Tenet's embarrassing 1994 scandal, for instance, a 1998 federal investigation was launched alleging, according to the subpoenas, Tenet's "connection with an investigation of Medicaid and/or Medicare fraud" at its Florida hospitals. The federal inquiry, like the one in 1994, centered on financial arrangements between the hospitals and doctors.[70] In 1997, the province of Ontario, Canada sued Tenet for allegedly bilking Canadian taxpayers out of at least $25 million for substandard treatment of patients. The government said agents for Tenet brought Ontario residents to its hospitals in the United States, provided improper care and then billed the Canadian province.[71]

The impact on patients of the hospital chain's profiteering can be seen by a 1997 $100 million settlement Tenet entered into with 700 former patients who claimed the company's physicians illegally imprisoned them in psychiatric hospitals in order to obtain claims payment from their insurance policies. The patients contended that they could not leave the health care chain's institutions until their insurance benefits had been exhausted. Patients said they were prevented from making telephone calls or talking to their family members. Many lodged charges of abuses, such as being placed in restraints for weeks on end or being forced to sit motionless for hours.[72]

When the Saints Come Marching In—With Money

HMO medicine lends itself to the hospital chain muscling out the community hospital and its values. But reckless budget slashing based on the profit motive is not the only issue.

Catholic Health Association, for instance, has 542 hospitals, 319 long-term care facilities and fifty-six health systems. It lays down another demand, according to vice president of the Association Sister Jean deBlois, "We will not partner with a hospital that does abortions."[73] A non-profit chain may be less susceptible to engaging in the profiteering of the for-profits, but access under the law is a different story.

Roe vs. Wade firmly established the *de jure* right to abortion in our civil realm—but as Catholic Healthcare West partners with more and more community hospitals, it imposes a *de facto* ban on reproductive services in its hospitals. The ban covers elective abortions, in vitro fertilization, direct sterilization of women and men, contraception, and 'morning after' pills. When hospitals that partner with this Catholic chain are the only hospital servicing a community, patients with rights under *Roe* are placed in a precarious situation that a community hospital would never have put them in.

One woman, a mother of two, who had an abortion at an outpatient surgery center because all the hospitals in her area were Catholic-affiliated, told the *Sacramento Bee*, "I was fearful that if something went wrong I wouldn't be at a hospital. I was unsure of the kind of care I would receive."[74]

From 1990 to 1997, there were eighty-four affiliations between Catholic and non-Catholic hospitals.[75] What has promoted this trend? Why would a successful community hospital affiliate with the Catholic Health Association? The answer again is managed care.

The larger chains control the contracts that ensure profitability.

"We began this process because we wanted to be in the best possible position to preserve our commitment to the community in this rapidly changing health care environment," said Marvin Reiter, Chairman of the Board of Community Hospital in Riverside, California, a long-time independent hospital that in August 1998 merged with Catholic Healthcare West after a lawsuit-laden fight against the merger. "We felt the only way to achieve that was by affiliating with a larger system."[76]

Two out of three of the city's hospitals are now Catholic Healthcare West facilities. As part of the merger, the hospital agreed not to provide any reproductive services.

Bruce Satzger, the administrator of Community Hospital, said the board "had to think long and hard about an affiliation process and how to stay and be viable as a hospital in the future." The merger, he believed, allowed the hospital to compete for big HMO contracts while lowering costs.[77]

In rural areas, the problem is exacerbated. In California's rural Lassen County, for instance, the one hospital is Catholic owned. Women who want tubal ligation, let alone abortions, must travel 100 miles over winding mountain roads to Chico, Redding or Sacramento.[78]

If You Can't Beat 'Em...

To fight for survival in the hyper-competitive medical marketplace, hospitals are also becoming their own HMOs. Cedar-Sinai, one of Los Angeles's top hospitals, for instance, applied to become licensed as an HMO.[79] One-time healing institutions will thus become organs of money management. Merger and acquisition in the hospital industry increased by 22% in 1997, according to a study by Irving Levin Associates of New Canaan, Connecticut. Since 1994, total transactions have increased by 109%.[80]

Communities have fought back against takeovers by large hospital chains. Many hospitals, however, have had to transform—and pick between the lesser of two evils just to survive.

Should they have to?

That question is not asked today in the halls of government or public forums. Hospital corporations assume they are calling the shots and civil society cannot fight them at any level, particularly not through the dictates of government. Attempts at reform have been stymied by industry lobbyists.

Bills to establish safe staffing levels and protect community hospitals in state legislatures have fallen victim to the cash-rich might of the for-profit hospital lobby.

Not-for-profit hospitals sit on assets worth hundreds of billions of dollars, so it's not surprising that big hospital chains have taken aim on these institutions. It is frightening, however, that most regulators have not been able to slow or stop them. Can community self-interest rebound before it is too late?

CHAPTER FOUR

The Financial Sting—
Paying More
For Less

Bob Ingram of La Canada, California lives on a fixed income and is disabled due to cancer. In May 1999, Ingram received a troubling letter from his wife's HMO, Prudential. "Your monthly premium will be increased by 21%," the letter read.

"Who can afford $8,000 per year in medical care with all the other expenses associated with going on with life?" asks Ingram. "When you don't have any more money coming in, and they are raising their premiums at this pace, it's mind boggling. You are cornered."

Managed care was premised on lower costs, but these promises now ring hollow.

Americans now face double digit premium increases and rising co-payments and deductibles to insure themselves. The nation's largest non-profit HMO, Kaiser Permanente, raised its premiums in 1999 by 12% for state employees and as much as 50% for individuals.[1] Humana raised premiums 11% to 12% for big employers and 15% to 16% for smaller groups.[2] The Federal Employees Health Benefits Plan, which covers all federal employees and is an important market barometer, had a 10.2% increase in premiums in 1999.[3]

Didn't HMOs contend that they could deliver quality medical care at reasonable cost? If patients have not been getting quality care, where did all the money go?

The final insult of corporate medicine is that it has been a financial swindle.

In Medicare, for instance, HMOs in 1998 began dropping senior patients in many counties because the companies' reimbursements were not high enough. In 1999, the HMOs told the federal government what they are now telling every other purchaser of health care—you will have to pay more for less.

Aetna testified before Congress in March 1999 that "If the current reimbursement structure is not adjusted, more Medicare-Choice organizations are likely to withdraw from areas served and beneficiaries enrolled in the remaining plans will likely experience premium increases or reduced benefits."[4]

In response, Congressman Pete Stark, ranking Democrat on the House Ways and Means Committee said, "As I've already described, we currently pay Medicare HMOs more than we should. We pay the plans more for the people they enroll than we would have paid if those people had stayed in Medicare fee-for-service. To rephrase that, the taxpayers would actually save money if we abolished the Medicare-Choice program today."[5]

To prove his point, Stark offered the following chart of overpayments to HMOs (see "Current Medicare Overpayments to Managed Care Plans," Page 101).

What incensed Congressman Stark most was that the HMO industry wanted a program of "premium support" that would require every Medicare recipient to choose an insurance program, with higher premiums charged to beneficiaries who pick traditional fee-for-service Medicare. The proposal is essentially a full employment act for HMOs because, as Stark says, "it is just a way to raise premiums on seniors and the disabled to force them into barebones, no-frills HMOs that will offer no extra benefits...If plans say they cannot offer extra benefits at a time when we are overpaying them, they certainly won't be able to do so if Medicare were to actually start saving money by paying them more accurately for the people they enroll. And, if plans cannot offer extra premiums, who would want to join a system that rationed their choices and services?"[6]

United States Senator Jay Rockefeller, Representative John Dingell and Representative Jim McDermott—who sat on the Bipartisan Commission On The Future of Health Care—agree with Stark and provide a larger context for American HMO medicine's failure: "We never seriously looked at the experience of foreign countries. All the other major industrialized nations (except Australia) have older populations than the United States, yet they

CURRENT MEDICARE OVERPAYMENTS
TO MANAGED CARE PLANS

(prepared by Rep. Pete Stark's staff)

SOURCE OF OVERPAYMENT	COST TO MEDICARE	SOURCE OF ANALYSIS
Overpayments due to BBA change that removed HCFA's ability to recover overpayments when health care inflation is lower than expected	$800 million in 1997 $8.7 billion over five years $31 billion over ten years	Congressional Budget Office
Overpayments due to lack of risk adjustment	5–6% overpayment to HMOs per beneficiary who is enrolled	Physician Payment Review Commission (now MedPAC) 1996 Annual Report
Overpayments due to inflation of Medicare's share of plan administrative costs	More than $1 billion annually	HHS Office of Inspector General July 1998
Overpayments due to inclusion of fraud, waste and abuse dollars from FFS payments. Managed care plans should better "manage" and therefore avoid such fraud, waste and abuse.	7% annual overpayment Annual savings with corrected 1997 base year would be: $5 billion in 2002 $10 billion in 2007	HHS Office of Inspector General September 11, 1998

are able to insure all their citizens, with reasonably good quality care, for about 30 to 50% less of their Gross National Product than we spend."[7]

The Congressmen quote a 1999 report of the National Academy of Social Insurance: "The United States...has the unfortunate distinction of spending relatively more per capita for the elderly while providing them with less comprehensive coverage with generally higher out-of-pocket costs."[8]

What happened to the claims that corporate-managed services can deliver quality medical care at reasonable cost? Where does all that money go?

One promise of managed care was that health maintenance and managed care organizations have a built-in incentive to keep patients well by providing preventive health care. Some of the best programs do try to keep patients well by providing alternative health care options and frequent screening rather than wait for serious problems to develop. Alternative medicine or health club membership can help Americans stay healthy. It is when patients become ill that the deficiencies of HMO medicine are clear. As evidenced by the stories and statistics in this book, corporate medicine has failed to exhibit caution in treating illnesses in the most timely and least expensive manner. The promise of managed care of long-term cost reduction has proven ephemeral.

Some 20 to 30% of our premiums now pays for overhead—to enrich industry executives and an army of bureaucrats—even as nurses are fired to save money and doctors are required to spend as much time with industry paperwork and obstacles as they do on treating patients. Numerous studies from sources such as the California Medical Association and the *New England Journal of Medicine* have documented the increasing money from our premiums going to the corporate bottom line.[9] Indeed, in "managed care" speak, any money spent on patient care is a "medical loss." This speaks volumes about the goal of corporate medicine—not to *lose* money on patient care.

In addition to rising deductibles and co-payments, the insurance industry is shifting every health care cost it can back on patients. Many Blue Cross patients, for example, recently found themselves forced into a bind: take much higher deductible policies or pay rate increases of up to 58%.[10] Many *insured* Americans find simple surgery can cost them thousands of dollars in out-of-pocket expenses. Orthopedic surgery typically requires serious rehabilitation and physical therapy. Any shoulder or knee surgery, for instance, can require months of physical therapy to avoid further surgery. Many managed care policies, even the more expensive preferred provider plans, typi-

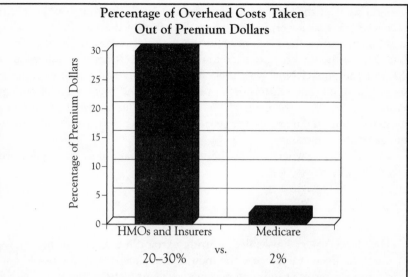

Percentage of Overhead Costs Taken Out of Premium Dollars

HMOs and Insurers   vs.   Medicare

20–30%   2%

*HMOs and Insurers Take Up to 20–30% of Premium Dollars for Their Own Profit, Other Overhead and Marketing Campaigns
Source: Medicare costs from letter by Bruce V. Vladeck, Administrator, Department of Health and Human Services, To Dr. Gordon Schiff, Department of Medicine, Cook County Hospital, October 21, 1994. HMO overhead costs from California Medical Association Knox-Keene Health Plan Expenditure Summaries.

cally place strict time limits (say thirty days)[11] on any physical therapy. So a patient can face the choice of more surgery or paying for physical therapy out of pocket. This absurd approach may lead to some patients having more surgery (presumably covered by insurance) to avoid paying for rehabilitation costs out of pocket.

These are only some of the effects as insurers becoming increasingly monopolistic, with growing power to rapidly escalate premiums in order to squeeze out more profit.

Another symptom of this power is the narrowing freedom that HMO doctors are allowed to exercise in writing prescriptions. Physicians are charted like race horses based on the costs of the prescriptions they write, sometimes regardless of the wellness or age of the patient population they serve. Patients are forced to pay for less effective over-the-counter medications rather than receive prescription drugs at a cost to the HMO. Some HMOs exclude the most effective prescription remedies in favor of cheaper, older drugs. Because of rising costs, employers, in fact, are scaling back retiree health coverage for pharmaceuticals.[12] Mental health coverage, too, has been squeezed with strict limits on therapy, and, perversely, because it is cheaper, a desire to shun therapy and instead prescribe medication.

And what of the uninsured? The promise by the architects of for-profit managed care was lower medical costs, thus expanded access for Americans without insurance. In 1988, prior to the national recession, managed care had 29% of the health care market and there were 36 million uninsured or 17% of the public. Now with a booming economy and near full employment, managed care controls 61% of the market and there are 43.4 million uninsured or 19% of the public.[13] The ranks of the uninsured are growing by close to a million Americans per year. Seventy-five percent of the uninsured are gainfully employed.

In this system, where the public increasingly pays more money for less coverage, who wins?

The Robber Barons of Health Care

HMO executives have piled up truly extraordinary sums of money for themselves. Even if we accept the industry's argument that executive compensation is a result of stunning new management techniques and the elimination of inefficiencies, the money in the executives' pockets formerly was spent on health care.

Does HMO executive compensation really reach the levels of the robber barons of old?

Former U.S. Healthcare CEO Leonard Abramson, now on the board of Aetna, made over $990 million when U.S. Healthcare was acquired by Aetna.[14] The merger was valued at nine billion dollars. This means over 10% of the companies' value ended up in his bank account. Remember the story of Betty Hale, forced to raise $30,000, one dollar at a time, to provide the downpayment on the breast cancer treatment that saved her life. Even so, she came out of it still owing $184,000. The money pocketed by Abramson could have paid for *four thousand* of these kinds of treatments!

Mr. Abramson may be the most striking example of appropriating our health care premium dollars but too many HMO executives live like sultans. Table 1 (Page 105) is illustrative.[15]

Even if we ignore stock options, look at just the top five 1997 salaries for the large publicly traded managed care companies in Table 2 (Page 105).[16]

Ironically, while Wiggins topped the 1997 list for pay, his company crumbled that year—recording consistent losses after computer problems caused it to lose track of billing records and medical costs. Too often, executive compensation and a company's performance bear little relation to one another.

Table 1

CEO	Firm	Pay '96	Stock mid-'97
Malik Hasan	Foundation	$17.2 mil	$166.4 mil
William McGuire	United Hlthcr	$14.7 mil	$74.7 mil
Leonard Shaeffer	Wellpoint	$14.2 mil	$16.5 mil
David Jones	Humana	$10.5 mil	$223.4 mil
George Jochum	MAMSI	$5.0 mil	$16.9 mil
Alan Hoops	PacifiCare	$4.7 mil	$26.9 mil
Stephen Wiggins	Oxford	$4.6 mil	$230.4 mil
Larry House	MedPartners	$2.5 mil	$108.5 mil

Table 2

		Salaries '97
Stephen Wiggins Chairman & CEO	Oxford Health Plans	$30,735,093
Wilson Taylor Chairman & CEO	CIGNA Corp	$12,456,169
William McGuire CEO	United Healthcare	$8,607,743
Ronald Compton Former Chairman	Aetna	$5,383,148
Eugene Froelich Executive VP	Maxicare	$4,720,482

Dr. Malik Hasan, recently forced from his position as CEO of Foundation Health, is a walking illustration of how to get rich from the current health care system. A neurologist by training, he quickly left his medical roots after he began a small Colorado-based HMO. Dr. Hasan embarked on a ferocious merger and acquisition binge that resulted in Foundation Health becoming one of the largest managed care organizations in the nation. Hasan had the dubious distinction of making the *Forbes* magazine list of "overpaid" executives during the nineties, the group of corporate chieftains who "made out far better than shareholders since 1993."[17] Even as Foundation's stock plummeted, his annual salary was in the millions. No blushing violet, Hasan stated, "we are being innovative, and we are helping to solve some very difficult and knotty problems. If we are successful, then I think we deserve not only this, but more."[18] Those "customers" of Foundation Health who were denied or delayed treatment to help amass the millions in pay and options may not agree with Dr. Hasan's definition of success. Dr. Hasan was also quoted about the problems of the uninsured and underinsured: "We are not in the business of social redistribution." Hasan claimed it is the not-for-profit companies that "have a responsibility they have not fulfilled" and they should be doing more to care for the indigent.[19]

Dr. Hasan also made no bones about profiting from the conservative's favorite health care idea, medical savings accounts. "We [for-profit managed care companies] would make out like bandits, but as a physician I have a serious concern about fragmenting the insurance pool...We are going into [MSAs] because these things are going to be a gold mine, let there be no doubt. They are a scam and we will get our share of that scam."[20] It's a dirty job, but someone has to profit.

What is so exceptional about overpaid CEOs? Every industry has them. One answer is that HMO executives like those listed above are among the most highly paid CEOs in the country. The *Crystal Report on Executive Compensation* found HMO chiefs' compensation outpacing their CEO counterparts in other industries by a factor of two to three. After analyzing the pay packages of 1,568 CEOs in thirty-one industries and accounting for company size and stock performance, the study found that HMO executives topped the list, trailed by CEOs of drug manufacturers and biotech companies, brokerages and computer companies.[21]

But does their pay, large though it is, really burden the system? The answer is yes. One study found that the stock-related wealth of just the top twenty-three managed care executives would provide:

- health insurance for six million people, *or*
- health coverage for 14% of the nation's uninsured or alternatively 18% of California's entire population.[22]

In 1996, analyst Don DeMoro added the estimated stock wealth of HMO executives ($6.9 billion) to the combined five-year profits of twelve select managed care companies ($8.8 billion) to the approximate amount of merger and acquisition activity in health care from 1992 to 1996 ($134 billion). This combined amount would provide comprehensive health insurance for 130 million Americans.[23] That's over half of the population currently insured.

In a democracy, how amounts of money this large are spent on a public commodity like health care ought to be the subject of major civic debate. Instead, the fate of precious health care resources is decided behind closed doors in corporate boardrooms.

As Dr. Eli Ginsburg notes, current government health care expenditures in the United States approximate 7% of the Gross Domestic Product. This is the same percentage that Britain spends to provide health care for all its citizens. When one adds all the money employers and individuals pay in an American system that still leaves more than 17% of the public uninsured, it is clear the profits currently skimmed from the system prevent more comprehensive approaches.[24]

Even one of the pioneers of HMO medicine has come to agree with this conclusion. Dr. Robert Gumbiner, the founder of Fountain Valley, California-based FHP, made a lot of money through his company, but insists that his primary concern as a doctor was his patients and providing access to affordable health care. His staff model HMO grew out of a physicians' group to service patients under the original HMO theory that all services would be under one roof at a reduced cost. In discussions in 1997, Gumbiner stated that he believes modern HMOs, that own no medical resources but simply contract with doctors and hospitals to provide care, should be regulated like public utilities. He charged HMOs had become too easily manipulated by the greed of corporate officers and Wall Street, causing patients to suffer.[25]

"The present orientation towards greed is a national catastrophe, as far as I can see," said Gumbiner. "The feeling is, it's okay to be greedy and it's okay to exploit your fellow man just to line your pockets. To me, there is something wrong with that...Quality and investment return are antithetical, because in order to generate short-term profits, the company cannot put money into research and development, new long-range concepts, management training, and all the things that will build a long-term successful organization. So people who strictly have investors' return as their motive are not interested in long-term corporate guarantees."[26]

Why did Gumbiner have a change of heart about the system he helped to found?

Gumbiner contends that following a bout with cancer he was forced from the helm of his company by venture capitalists who conspired to defraud FHP shareholders of over $200 million during the 1997 sale of FHP to PacifiCare. He alleges numerous violations of the federal Securities and Exchange Act.[27]

The allegations, made in conjunction with the lawsuit filed in a Los Angeles federal court, paint a troubling portrait of a handful of insiders seizing control of a health maintenance organization and strip-mining it of its value to long-term shareholders, patients, medical personnel and the public. According to the allegations, "dressing up" FHP for sale involved the dismantling of its medical infrastructure and forward-thinking medical programs in order to reduce overhead costs and make the HMO attractive to any new suitor. Gumbiner revealed that corporate officers not only fired one-third of FHP's doctors to make the company attractive to potential buyers, but went so far as to round up all the potted plants at the HMO and put them in a dark room to die rather than paying for a housekeeper to water them.

The FHP-PacifiCare consolidation was only one in a series of HMO mega-mergers in the 1990s demonstrating that money, not patient care, is the driving motivation of the new medical regime.

That Vexing Problem:
What Do We Do With All the Money?

As managed care companies squeezed more profit from premium dollars, the HMOs piled up so much money that by the end of 1994, Margo Vignola, a Solomon Brother's analyst, estimated the nine biggest publicly traded HMOs were sitting on $9.5 billion in cash. Using this money from premium payments, they soon began to buy up smaller competitors. "Our problem is what to do with the money that comes in, not whether we have enough cash," said Alan Bond, the treasurer of Health Systems International.[28] At that point, the HMO had $475 million in cash in the bank with $15 million pouring in every month. A spending spree soon ensued in the managed care industry, not one that would help patients, but one designed simply to make more money for management and shareholders. Eighteen of the largest for-profit HMOs and managed care companies have now been reduced to six gigantic companies: Aetna, CIGNA, United Healthcare, Foundation Health Systems, PacifiCare and Wellpoint Health.[29] (Kaiser, a non-profit, is the only other HMO in this company.) As Robert Hoehn, director of stock research at Solomon Brothers, recently noted, "The industry in the 21st Century will comprise a few diverse large companies who have pushed out the niche players."[30] While this now seems inevitable, effective anti-trust action could prevent this course.

Unfortunately, the Clinton Administration has been asleep at the switch, failing to break up any major HMO merger to date.

Acquisition and consolidation in the managed care industry is what led to inflated executive compensation packages at the top. Like many industry consolidations, mergers in health care limited choice and drove down services, as the cost of the acquisition had to be absorbed. Health care consolidation has meant riches for the few and downsizing for the rest of us. As the California Medical Association noted during the merger of PacifiCare and FHP, numerous studies indicated few new efficiencies in managed care mergers but merely fewer dominant companies that increased prices and cut services.[31]

For a while this game of musical chairs was possible because Wall Street investors kept bidding up the shares of certain managed care companies. These companies with inflated share prices gobbled up each other as well as community hospitals and non-profits. But then the zero sum financial nature of managed care became increasingly clear, as many companies reported losses and one time "write-offs." Kaiser Permanente lost $270 million in 1997. Stock prices for corporations like Columbia/HCA and Oxford Health collapsed, the latter plummeting by 70%. An August 1998 merger between Humana and United Healthcare to create the largest managed care organization failed when stock prices took a nose dive. Foundation Health Systems, Mr. Hasan's source of wealth, saw its stock drop from thirty-two to five by February 1999. This slump in stock prices may not be short-lived. As Joseph Nocera, editor at large of *Fortune* magazine, observed: "Consider the root cause of the swoon in health stocks. After years of cutting costs with impunity, managed care companies are forced—in no small part as a reaction to intense criticism from doctors and patients—to pay more for treatment."[32] But industry analysts do not discount the role that mismanagement, waste and greed in the race to grow at all costs has had on corporate stability.

A Looming Bailout?

Merger mania has begun to increase prices and restrict choice for patients. The glory days for HMO stocks seem past, now that all the low-hanging fruit has been picked. New profits can be squeezed only from doctors' fees, patient services and raising premiums. In fact, in the spring of 1999, some of the largest companies, like PacifiCare and Aetna, posted significant profits from their premium increases and decision to dump more costly Medicare patients.[33] The depressed stock prices of some of the weaker companies left them as easy pickings for the largest companies.

Where will all these mergers lead? A peculiar possibility is the creation of health care organizations that are "too big to fail." This will be the ultimate perversity, the taxpayer being called upon to subsidize the avarice of top managed care management. This is not just a far-fetched worse case scenario; it already occurred in New York when the taxpayers provided funds for Empire Health in 1993. In New Jersey, an HMO called HIP recently had to be taken over by the state. In 1999, the state of California seized a physician-run medical management company, MedPartners, that served 1.3 million patients. On paper, the company itself had no employees, or assets regulated by the state, only the value of its parent corporation, which said it had no obligation to debtors.[34] A similar failure of San Diego-based FPA Medical Management Corporation left doctors on the hook for tens of millions of dollars in bills for services already rendered.

Sound familiar? Is it like the Savings & Loan bailout, which cost taxpayers up to $400 billion to rescue after quick-buck operators of these deregulated operations went down in fraud and flames? As Michael Schrage, a consultant at MIT noted, "HMO networks will not go bust lending money to aspiring Texas mall moguls or Arizona real-estate developers. The issue here is not bad loans and rising interest rates, it's balancing promised business performance with promised quality and quantity of care. That is becoming ever harder to do."[35] In addition, many HMOs are heavily leveraged and an economic downturn or prolonged stock slump could lead to further bankruptcies.

State and federal regulators have often been slow to look at the impact of mergers on the health care of patients, even as the twin goals of market return and quality medical care now appear mutually exclusive. HMOs cut back to maintain profits in a number of ways—fewer referrals, less treatment, less caution with regard to patient health. Moreover, accountability also suffers. Why worry about fines or sanctions if you hope to sell your company before the lethargic regulatory environment catches you?

The corporate logic favoring monopoly is pushing towards a few giant health care concerns that manage the care for most Americans. To get a snapshot of where the country stands in this spiraling trend toward monopoly, one need go no farther than Aetna's proposed buyout of Prudential's health care business. Despite the slump in profits, or perhaps, in some cases, propelled by it, consolidation continues:

- Aetna currently provides care for one in every twelve Americans; after the merger it will be close to one in eleven.

- 38% of the HMO market in New Jersey will be controlled by the company and over 50% in other small markets. "Our concern is that when a doctor's practice is more than 20% with any carrier, it becomes almost impossible to say something is unacceptable," said Dr. Greg Bernica of the Harris County Medical Society in Texas.[36]

- Aetna will control 39% of the market in Philadelphia, 30% in Atlanta and 33% in Orlando, Florida.

As competition disappears, one impact of this concentration will be increased premiums. Professor Glenn Melnick, a specialist in health care finance at USC, stated the relationship like this: "When the number of competitors goes down, the level of price competition also goes down."[37]

One can also expect less generous benefit packages and lower levels of basic care for the money. As health care expert Charles Blankersteen noted, "Choice in the marketplace is rapidly diminishing, customer service and value are less than spectacular. Who bears the cost of these acquisitions? My bet is the people who buy the services."[38] In other words, you and I do.

Aetna has yet to integrate the last two companies it absorbed, New York Life in 1998 and U.S. Healthcare in 1996. Three years after the merger, doctors and patients of U.S. Healthcare continue to have problems with service. Perhaps what is most telling about Aetna's ongoing consolidation are the patients' and doctors' views. According to a 1998 survey in *U.S. News and World Report*, Aetna ranks last among insurers in customer satisfaction in nine states (Connecticut, Georgia, Illinois, Maryland, Massachusetts, New Hampshire, New York, Texas and Virginia). In five of these states, Aetna is among the biggest three insurers.[39] In California, Aetna was ranked dead last in an opinion survey of doctors conducted by the Pacific Business Group on Health Negotiating Alliance.[40]

One consequence of being the biggest company is that patients and physicians have little leverage to maintain the quality of care. The stranglehold such a company has over physicians is profound. Aetna has employed gag orders on doctors to prevent informed choice by patients. The company has been charged by regulators in New York and Florida with the failure to comply with state laws.[41] Four hundred doctors in Texas, 600 in San Jose, California and over 500 in Southern California have walked out recently due to Aetna's cut-rate reimbursements and contract clauses.

Aetna has tried to foist upon doctors the requirement that they either sign onto all Aetna's plans or they not be allowed to do business with any of its plans. With this "all or nothing" approach, the insurer tries to force physicians who accept any form of insurance from the company to accept all forms. As Dr. Howard Weiner, head of a 1,200 member physicians association noted, "This policy in essence drives the market to all HMO care."[42]

Concerned about Aetna bullying doctors in this way, lawmakers in Texas, Illinois and Rhode Island are considering bans on such all-or-nothing clauses. The North Dakota Senate has passed a prohibition and the Nevada Insurance Commissioner has stopped the practice. Physician concerns about only participating in plans that allow them to meet both their ethical and financial goals, since some plans have higher reimbursements and fewer restrictions on treatment options and referrals, have fallen on deaf ears at leviathan Aetna.[43]

Why should Aetna listen? It has expanded because of its callousness towards physicians' concerns—which has enabled the company to cut costs and conserve cash for purchases.

Financial Failure of The HM-itos

One of the newest problems is that HMOs have foisted onto physician-run medical groups responsibility and risk they are incapable of handling.

The State of California takeover of the financially bereft, physician-run medical group, MedPartners, dramatizes the newest vice spawned by HMO medicine—physicians practicing insurance without a license. When HMO bureaucrats with MBAs started to tell MDs what to do, the physicians' political establishment responded. It created another mid-level bureaucracy run by physicians, called the medical group, to manage risk, like an insurer does.

Like the HMO, the medical group receives a "capitated" rate, only from insurers instead of employers. Like the HMO, the financial incentive for the medical group means the less done for patients, the more it makes. The arrangement has won the medical groups the designation "HM-itos" among insiders.

The medical group system was once touted by some as a middle ground for managed care because doctors purportedly had control again. But as the financial collapse of MedPartners and FPA show, these groups can be financially unsound.

William Sage, who teaches health policy at Columbia University Law School, says, "The entities that are most vulnerable tend to be contractors that have been the most aggressive in terms of growing their companies."[44]

In fact, HMOs have paid to physicians capitated rates that are so low that it would be virtually impossible to take care of patients' real medical needs. In one case, doctors are reported to have received as little as $6 dollars per patient per month from an HMO to manage all their needs.[45]

Because there are so many doctors and so few HMOs, doctors have little leverage in their negotiations. If a medical group receives an HMO contract, among so much competition for them, the group has probably agreed to take whatever reduced-rate the HMO will pay.

When an HM-ito like FPA or MedPartners fails, it is the patient who pays with disruption to the continuity of care. "It's high anxiety," said Edward J. Gold, an oncologist who had patients with the failed HIP Health Plan of New Jersey. "Many patients are afraid. They don't know what's going to happen."[46]

The *Los Angeles Times* reports that the parents of twins recovering from premature delivery were told by their HMO that the children must be moved crosstown from one hospital to another because of the bankruptcy of FPA. FPA's failure forced the primary-care doctor to switch medical groups. That led the doctor to affiliate with a new hospital.

"The Raffertys did not want to break the close ties they had developed with the medical staff at the hospital, especially when it would mean putting Paige and Hannah in the care of people less familiar with the twins' histories," reported Stuart Silverstein and Davan Maharaj. "But the HMO told the Raffertys that they might be responsible for all future hospital-related costs—expenses that wound up totaling hundreds of thousands of dollars—if they refused to allow the babies to be transferred."[47]

Moreover, so much money is spent on bureaucracies to manage risk that the dollars actually spent on patient care has dwindled to a pittance. The irony is that the mounting administrative costs of insuring, not caring, for patients is what is driving health premiums up.

If the HMO takes 20% right off the top for its own business costs, overhead and profit, what does a medical group take? What is paid to the medical group may be reported as a "medical loss" by the HMO (i.e., dollars spent on treatment), but the medical group must then take from this remaining money its administrative costs. These include a burgeoning number of "medical directors" whose job is to say "no" to other physicians who request care. They track and compare the costs of doctors' prescriptions and treatments in fancy bar graphs. Then with remaining dollars the medical group must buy reinsurance, so-called stop-loss insurance, to cover the cost of any catastrophic care that, for instance, a cancer patient may need. In perhaps the biggest financial scam in the system, medical groups are said to even buy stop-loss insurance from the same HMO that passed them the full-risk capitated rate in the first place. So the HMO profits twice.

Climbing out of the Spiral:
Health Care Professionals and Others Fight Back

This trend of consolidation and its deleterious effects are becoming clear to many. Princeton health care expert Uwe Reinhardt echoed Wall Street analyst Hoehn, noting, "The health system is stumbling toward a bilateral monopoly of insurance companies and provider groups in every market. If only one provider is left in a community, it will send the bill to the consumer by raising premiums. The government can then say, 'You have converted health care into a public utility, we need to regulate you.' "[48] Indeed, if there is to be a role for profit-making monopoly health care in our future, it will have to be regulated much like an electrical utility. A reasonable amount of administrative overhead and return on investment would be allowed in return for strict compliance with public standards. This, of course, will be derided by some as socialized medicine, but it merely acknowledges that the market must be regulated in health care. As Professor Reinhardt notes, "If these plans keep buying each other up, there is no longer competition, because executives of the plans can regulate everything they want in one golf game."[49]

How did we get to this point in the monopoly spiral? Large employers clearly were looking to control their health care costs. The strategic underpinning and promises of managed care were promoted by corporate think tanks. Miracles were promised from market-based solutions. Employers signed on. Without full public debate about the wisdom of managed care, Americans now find themselves pushed into HMOs by their employers. Sixty percent of Americans insured through their employers have no choice in health plans and another 20% have only a choice between two plans.

In reaction to a system designed for profiteering that has been squeezed on many fronts, doctors and nurses have rebelled, increasingly unionizing to confront the HMO bosses. The historic approval of a doctor's union by the American Medical Association in June 1999 is instructive. Americans should realize that the concerns of doctors should be their own.

What stands in the way of a few corrective regulations? One unfortunate answer is the employers who pay for much of the insurance. The mantra the insurance industry and the Washington, D.C. trade associations employ today is, "Regulation will lead to increased costs and less coverage." This statement by some corporate employers that increased regulation will drive up costs indicates the often shredded nature of the social compact between employers and employees. It is emblematic of the times that most employers side with for-profit insurers rather than their own employees in health care decisions. If top executives were forced to endure the vagaries of managed care then perhaps we would see real change. Many in top management, however, enjoy gold-plated fee-for-service policies—the kind that used to be available to everyone. Allen Meyerson of the *New York Times* noted, "Many of the nation's largest corporations—including Atlantic Richfield, Charles Schwab, RJR Nabisco, SBC Communications, Gannett—are leading more by precept than example."[50]

The increasing complaints of employees have led some companies to join their employees in the search for increased quality health care. Some employers are indeed rethinking their allegiance to these insurance companies. Bruce Bradley, director of managed care plans for General Motors, noted recently he was, "very concerned that the health care industry is moving away from local delivery and HMOs are becoming more like insurance companies."[51] It behooves our large employers to look at quality of care not just cost in seeking medical care. The managed care industry is merely an expensive middleman. Companies can begin to contract directly with non-profit hospitals or organizations of doctors.

In the meantime, corporate medicine continues to exact its financial toll not only on resources for patient care, but on academic medicine and charity care as well.

Two March 1999 studies published in the *Journal of the American Medical Association* found that in regions where managed care saturation is greatest, physicians are less likely to give the poor free care and academic institutions are less likely to spend their money on scientific research. Ten thousand physicians and 2,000 faculty members were surveyed. Dr. David Blumenthal, director of the Institute for Health Policy at Massachusetts General Hospital and author of the medical-school study, said the results show that where HMO medicine predominates, the ability to work toward "the common good" evaporates.[52]

America's great teaching hospitals and medical school physicians are the envy of the world. The current regime of financing has, however, helped strangle research and left elite physicians with ponderous paperwork fighting insurance companies to pay for required treatment in their clinical practices. The medical school mission is not merely to make money, but to train physicians and conduct cutting-edge research, as well as treating the poor. Urban medical schools frequently end up treating complicated cases from publicly supported hospitals. This is not a recipe for making money. Financial gain should not be the mission of our advanced medical institutions. Academic medicine should not be merely advanced clinics forcing physicians to see patients in a rushed manner. This is the case in many medical schools today.

If our society is going to commit less in public dollars to academic medical centers because we are training fewer doctors, then the money must come from somewhere. One solution could be a dedicated tax on HMO profits to support regional academic medical centers. The health care system benefits greatly from these institutions. As Dr. Harvey Shapiro notes, "Some type of per head tax on HMO revenues should be assessed to develop a trust fund for academics and other functions such as independent oversight, technology assessment, and standards-setting boards."[53]

Medical schools often treat patients with the most difficult and complex diseases or conditions. In addition, any effort to transfer risk to physicians via capitation or any other schemes will naturally hurt physicians who employ their skills treating the sickest patients. According to a recent report by the Commonwealth Fund, medical schools and their clinics make a unique contribution to communities by delivering highly specialized care. For instance, although academic medical centers are only 2% of all community hospitals, they are 47% of trauma units, 46% of burn units, and 31% of HIV/AIDS units.[54] Managed care plans push patients away from academic medical centers, because of higher costs. This deprives these centers of clinical revenues which helped subsidize complex patient care and the disproportionate number of Medicaid and charity cases these hospitals take as referrals.

Teaching hospitals provide nearly 40% of the nation's charity care. How have the financial pressures impacted academic medicine's mission? "It's a total crisis, a complete crisis," said Neil Rudenstine, the president of Harvard in April 1999. "I think anybody who would call it less than that would really just not know what's going on. I'm not quite sure what the cumulative deficit of our four or five closely related hospitals is, but it's certainly well over $100 million, and we haven't even finished the year yet."[55]

UCSF Stanford Health Care lost $50 million in 1999 and expects to layoff 2,000 of its 12,000-person staff. Peter Van Etten, the center's chief executive, said, "I have to say the services we will provide can't be of the same quality that we would provide with 2,000 more people."[56]

Academic hospital downsizing has also sparked an unprecedented push towards discouraging doctoring. The nation has more than 700,000 physicians. As a result, the federal government has, for the first time, agreed to pay hospitals around the nation hundreds of million of dollars *not* to train doctors.[57] Hospitals that limit their number of residents receive more federal funds. The idea is to give hospitals an incentive to save money.

Academic medicine has also been hurt by declines in medical research despite increased funding of the National Institute of Health in the nineties. The Administration, though, is proposing only a 2% increase in FY 2000. The United States now spends less per capita on medical research than England, Denmark and France. Research is too often conducted by pharmaceutical companies hoping to cash in with exorbitant prices on lifestyle enhancing drugs. Unchecked corporate medicine will certainly facilitate this transition. The patent offices of drug companies are working overtime. While private research can be very important, many of the most critical American medical breakthroughs have relied on public research dollars, which are now evaporating.

The Political Muscle of the Insurance Industry

Where does an increasing amount of HMO cash go? Unfortunately, to Capitol Hill lobbyists and Madison Avenue spin-doctors.

Growing monopolies mean more than rising premiums, constraining doctors, cutting care, and foisting costs onto patients. It also translates into political power. The insurance industry has added hundreds of millions in profits during the rise of managed care and is spending significant sums of this money to preserve its dominion. It defeated the Clinton health plan through its misleading "Harry and Louise" ads and millions in lobbying dollars. It is laughable that the centerpiece of the insurance industry advertising campaign concerned the inability to consult with your family physician under the Clinton plan. The proposal may have been overly complex and bureaucratic, but the industry has since limited coverage, choice and access to specialists in a manner never envisioned by the Administration. Today, "Harry and Louise" would be cast as a woman unable to get a mammogram annually and a man unable to schedule a cardiogram—the victims of corporate bureaucrats, not government employees.

The Patient Protection Bill introduced by Senator Edward Kennedy and Congressman John Dingle and endorsed by President Clinton is the best opportunity to reduce the industry's power over health care decisions. It would, among other things, hold the insurance companies legally account-able for denying medically necessary care. In March of 1999, the Business Roundtable launched yet another round of multi-million dollar television advertising against the plan during the NCAA basketball championships. The ads compare reforms allowing patients the right to sue their HMO with playing roulette and refer callers to the HMO industry's 1-800 hotline to send a message to Congress. Another multi-million dollar ad campaign is underway at this writing in the summer of 1999.

Republicans, who by and large oppose liability for the insurance industry, read the 1998 polls and did offer cosmetic reforms. The party made no real attempts to pass even these reforms, preferring to defeat the Democratic pro-posals and attempt to increase the strength of anti-reform forces in the 1998 election.

The message was not lost on the insurance industry in 1998. The industry certainly responded with its wallets. Direct contributions to candidates from the health insurers doubled between 1994 and 1998. Certain favorites like Republican Congresswoman Anne Northrup reportedly received more than 10% of their total contributions from the industry in return for leading the fight against increased patient protection. The industry was also active in so-called issue ads. The American Association of Health Plans spent a consider-able sum against the Senate challenge of Democrat John Edwards in North Carolina who campaigned heavily on behalf of patients rights. The ads vilified trial lawyers and stated Americans would lose their health care if patient pro-tection measures passed. The voters thought otherwise, and Edwards won a narrow victory.

Frank Pallone, a six-term New Jersey representative, also learned the dangers of opposing the insurance industry. A front group, Americans for Job Security, spent over $1.2 million trying to defeat Pallone after his aggressive promotion of the Patient Protection Bill. Over one million of the organization's $7 million advertising campaign against pro-HMO reform Democrats was reported as a grant from the insurance industry. Pallone still won handily.

One estimate of total industry spending during the first six months in 1998 for direct lobbying to defeat managed care reform topped off at $60 million. This averaged $112,000 per member of Congress. This outrageous sum of money, of course from patients' premiums, does not include direct candidate contributions nor $11 million in "feel good" advertising. This figure dwarfs the estimated $40 million spent by the tobacco industry to defeat federal anti-smoking legislation. The chief spokesman of the Texas Medical Association questioned why the health plans do not spend premium dollars on medical care: "If this were about patient care, they would shift the money into patient care aspects, therefore dissipating some of the consumer insurrection. What this is really about is control and power. It speaks volumes about their intent."[58]

The industry has already announced its plans to spend millions of dollars in New Hampshire and Iowa to affect the outcome of the presidential primaries in 2000 and will no doubt spend tens of millions in 1999 and 2000 in the renewed effort to prevent federal and state regulation. The industry, with allies such as the Chamber of Commerce, is intent on maintaining a stranglehold on the health care of the American public.

Corporate for-profit medicine has as its core principle interests inimical to any American who is seriously ill or injured. Unfortunately, over the course of time, this is the fate of almost all of us. The message from the industry to its captive customers is clear. Profits will be protected at all costs. Unless the public rallies to support meaningful reform, the industry will continue to curtail medical care to maintain profits. One of the founders of the HMO concept was Paul Ellwood, MD. He recently noted, "For those of us who devoted our lives to reshaping the health system trying to make it better for patients, the thing (managed care) has been a profound disappointment."[59]

CHAPTER FIVE

Getting Away With Murder

Why You Can't Sue Your HMO

"They let a clerk thousands of miles away make a life-threatening decision about my life and my baby's life without even seeing me and overruled five of my doctors," said Slidell, Louisiana resident Florence Corcoran. It is a story that echoes so many tragedies recounted in this book. But as with many of the other stories, there's a twist—a second tragedy. "They don't get held accountable. And that's what appalls me. I relive that all the time. Insurance companies don't answer to nobody."

Corcoran faced a high-risk pregnancy. Her obstetrician ordered her hospitalized, as she had been in a previous high-risk birth. Yet her managed health care company, United Healthcare, overruled her doctor and denied the hospitalization, even though it had a second opinion agreeing with the doctor's advice. Instead, Corcoran's insurer ordered home nursing for ten hours each day.

During the last month of Corcoran's pregnancy, when no nurse was on duty, the baby went into distress. Denied the monitors and care she would have had in the hospital, Florence Corcoran's baby died.

Mrs. Corcoran filed a wrongful death action in Louisiana state court, alleging medical malpractice. But because of a legal loophole that exempts health insurance companies from such lawsuits in instances where the plaintiff receives insurance through her employer, as Corcoran did, her managed care insurer could not be held liable!

The case was dismissed, but not for lack of merit. Fifth Circuit Court of Appeal Judge Carolyn Dineen King wrote that "the basic facts are undis-

Florence Corcoran

puted," but "the result ERISA [the federal Employee Retirement Income Security Act] compels us to reach means that the Corcorans have no remedy, state, or federal, for what may have been a serious mistake." She continued, saying ERISA "eliminates an important check on the thousands of medical decisions routinely made. With liability rules generally inapplicable, there is theoretically less deterrence of substandard medical decision making."[1]

"If I go out on the street and murder a person, I am thrown in jail for murder and held accountable," said Corcoran. "What's the difference between me and this clerk thousands of miles away making a life decision which took the life of my baby and she gets off scott-free and keeps her job?"

This is the dirty little secret that lets HMOs walk away from responsibility for denying or interfering with medically appropriate treatment.

Corporate health providers that administer employer-paid health benefits are above the law. How big is this loophole that Florence Corcoran and her baby fell through? Fully 125 million Americans with employer-paid health coverage in the private sector are unable to sue their HMOs or insurers for damages—no matter how egregious the HMO conduct or serious the consequences of the treatment denial. HMOs can operate with virtual impunity.

How did they get this shield of immunity?

In 1987, creative insurance-industry lawyers convinced a majority of the Justices of the U.S. Supreme Court that the federal Employee Retirement Income Security Act of 1974 or ERISA put the industry above state common law—under which damages are available to injured consumers.[2] How did they convince the highest court in the land? Company lawyers argued that the corporation was not technically in the business of insurance but merely an administrator of employee benefits. This meant that it could not be held accountable under state laws, but was subject to ERISA's federal scheme, which provides little remedy, as discussed in more detail below.

The *Pilot Life Insurance v. Dedeaux* case did not involve an HMO, but rather a disability insurer. But as managed care became ascendant, the precedent stuck.

If a patient who is denied doctor-recommended care by his HMO tries to file a case in state court, where damages are available under state common law, HMO lawyers will have the case "removed" to federal court under ERISA's rules. HMOs or insurers that lose the federal ERISA grievance only pay the cost of the procedure or benefit they denied in the first place, no other damages or penalties. Thus there is no financial incentive for the HMO to provide timely treatment. And that is the good news. The bad news is that companies are obligated to provide the cost of the benefit only when the patient survives long enough to receive it. *If the patient dies before receiving the treatment, the insurer or HMO pays nothing.* Because there is no meaningful penalty for denying medically necessary treatment, there is no incentive to approve costly care.

Imagine that the penalty for bank robbery was limited to giving back the stolen money. No jail time, no fines, just pay the money back—and only if you are caught. To top it off, the repaid money would be interest free. Would bank robbery increase under such conditions? That's the situation HMOs and insurers enjoy under ERISA.

For this reason, even conservative judges have condemned ERISA's injustice and pleaded for Congress to clarify accountability for HMOs.

California's conservative Federal Judge J. Spencer Letts wrote in 1997, when he was hamstrung by ERISA's ban on damages, "This case reveals that for benefit plans funded and administered by insurance companies, there is *no* practical or legal deterrent to unscrupulous claims practices. Without these practical incentives there is no counter-balance to insurance companies' interest in minimizing ERISA claims."[3] (emphasis added)

Federal Judge William Young, appointed by Ronald Reagan, also recently expressed his frustration with ERISA's prohibition in a Massachusetts case: "Disturbing to this Court is the failure of Congress to amend a statute that, due to the changing realities of the modern health care system, has gone conspicuously awry from its original intent. This court had no choice but to pluck [the] case out of state court...and then, at the behest of Travelers, to slam the courthouse doors in her [the wife's] face and leave her without any remedy. ERISA has evolved into a shield of immunity that protects health insurers...from potential liability for the consequences of their wrongful denial of health benefits."[4]

These judges are reacting to violation of a basic tenet needed to make a market function: fundamental fairness.

When good companies are not rewarded and bad ones are not punished, the market is not free to compete on the basis of quality. ERISA's shield of immunity supplies a powerful incentive to ignore the most basic ethical considerations in providing care: low quality actors come out ahead because they make the most profits by providing the least and worst care. Competition is then almost exclusively focused on cost-cutting—a structural recipe for the crisis of quality we now have under HMO medicine. Insurers find this loophole so lucrative that they even teach their claim handlers to respond differently depending on whether the claim is subject to the ERISA loophole or not. In some cases, the shield of immunity does not apply and patients can sue their HMO, a circumstance that will be discussed shortly. An internal Aetna videotaped training session, discovered during a 1998 Alaska lawsuit, shows how insurers and HMOs can teach claim handlers to treat ERISA and non-ERISA claims differently.

The videotape of company lawyers training Aetna claims managers shows they consider liability exposure as a determinant of whether or not to pay a policyholder's claim.[5] As the Associated Press reported, "The topic is long-term disability claims, not health insurance, but the company says its policies do not differ."[6]

Early in the training video, Aetna's in-house counsel Jeffrey Blumenthal clarifies the difference between ERISA and non-ERISA cases: "We have an obligation, certainly, in a non-ERISA setting, under State law, to conduct what is called a reasonable investigation."[7] The implication is that in the no-liability ERISA case, no investigation is necessary.

Aetna is far more cautious about cases in the one state where HMOs and insurers are liable for their actions. Blumenthal notes of a new state liability law in Texas, meant to apply to all patients: "In the state of Texas, the State Court—in that scenario, we could be subject to—we'll get into more of this later—to back pay and damages, to punitive damages, to a whole range of extra-contractual liability that could be many, many millions of dollars."[8]

Another attorney adds about ERISA, "It is a very important distinction...one you have to know when you're processing a claim."

Still another attorney says, "As a practical matter, you really may have to do more on a non-ERISA plan to protect against some of the exposure we're talking about."[9]

Later, realizing what's been said, and trying to cover it up, Blumenthal said, "Well, let me just say that in the non-ERISA context, none of you will ever have to testify, 'Well, you know, we do more in the non-ERISA context than the ERISA context because our lawyers tell us there's—punitive damage exposure.' That—that would be a cry to Congress to enact legislation to repeal ERISA, there's obviously attempts to do that."[10]

Writing about Blumenthal's blundering disclaimer, *Orange County Register* columnist Dan Weintraub says, "It would be ironic if Blumenthal's statement—as recorded on Aetna's own tape—becomes the cry that Congress finally heeds...The picture is grainy, the lighting is weak and the sound fades in and out. But the message in a newly disclosed videotape could not be clearer: Aetna Inc. treats people who can sue for punitive damages better than those who can't."[11]

The tape and evidence in the case also show that following the *Pilot Life* decision, Aetna dropped its field investigation force, (the people who 'worked up' documentation of legitimate claims so they could be paid) and increased its claims personnel caseloads to four to four-and-a-half times the industry average. This made it harder to document a claims file for payment. The burden of proving that a claim should be paid shifted from the company to the patient.

After viewing the tape, national columnist Jane Bryant Quinn wrote, "The tape shows that, instead of gathering evidence itself, Aetna tells the sick person to handle it. If he or she doesn't present exactly the proof Aetna wants, or presents it after the final deadline for claims, too bad."[12]

In the training video, one long-time Aetna employee spells out the differences in company policy before and after the shield of immunity from prosecution was erected by the *Pilot Life* case in 1987. The twenty-year veteran of the Department says, "We used to investigate 100% of our cases practically, and that was called 'overkill.' But now we investigate a far, very tiny percentage of that...And what we're finding today is that the claim investigator does not have the [time]—because of the 8[00] or 900 case load versus 200 for competitors, and go out and solicit all these [materials]...the question is having the time to go out and investigate and work up that file the way it's supposed to be."[13]

Investigations Stop After *Pilot Life* Ruling

While Aetna initially told the Associated Press that the procedures at issue applied to HMO claims too, company spokespeople subsequently retreated from that position, later writing, according to Quinn, that "the interpretation of the videotape is inaccurate, but because of the misperception, Aetna would change its system." Nonetheless, testimony and documents in the case at issue, *Fisher v. Aetna*, and another Alaska case brought to light the following startling revelations about Aetna's claims handling in wake of the the *Pilot Life* decision. They show how for-profit insurers and HMOs can change their policies when given shields of virtual immunity. After the 1987 ruling:

- Aetna abolished its claims-handling guidelines—leaving analysts without guidance about how to fairly treat claimants. Trial testimony demonstrated that the previous guidelines worked and were essential for analysts to treat claimants fairly. Industry experts characterized the elimination of the guidelines as outrageous.[14]

- Aetna eliminated field representatives in 1989, and by 1992, had none. Field representatives are the people who ordinarily investigate a claim by talking to the claimants, the doctors involved in treatment, the claimants' friends, and co-workers. Field representatives are often necessary to fairly investigate and evaluate a disability claim. Trial testimony reveals that Aetna no longer interviews claimants and rarely contacts friends and co-workers or the treating doctors (except to get medical records).[15]

- In the early 1990s, Aetna began asking its analysts to reduce the use of Independent Medical Exams (IME). These are exams by independent doctors to gain another perspective on whether or not someone is disabled. Instead of IMEs, Aetna placed increasing reliance on its inhouse doctors.

- By the mid-1990s, Aetna-based evaluations of its analysts in part on their ability to reduce investigations and reduce payments on claims.

The training tape makes clear that the burden of proving a claim falls on the consumer. This is an enormous advantage to the insurer since at this point the patient, who must supply all necessary information to the investigator, is often weak with illness or in an otherwise medically compromised condition. It is hardly the time for someone to vigorously vindicate their rights.

The adjusters know how difficult it is for a disabled person to handle those burdens and that the claims personnel is in the best position to gather information and investigate claims. In the video, they put it this way:

> Trainee: If we're trying to be very specific about what kind of—wouldn't it be better, you know, by law, if it should go to court or whatever, [for the analyst] to do the requesting [of the medical records] themselves.[16]
>
> Another trainee: If you are concerned with all that money going out, why couldn't some of the money be allocated to perhaps set up a special (indiscernible), reviewing these claims (indiscernible)—she has a better handle on, really what our claim load is more so than you do. How come time can't be spent on people that can really go out and research all these medicals that are just sitting there in the file?[17]

Aetna lawyers claimed "management" rejected those ideas.

Medical Apartheid

The most tragic consequence of the Aetna system is not just that consumers shoulder the burden of proving their claims, but the caste-like system that results. Two patients with precisely the same medical needs are treated very differently by the Aetna claims system— simply because one is subject to the ERISA loophole and one is not.

Patients with employer-paid health care in the private sector have become second class citizens in the minds of insurers and HMOs because these working Americans have no recourse to receive damages against the companies.

The ERISA law applies only to private industry benefits. Americans who buy their own health insurance, employees who received health insurance through church or government employers, and Medicaid and Medicare recipients, are not subject to the ERISA loophole and can sue their insurer for bad faith and punitive damages.

The non-ERISA claims that are subject to liability, according to the training video, receive an extra level of review and are all considered by the Specialty Review Team. The ERISA claims can be denied without going to the Specialty Review Team. There is no need for scrutiny, because there is no remedy for the patient if a legitimate claim is denied.

The lack of remedies for patients with employer-paid insurance benefits in private industry following the *Pilot Life* decision allows HMOs and insurers to breach the code of good faith and fair dealing with impunity. The Aetna evidence—which the company tried to keep under seal—shows how insurers can respond when their insureds have no remedy.[18]

Unfortunately, Aetna does not appear to be alone.

How to Evaluate a Claim in Six Minutes

Los Angeles Times columnist Ken Reich noted that, after two columns on patient complaints at Prudential HealthCare, eleven of Prudential's very own employees wrote or phoned saying they were troubled about the way PruCare deals with claims.

"Emphasis at the L.A. center is on individual production rather than quality," e-mailed one employee at the company's new Los Angeles National Service Center, one of four such centers nationwide. "Currently, an examiner is expected to 'finalize'—that is, pay or deny—82 claims per day. This is roughly one claim every five to six minutes, which leaves little time for careful consideration of difficult issues...Productivity is reported on weekly scorecards, and the cumulative scores are posted, by name, for all examiners to see. Few want to be in last place."[19]

The employee continued. "Credit is given only for either successfully paying...or denying a claim. Leaving it pending for more information or referring it to someone with more experience...results in zero credit to the examiner for the time spent. Some of these examiners intentionally deny claims that could be processed correctly so they may meet the standard for production. They...rationalize that the provider or member will appeal the denial and eventually get paid correctly. This ultimately results in additional delays and an unnecessarily increased workload."

Patients Pay The Price

Congress and state legislatures are still grappling with the growing toll of ERISA casualties.

Stephanie Ulrich, the woman discussed in a previous chapter who had an aneurysm, was not admitted for an angiogram, and was almost shunted to a nursing home, is one example of an ERISA casualty. And ERISA prevented the widow of Glenn Nealy, the cardiac patient who could not get to an HMO cardiologist (Chapter One), from ever collecting a dime.

These patients, like the other 125 million Americans with private sector employer-paid insurance benefits, all are subject to the ERISA loophole and have been unable to hold their HMOs and insurers accountable for damages.

There is little question that one reason these patients have been treated so callously is their lack of a remedy. Judith Packevicz, whose doctors recommended a liver transplant denied by her HMO (Chapter One), was also an ERISA victim—of a sort. Packevicz first filed her case in federal court under ERISA law, not for damages but simply to force the HMO to provide treatment. But because she received health care through her public employer, the City of Saratoga Springs, she soon discovered that the shield of immunity did not apply to the HMO and she could file in state court and receive damages. Once she did refile, within a few days, her HMO relented and told her it would reevaluate her situation and, ultimately, agreed to pay. This was the good news. Unfortunately, it was too late. Packevicz died before she could benefit from the transplant that might have saved her. She was a victim of the HMO immunity shield even when it did not apply to her.

Ulrich's story is also very instructive. She had two HMOs—one through her mother's private employer, and the other through her own public employer. In the end, the health care company hired by her public employer, the non-ERISA carrier, paid its share of the bills. The private-sector, ERISA claim was never covered.

At least Ulrich received her care. Others have been less fortunate.

In 1991, Phyllis Cannon was diagnosed with acute myeloblastic leukemia. When she went into remission, her doctor urged that she undergo an autologous bone marrow transplant (ABMT). Yet her insurer, Blue Lines HMO, delayed authorization for three months, by then the cancer had returned and Mrs. Cannon could no longer benefit from the treatment.

Her HMO claimed that Cannon's bone marrow transplant would be "experimental," even though this procedure was a covered benefit under Cannon's policy. She died just weeks later. Because Mrs. Cannon received

Jerry and Phyllis Cannon

health insurance through her employer, the ERISA loophole required Blue Lines to pay no price for its delay and gave Phyllis' husband, Jerry Cannon, no compensation for the death of his wife.

When he brought the case to court, the judge was sympathetic. But noting the problem of ERISA's broad preemption of remedies for wrongful death, Judge John Porfilio, of the Tenth Circuit Court of Appeal, ruled in Cannon's case that, "Although moved by the tragic circumstances of this case, and the seemingly needless loss of life that resulted, we conclude that the law gives us no choice but to affirm"[20] that Mr. Cannon has no remedy for his loss.

In the fee-for-service age, traditional insurers may not have paid bills for services already rendered. This often drove people into bankruptcy. But because the patient had already been treated, the issue was only money.

Under HMO medicine, the shield of immunity can be a death sentence. When treatment itself is withheld, patients die.

The HMO Shell Game:
When is an Insurer not an Insurer?

Consider the tragedy of 34 year-old Stephen Parrino who was diagnosed with a brain tumor. His HMO, lacking expertise in the area, referred Stephen to California's Loma Linda University Medical Center. There Parrino underwent successful surgery to remove the tumor.

Stephen's treating physicians at Loma Linda immediately ordered that he undergo proton-beam therapy no later than seven to ten days after the surgery. Proton-beam therapy is recognized as appropriate and necessary by the medical community for the prevention of tumor reoccurrence. The therapy is extremely expensive, and Stephen could not pay for it on his own.

When Loma Linda contacted Stephen's HMO to request that the company authorize the treatment, the HMO responded that it would not pay. Stephen called his HMO's customer service department. The HMO claim reviewer explained that the company would not pay for the treatment because it was "experimental, unapproved and not medically necessary" and thus "did not fall within managed care guidelines."

According to Stephen's father, Nick Parrino, Loma Linda Hospital told Stephen, at the time of his denial, that proton radiation was being paid for by fifty-two insurance companies, Medicare and Medicaid.

Even though the HMO had originally referred Stephen to Loma Linda, the company now rejected Loma Linda's judgement that the treatment was "medically necessary." And the specialists specifically said the proton-beam therapy must be given no later than two weeks following brain surgery to be effective.

During repeated calls to the HMO claim reviewer, Stephen threatened a lawsuit if the company did not authorize the treatment within the seven to ten day time period. He continued calling during an almost two month period, but was informed that authorization had been denied. The HMO claim reviewer did say he would ask for a second opinion from a doctor at the USC Kenneth Norris, Jr. Cancer Hospital.

Seven weeks after the surgery had been completed, the USC doctor seconded the opinion that the proton-beam therapy was "medically necessary" for Stephen. He put in the request for authorization to Stephen's HMO.

Two weeks later, Stephen had a CT scan at Loma Linda. He was informed that his brain tumor had reoccurred in the same place it was removed. The very next day, Stephen was informed by his HMO that he had been approved for the proton-beam therapy. But the delay had sealed Stephen's fate.

Stephen underwent a second surgery at Loma Linda during which the surgeons found the tumor more difficult to remove than during the first surgery. The recurring tumor spread to the rest of Stephen's body, including his lungs. Stephen was diagnosed with metastatic cancer.

Stephen subsequently brought suit against the HMO in state court, alleging that the denial of his initial claim for proton-beam therapy was improper. Claiming ERISA preemption, the HMO had the action removed to the U.S. District Court for the Central District of California. Stephen requested a remand motion, but the District Court denied it and dismissed each of his cause of actions.

With no timely remedy against his HMO, the recurring tumor killed Stephen Parrino. Stephen's estate appealed the decision, arguing that the removal to the District Court was improper. However, on appeal the Ninth Circuit found, "Because Parrino was a participant in an ERISA plan, and at least some of his claims fall within the scope of [ERISA], they are completely preempted." The U.S. Supreme Court refused to hear the case on appeal.

The family is left with no remedy. The Parrinos are double victims—first losing Stephen when the HMO denied needed care, then by a system that denies patients and their survivors legal recourse.

It is a cruel irony. HMOs evade accountability for failing in precisely the role they claim to succeed at: managing care, not delivering it.

Wronged patients and their loved ones can take doctors to court for medical negligence. Such cases of quality-of-care violations are not preempted by ERISA. But when the families of patients like Stephen Parrino try to take their HMO to court, the HMO claims that it did not deny medical treatment—but rather simply denied coverage—and therefore cannot be sued for medical malpractice. HMOs that administer employer-paid benefits know that they cannot be taken to court, either, for breaching the duty of good faith, because such state lawsuits are superseded by ERISA under the reasoning of *Pilot Life*.

Are HMOs insurers or caregivers, money managers or care managers?

Tragedies such as Stephen Parrino's occur because HMOs hide behind many fictions, depending upon which is convenient.

On television, HMOs advertise that their doctors and treatment are the best. In court, HMOs claim they do not deny medical treatment, simply coverage, and therefore cannot be held accountable for negligence. In advertisements, HMOs promise patients that they will be protected when they are sick. But when a patient with employer-paid health care tries to sue an HMO for bad faith, the company claims it is not an insurance company, but simply an administrator of employee benefits, so, under ERISA, it cannot be held accountable for damages.

For patients with employer-paid health care, who are precluded from receiving damages over a benefit dispute (coverage decision), HMOs deny treatment under the coverage tag and the ill have no remedy.

For other patients, who can receive damages over an insurance company's bad faith, the HMO decision is presented as a medical determination. In the best case, the patient is told an "expert" has reviewed the file and the proposed treatment is not medically appropriate. In the worst case, the patient is never even told that there is any treatment available. Catch 22 is alive and well in the HMO industry. Often, no formal denial is ever made because a written denial is typically a trigger for a state review process.

This shell game keeps too many patients on the HMO industry's death row—facing a denial of care but having no clear remedy.

Two hundred years of carefully crafted state common law has evolved to hold all sorts of wrongdoers accountable for all types of negligence. At the urging of both Democrats and Republicans, Congress has taken up returning actions against HMOs that improperly administer employee-employer benefit claims to the province of state common law. Unfortunately, in 1998, Republican leaders who have traditionally been aligned with the insurance industry, buried ERISA reform efforts in committee. Naturally, members of Congress have gold-plated insurance programs.

How closely have GOP leaders collaborated with the insurance industry to thwart reformers in their own party? An internal October 1997 memo from an HMO industry lobbyist to her colleagues said Senate Republican Leader Trent Lott and his aides had indicated that, "Senate Republicans need a lot of help from their friends on the outside" to stop ERISA reform, and that insurance industry lobbyists should "Get off your butts, get off your wallets,"[21] meaning pump money into anti-reform efforts and politicians. Still, rank-and-file Republican reformers, while temporarily silenced by party leaders, will rise again.

Conservative Rep. Charlie Norwood of Georgia said: "One of the primary reasons I sold my dental practice in 1994 to run for Congress was to make sure the Clinton plan was dead for good. The Wall Street variety of Republican seems to think that Clinton Care is just fine, as long as corporations run the show instead of the federal government. Health insurance is the only industry in this country that enjoys a federally mandated shield against liability for its actions, and that's at the root of the horror stories of managed care."[22]

ERISA reform is bipartisan, in part because it deals with an issue of fundamental fairness and the failure of the free market to be truly "free." Placing trust in 200 years of carefully-crafted state common law is a non-regulatory, localized, state-based approach supported by conservative ideology and free-market philosophy. Conservatives, who love state control in other areas, should not insist on federal uniformity in health care.

But corporations do not like proposals that would impose liability on HMOs. They claim it would drive up health care costs. This argument is but a fig leaf. Two July 1998 studies show ERISA reform would be both health enhancing and cost effective.

- In a study of one million public employees in California, people who can sue their managed care plans already, the Kaiser Family Foundation found the cost of lawsuits and settlements minimal—no more than thirteen cents per member, per month.[23]

- The Congressional Budget Office reported that giving patients the right to sue would add only 1.2% to health care premiums, including costs of so-called defensive medicine. That's less than half the minimum estimate of the HMO-industry lobby.[24]

But the greatest evidence that ERISA reform is both cost-effective and health-enhancing is from Texas.

In 1997, Texas became the first state in the nation to offer its citizens a way around ERISA, by allowing HMOs to be taken to court for what is a new cause of action for corporate medical negligence. The Texas law skirts ERISA's preemption because the law provides damages for quality-of-care violations or medical negligence—which Courts have upheld as within the state's province—instead of damages for bad faith and other contract-based benefit disputes which have traditionally been preempted by ERISA.

The Texas law, enacted under Republican Governor George W. Bush[25], holds HMOs accountable when they have "exercised influence or control which result in the failure to exercise ordinary care." While HMOs claim states cannot pass such laws, a legal challenge to the Texas statute by Aetna was rejected in September 1998 by U.S. District Judge Vanessa Gilmore, who set aside arguments that the Texas "right to sue" statute violated the 1974 federal law governing employee pensions.

The Court wrote: "In this case, the Act addresses the quality of benefits actually provided. ERISA 'simply says nothing about the quality of benefits received.' Dukes, 57 F.3d at 3576…the Court concludes that the Act does not constitute an improper imposition of state law liability on the enumerated entities."[26]

The Texas experience shows that such a liability law does not raise health care costs or result in litigiousness. The law's author, Texas State Senator David Sibley says, "When the state of Texas passed its state legislation holding managed care organizations accountable, the managed care industry said it would cost over a billion dollars. When an actuarial analysis by Milliman & Robertson for a Texas HMO was performed on the impact of the bill after it was passed, the cost was estimated to be far less—a mere thirty-four cents per member per month (about 0.3%)." This estimate is from the industry's accountant.

"The law became effective on September 1, 1997 and since then not a single case has been filed," Sibley noted in June 1998, and since only a few lawsuits have been filed. "When asked about the impact, Texas physicians say they have not heard of any litigation but believe they are now receiving more attention from managed care reviewers when requesting necessary medical care for patients."[27] Thus rather than spark a litigation explosion, the exposure to liability deters HMOs from withholding care and, instead, encourages them to provide quality services. It helps prod the corporate conscience.

Carol Cropper writes in the *New York Times*, "What lessons does Texas offer? The short answer is that the spotty early evidence does not support a lot of the dire warnings on Capitol Hill about a landslide of litigation." Cropper also cites a Texas Department of Insurance report which found that between September 1997 and March 1998 the increase in total spending per member per month of full service HMOs was only 0.1%.[28]

The implications are clear. Unless there are consequences to an HMO for denying expensive treatment, no matter how sorely the treatment is needed or how justified by medical science, the financial calculus of "managing care" will weigh toward withholding and delaying costly care.

The American public certainly understands the principle at work. Nearly eight out of ten Americans support having the right to sue HMOs, even if it means a $1–$10 increase in premiums per month, according to a poll com-

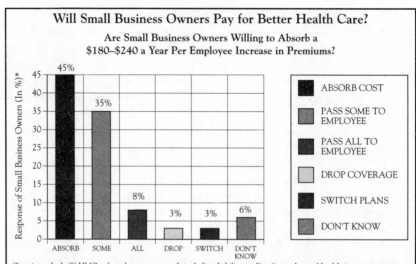

Will Small Business Owners Pay for Better Health Care?

Are Small Business Owners Willing to Absorb a
$180–$240 a Year Per Employee Increase in Premiums?

Question asked: (If HMO reform laws were passed, including liability, and)... "your share of health insurance premiums increased by 15 TO 20 DOLLARS per month for a single employee, would your company (organization) be most likely to...?"
*The survey results in the chart are based on the responses of 294 out of 800 heads of companies and organizations with fewer than 100 full-time employees surveyed between March 18 and May 9, 1998. The sample of 294 were those who offered health insurance benefits to their employees.

Source: Kaiser Family Foundation/American Small Business Alliance Education Fund Survey, June 17, 1998.

missioned by the American Psychological Association and reported in *USA Today* in June 1998.[29]

How can the ERISA loophole be closed? By legislative action.

Congress has the power to end ERISA's preemption of state consumer protection laws and states can specifically skirt the ERISA loophole and hold HMOs accountable for their decisions by creating a new "corporate negligence" law for HMOs, such as the one in Texas.

Most states have "corporate practice of medicine" laws that say corporations cannot practice medicine. That is how HMOs claim in court that they don't practice medicine, only provide coverage. Yet HMOs do deny treatment and overturn doctors' decisions. HMOs do dictate limits on medical treatments and care. New state laws, like the one in Texas, could require that HMOs be held accountable for reckless health care decisions.

The return to state laws is particularly needed because under state common law, HMOs, like other corporations, must act with good faith and obey the covenant of fair dealing. But until Congress and state legislatures act, patients will continue to be at the mercy of HMOs and insurers.

For every year of delay, ERISA casualties mount.

- Rhonda Rae Fleming Bast's HMO delayed her bone marrow transplant and she died. Three years later, Rhonda's husband and son filed suit against the HMO. However, because Rhonda received her health care through her employer, the state law claim was preempted by the federal ERISA law. Deciding that the wrongful death claims of the Seattle resident's family were preempted by Congress, the Appeals Court said without Congressional action there was nothing it could do.

- "Until this day, my HMO refuses to pay for the procedure that saved my career and my quality of life," says Debra Moran, of Winfield, Illinois. "If the HMO knew they would have to pay damages, I don't think they would ever treat me this way. I thought I had more rights, but instead I am paying huge credit card finance fees to pay off this procedure. I mortgaged our future and our house, as well as our 401k, to pay for this surgery." Moran's managed care ERISA nightmare began in July 1995 when she developed pain in her hand, wrist, elbow, shoulder and neck. The pain came from two related conditions that impair circulation and neural transmission. As the conditions worsened, the pain grew. The Winfield, Illinois resident could not cook, clean, or go to work. She continued to get a run-around from her HMO. Debra was forced to find out about her condition herself—through research and an out-of-pocket evaluation by a specialist in Virginia. The specialist recommended surgery to repair the nerve and restore circulation. Unfortunately, the HMO denied payment for this $100,000 procedure, claiming it was not medically necessary, even though Debra's pain was medically documented and her primary-care doctor at the HMO backed her up. ERISA's standard for proving an "arbitrary and capricious" denial to recover even those costs is much higher than the "medically necessary" standards under state law. Even if she does prevail and the HMO has to pay for the treatment, the HMO will still pay no damages.

- In Baltimore, Maryland, Michelle Leasure-Firesheets, a disability advocate with incontinent ostomy (no bowel control), was denied ostomy supplies which are 100% covered under Maryland law. Michelle has systemic lupus which compromises her immune system. Still, her insurer expected her to wash out her colostomy bags and reuse them for five days each. The stress from the denial of supplies may have contributed to a stroke requiring a hospital stay. Ironically, she could get benefits if she went on welfare, but she wants to work. She has no remedy under ERISA.

- Madison Scott was born prematurely but otherwise healthy in Orange County, California. She required monitoring to prevent Retinopathy, which can cause blindness. Her parent's HMO delayed treatment and refused referrals for Madison until her eye condition became serious. After five failed surgeries it was determined that Madison, at three months of age, was completely and permanently blind. The HMO faces no liability due to ERISA.

- Three year-old Kyle Morgan of Bakersfield, California began having ear problems at six months of age. His HMO withheld tests and treatments that could have detected Kyle's cholosteatoma. Now the bones in his ears have had to be removed due to destructive infections and Kyle has suffered hearing loss. Kyle's hearing loss looks like it will continually worsen into adolescence and he will require monitoring every year to check for more potential problems. Kyle's family has no legal remedy.

- Nine year-old Alex Giles of Houston, Texas was athletic. However, he fainted on numerous occasions while exercising. Though fainting during exertion is a serious medical indication of a cardiac condition, Alex's managed care doctor never studied the boy's medical history or ordered any diagnostic tests. Alex's mother was simply told to give him Gatorade. After more fainting spells and further disregard from his plan doctor, Alex tragically died undiagnosed. The HMO argues that ERISA preempts Alex's family's claims, though Alex's family is attempting to take the company to court under Texas's HMO liability law. To date, the HMO has lost its appeals.

- Frank Wurzbacher is a retiree in Covington, Kentucky who had surgery for prostate cancer. He took monthly lupron injections to keep the cancer from returning. After a new insurer took over his health plan, Frank's coverage was cut back and he could no longer afford the injections. The only alternative he could afford, according to his doctor, was castration. Frank tried unsuccessfully to get his insurer to change its mind. Frank had the castration procedure done, only to return home to a mailed notice that he could receive the injections. His company had decided a month prior, but administrative snafus prevented the information from getting to Frank. Wurzbacher's benefits are subject to ERISA.

- Bobby Kuhl suffered a major heart attack that required specialized surgery. His HMO refused to refer Bobby to a qualified hospital for the procedure, but later relented. The delay cost Bobby the chance for surgery, because of deterioration to his heart. Later, the HMO refused Bobby evaluation for a heart transplant. Bobby managed to get himself placed on a transplant list, but died waiting. A federal court refused Bobby's family a remedy due to ERISA.

- Ariday Dearmas was injured in an auto accident and taken to her HMO hospital in Miami, Florida. Because of a lack of "in-network" HMO doctors, she was transferred to four different hospitals in three days. She suffered irreversible nerve damage as a result, but her family cannot hold the HMO accountable in court.

- Norco, California resident Melody Johnson tragically died at 16 from cystic fibrosis after her HMO denied referrals to a Cystic Fibrosis Center and attempted to treat her condition without adequate expertise. Her HMO has not been held accountable due to ERISA.

- Complaining of depression, Los Angeles resident Douglas Hovey visited his HMO. The company downplayed his condition, blamed it on sexual dysfunction and prescribed antidepressant drugs. With persistent symptoms and suicidal thoughts, which occurred only after he was placed on the antidepressant, Douglas continued to receive only drug treatments from his HMO. Finally, after his HMO doctors refused to continue seeing him because of a lack of resources, Douglas, in the ultimate act of alienated defiance, committed suicide at the age of 23. His family has no remedy because of ERISA.

- Serenity Silen's HMO delayed diagnosing her acute myeloid leukemia, complicating the possibility for a cure. After numerous instances of misdiagnosis, dangerous oversights in Serenity's care and a denied authorization for a bone marrow transplant, her parents were forced to transfer her to a more qualified hospital. They found themselves in a fight with the HMO to get coverage paid for at the new facility, where care was taken to alleviate her pain and, according to her mother, she found renewed strength in her final fight against leukemia. Unfortunately, Serenity succumbed to the disease at sixteen years of age in October 1998. Due to ERISA, the HMO is liable for no damages in her death.

- Refused treatment by his HMO for a tumor the HMO said was terminal, Bill Beaver of Pollock Pines, California searched out life-saving treatment from John Hopkins Hospital, which spared his life for four years but for which his HMO refused to pay. (Chapter One) Because of ERISA, Bill was prevented from recovering damages, or even the cost

Serenity Silen

of the treatment—he couldn't even find an attorney to take his case.

• Simi Valley, California resident Janice Bosworth was one of a group of breast cancer patients initially denied bone marrow transplants by Health Net who ultimately died. The two other women in the group, Nelene Fox and Christine deMeurers, had health care coverage through public employment, and were not subject to ERISA. Their families won multi-million dollar judgments after their deaths. But Bosworth had her health care through her private employer, which, ironically, was Health Net, the HMO initially denying her the life-saving care. As noted in Chapter One, she finally secured the transplant for herself, but did die two years later. Bosworth's surviving husband and son, subject to ERISA, have been unable to recover damages from the HMO for Janice's death.

These are just a few of the cases where patients and their families were denied recourse.

Till Delay Do Us Part

Certain medical malpractice cases, unlike bad faith cases, can survive ERISA challenges if the patient can prove that the HMO had knowledge of repeated negligence or was involved "vicariously" in the quality-of-care violation. This would include negligence in running a substandard hospital or contracting with incompetent doctors. It would also include HMOs that indemnified the doctors it employed against a lawsuit, as Kaiser does. Where state law permits, these patient claims are often pushed into mandatory binding arbitration. In these secret proceedings, controlled by private lawyers and retired judges who depend on repeat business from the HMOs, cases are screened from the open forum of public opinion. Forced arbitration is costly, unfair, and conceals quality-of-care violations.

Most patients do not even realize they have signed away their constitutional right to a jury trial in their HMO enrollment agreement. They only find out after becoming sick or injured when they try to go to court.

How have HMOs skirted the courts and required patients to submit to binding arbitration? Where state laws allow, most HMOs and managed care plans *require* the consumer to give up their right to sue in cases of malpractice or in disputes over quality of care—*as a condition of coverage*.

Arbitrations are private. Decisions and evidence presented are never published. Repeated violations of quality-of-care standards are thus hidden from public view. Since no precedent is set, the next victim must start from scratch in making her case against the HMO.

It gets worse. While many patients are in a race against time for treatment, the arbitration system is frequently lengthy and sometimes deliberately drawn out by HMO attorneys.[30]

Kaiser doctors misdiagnosed Wilfredo Engalla's lung cancer as colds and allergies. By the time he was diagnosed properly five years later, the cancer was terminal. Engalla's family filed an arbitration claim against Kaiser for medical malpractice and, after waiting more than six months for an arbitration hearing, charged Kaiser with deliberately stalling to reduce any damages.[31] By intentionally stalling, Kaiser could avoid liability after Wilfredo's death, as the dead can collect no compensation for their pain and suffering.

The case, ultimately heard before the California Supreme Court, became a national example of how HMOs can and will delay when able. Ironically, because the case went to court rather than arbitration, court-ordered data showed the systemic nature of the delays at Kaiser and the fact that Kaiser arbitration is more prolonged and costly than court cases.

Kaiser's service contract with its members promised an arbitrator would be appointed within two months. Pursuant to a court order, Kaiser's own statistician Michael Sullivan produced data regarding delays in Kaiser's arbitration system:

1) Kaiser's statistician's data showed that during the later part of the 1980s, on the average, it took 863 days (almost two-and-a-half years) to reach a Kaiser arbitration hearing. With the advent of fast track in our courts, the court system would prove significantly quicker. More importantly for the Court was the gap between Kaiser's promise of sixty days until the appointment of a neutral arbitrator and its practice of taking years to resolve disputes.

2) Statistically, delays occur in 99% of Kaiser medical malpractice arbitrations; in only 1% of all Kaiser cases is a neutral arbitrator appointed within the sixty-day period provided by the provision.[32]

More recent data from Kaiser shows the company did not improve its record in the 1990s. The average time for an arbitration case to come to a hearing was: 3.2 years (1992), 2.9 years (1993) and 3.1 years (1994).[33]

Ruling in the *Engalla* case, a conservative California Supreme Court found, "There is evidence that Kaiser established a self-administered arbitration system in which delay for its own benefit and convenience was an inherent part, despite express and implied contractual representations to the contrary."[34]

The six to one ruling held that if a patient can show that an HMO unreasonably delayed arbitration when it promised otherwise, it is essentially fraud, and the patient or next of kin can seek justice in court. The long-term problem remains, as Kaiser can simply rewrite its service contract to specify a longer period of time until arbitration must begin to avoid future liability.

According to the Engalla's oldest daughter, 28 year-old Aina Engalla Konold, "My dad had hoped to have his day in court. Kaiser knew he was dying. He was their patient and he was on oxygen when they took his deposition. But Kaiser only stalled and made us wait until after my father had died. He never got to tell his story or see the result of his case."

Patricia Engalla, 21, commented: "My father was always so responsible. He believed everything they told him. How was he to know?"

The HMOs promised binding arbitration would be more expeditious and less costly. Evidence suggests that, as part of the HMO strategy, the promises have failed on both accounts.

Arbitration is usually more costly than a trial and consumers cannot recover their legal costs, while the awards made by arbitrators are generally 20–50% lower than awards made by jurors. For instance, Linda Ross, whose mother died of a misdiagnosed and untreated pulmonary embolism in a Kaiser hospital in Fontana, spent nearly $22,000 in legal fees over the course of three years. When the case was finally heard, Ross was awarded only $150,000, significantly less than what a jury likely would have awarded, even though the arbitrators unanimously agreed on Kaiser's liability.[35]

Litigation costs, of course, mount during a prolonged waiting period to reach arbitration. In addition, the costs of arbitration are exponentially greater than a case that goes to trial. Filing fees for superior court litigants are $183. In the American Arbitration Association system, filing fees range from $500 to $5,000. Arbitrators generally charge $100–$400 per hour,[36] whereas court costs amount to approximately $350 per day, according to one witness at a recent state hearing on the matter.

Due to the prolonged proceedings, arbitrations have become a cottage industry for retired judges and lawyers. The *Los Angeles Times* reports, "Even a part-time arbitrator can earn close to $200,000 in annual fees, according to those familiar with the system."[37]

The system also appears less than impartial. Arbitrators who rule against health plans and award substantial damages to the patient rarely find themselves asked to arbitrate future disputes, giving them a strong financial self-interest in securing favorable settlements for health plans.[38]

If patients survive ERISA's draconian restrictions, they are too often stuck in arbitration. In Adrian Broughton's case (Chapter Two), a California Appeals Court allowed the unfair business practice lawsuit despite the family's arbitration agreement with CIGNA. The Court found that because the claim against the HMO was that a door-to-door marketer fraudulently induced the patient's mother into joining the HMO, the mother was not bound by the arbitration clause. But Broughton was the exception, not the rule. (The HMO has appealed the decision and the California Supreme Court has agreed to hear the appeal.)

In response to the growing backlash against mandatory arbitration caused by HMO abuses of the process, the American Arbitration Association changed policy in 1998. Following the Engalla decision, the nation's largest and most powerful association of arbitrators decided not to conduct any further forced HMO arbitrations.[39] In a joint statement with the American Bar Association and American Medical Association, it condemned the forum of arbitration for health disputes.

Unfortunately, the system refuses to die, as new arbitrators are hired to replace those who bow out over ethical concerns.

It is clear that the managed care industry uses arbitration not for expedient justice, but as a means to gain the upper hand over those who challenge them.

Patients should not have to sign their seventh amendment right to trial away when they sign up for an HMO. Until all states pass laws preserving patients' right to trial, however, the playing field of justice is dramatically tilted against the injured patient and in favor of the HMO corporation.

Putting a Lid on Justice

The tragic story of two year-old Steven Olsen, whose brain injury went untreated because of a hospital's refusal to administer a CT scan, which in turn led to cerebral palsy and blindness, was recounted in Chapter Three. The injustice does not end with Steven living in a world of darkness. His hospital and doctors were sued for medical malpractice. The jury found that his treatment was below the community's standard of care, and for his life of pain and suffering awarded him $7 million. But unfortunately for Steven, his parents, and even the jury, a California state law puts a cap on such awards, and a judge slashed it to $250,000.[40]

"The jury can not be told about the arbitrary cap for Steven's compensation, which the doctors and insurers lobbied state legislators to become California law," said San Diego resident Kathy Olsen, Steven's mom. "The judge was forced to reduce the decision made by a jury of our peers. I know that this law cannot be changed for my son Steven. But I do feel that if another child is injured like [the way he was], that he should get what he is rightfully due."

The jurors found out that their verdict had been reduced not by a judge but by reading about it in the newspaper. Jury foreman Thomas Kearns responded, writing a letter to the *San Diego Union Tribune*:

> I served as foreman of the Steven Olsen jury ("Capping the cost of suffering," P A1, May 10, 1995). During some three weeks, we heard evidence and testimony in this tragic case. We viewed a video of Steven, age 2, shortly before the accident.
>
> This beautiful child talked and shrieked with laughter as any other child at play. Later, Steven was brought to the court and we watched as he groped, stumbled and felt his way along the front of the jury box. There was no chatter or happy laughter.

Steven is doomed to a life of darkness, loneliness and pain. He is blind, brain damaged and physically retarded. He will never play sports, work or enjoy normal relationships with his peers. His will be a lifetime of treatment, therapy, prosthesis fitting and supervision around the clock.

Medical testimony revealed that a facial injury to Steven, suffered in a fall, resulted in complications. The attending physician correctly listed "CNS abscess" in her differential diagnosis, but failed to order a brain scan, choosing instead to go with her instincts and treat him for meningitis. Three days later, Steven's brain herniated from the abscess. The physician had not met the standard of care.

After summation, our jury delivered a just verdict, and in accordance with the judge's charge, a fair award which included $7 million for pain and suffering. I only learned of the $250,000 cap on pain-and-suffering awards from your newspaper, as the judge saw fit to keep this information from the jury.

Our medical-care system has failed Steven Olsen, through inattention or pressure to avoid costly but necessary tests. Our legislative system has failed Steven, bowing to lobbyists of the powerful American Medical Association (AMA) and the insurance industry, by the Legislature enacting an ill-conceived and wrongful law. Our judicial system has failed Steven, by acceding to this tilting of the scales of justice by the Legislature for the benefit of two special-interest groups.

America deplores the frivolous lawsuit. Dubious "whiplash" and "backache" claims waste time and resources of the courts. Some limit on awards in such cases is reasonable. However, our "one size fits all" awards-law equates in terms of upper limitation the most minor of malpractice conditions with the catastrophic situation of the magnitude of that which has befallen Steven Olsen.

I think the people of California place a higher value on a human life than this. Let us change this egregious law.

THOMAS J. KEARNS
San Diego[41]

Similar caps to the one in California have been enacted across the nation at the behest of lobbyists working for the medical-insurance industry. Pioneered in California, campaigns have foisted these restrictions on the public in twenty states.[42] The campaigns have succeeded only by perpetuating fictions, which were used again by House Republicans under the banner of "HMO reform" in 1998 to pass legislation aimed at eroding the same patients' rights to fully recover in malpractice cases.

Two decades ago, skyrocketing premiums for medical malpractice insurance whipsawed California doctors and hospitals into supporting anti-consumer restrictions on the rights of patients. The most grotesque component of the 1975 Medical Injury Compensation Reform Act—MICRA—was the $250,000 cap on compensation for pain and suffering which, because of inflation, now limits victims of malpractice—no matter how egregious—to the equivalent of $50,180 in compensation in 1976 dollars.

It might seem logical that a cap on awards such as MICRA, when implemented, would lower health care costs. In fact, medical malpractice costs are less than 1% percent of all health care costs—an insignificant component. Despite California's cap, medical malpractice premiums are a slightly higher percentage of health care costs in the state (0.86%) than in the nation (0.69%). The cap has not reduced overall health care costs, which are among the highest in the nation, and has not reduced per capita medical malpractice premiums below the national average.[43]

MICRA did, however, boost the profits of the malpractice insurance companies.[44] In 1995, for every dollar of premiums malpractice insurers received, they paid malpractice victims a pitiful forty-one-and-a-half cents on average. Nearly the same amount—forty cents of every dollar—was paid to the insurance companies' own defense lawyers. MICRA has proven another windfall for the insurance industry.

Caps on pain and suffering reduce the deterrent effect of the medical malpractice liability system and the quality of health care. Dr. Troyen Brennan, co-author of the landmark study of medical malpractice by the Harvard School of Public Health, reports that restricting injured patients' rights to recover damages will reduce deterrence and increase the rates of medical injury. According to Harvard experts, 80,000 patients already die each year in hospitals alone due to medical negligence.[45]

MICRA's low limits on how much victims recover, as well as on how much victims can pay for legal representation, have driven consumer attorneys away from taking malpractice cases. The few court victories, like the Olsen's, ultimately have great reductions on hard-won compensation.

HMO medicine may have put the doctors' lobby in conflict with the HMO and insurance industry. But when it comes to limits on malpractice victims' rights, the doctors' lobby long ago made an alliance with the insurance industry to limit physicians' liability for medical negligence.

Harry Jordan is a classic illustration of the failure of such laws.

Jordan, a Long Beach California man, was hospitalized to have a cancerous kidney removed. But the surgeon took out his healthy kidney instead. A jury awarded Jordan more than $5 million, yet the judge was required to reduce the verdict to $250,000 due to California's cap on "non-economic" damages—plus a mere $6,000 in "economic costs". Jordan, who lived on 10% kidney function for more than a decade after the case, could no longer work, though the jury (which could not be notified about the "non-economic" cap) did not take this into account. Jordan's court costs—not including attorney fees—amounted to more than $400,000. His medical bills, which were frequently denied by insurers, totaled more than $500,000. He paid, until his death in the late 1990s, $1,700 *per month* in health insurance.

In the age of mismanaged care, the stakes are different. It is not just a slip of a scalpel that can be subject to MICRA-like limits, but the mismanagement of HMOs.

The Poison Pill

Responding to demands across the country for ERISA reform, the industry has promoted this poison pill of damage caps on HMO liability.

When multi-billion dollar corporations enjoy liability caps, the financial calculus for HMOs deciding whether to grant treatment will more often than not weigh on the side of denial. Under market-oriented medicine, only the threat of costly lawsuits will force Wall Street-driven HMOs to provide timely and adequate treatment.

Even the American Medical Association, which long fought for medical malpractice damage caps on physician liability, now recognizes this. In 1998, the organization took a courageous stand, insisting that the caps not apply to HMOs if the ERISA shield is lifted. The AMA also asked that the legislation federalizing the caps on doctors not be attached to the ERISA reform bill, knowing it was a poison pill.

Physician and Texas State Senator David Sibley wrote: "In Texas, civil liability for damages of a 'physician or health care provider' is limited...akin to California's MICRA. For the purposes of SB 386 [the Texas HMO liability law], however, we determined that managed care companies should not be treated any differently than other profit-making business enterprises that are subject to liability under traditional tort laws.

"Because HMOs and managed care companies (including doctor-run medical groups) often apply a financial filter to determine treatment denials, their liability must not be artificially limited by a compensation cap. Such restricted responsibility would mitigate against approval of the most expensive treatment, such as cancer care. Under the Texas law, physician-run medical groups are considered managed care entities and do not fall under the compensation cap applicable to sole practitioners."[46]

The few California cases where MICRA has applied to HMO patients lucky enough to find a medical negligence cause of action reveal disastrous public policy outcomes. Some of the patients whose stories are told in previous chapters went on to be victimized again by MICRA's draconian limits.

- Recounting her nightmare with California's medical malpractice cap, Suzanne Lobb (Chapter Three), whose husband died unattended at a Kaiser-owned hospital, says, "My husband's death ended my life as I had known if for twenty-eight wonderful years. Our family has been devastated by this loss. Not only have we been betrayed by a health care provider that promised to protect us, but [by] our legal system as well. Within a couple of weeks, I had obtained a copy of my husband's medical charts. It was not difficult to see his life literally slip away on paper. My next visit was to an attorney's office. I, like most people, was unaware of the law in the state of California which limits the award for medical malpractice. I was shocked and distressed that a hospital could be this negligent and be so protected. To an HMO as large as Kaiser, a maximum $250,000 award for pain and suffering is a mere slap on the wrist. They can afford to cut costs and take chances with lives because this law makes it affordable for them to do just that."

- Kevin McCafferey (Chapter Two), whose son is crippled because no doctor was present during the high-risk delivery at Kaiser, said, "My lawyer informed me that suits against my HMO are decided through arbitration. I asked what this meant and he told me that there would be no jury involved. An arbitrator would decide the case. Furthermore, he informed me that there were set limits determining the size of the award in these type of injury suits. They were typically a lot less than those awarded by a jury in other states, but in California this was the law. When I asked about factoring in lost wages for Colin, or emotional stress caused to the parents, he said it was too difficult to prove. Lost wages are difficult to prove unless someone is actually working. I thought this unfair. It seemed as if they were penalizing Colin because he was a baby and because he happened to be born in California. My lawyer also told me the whole arbitration process was kind of rigged in the HMO's favor. The arbitrators were typically retired judges seeking means to supplement their income, and many relied on my HMO for a steady stream of cases. Given this fact, it made it difficult for an arbitrator not to favor the HMO, since the HMO would cut them off if there were too many adverse decisions. Ultimately, since there was not much choice in the matter, we settled for $250,000. The settlement was in the form of a structured annuity, which probably can be purchased for less than the cash value. Although it was better than nothing, I still don't think it's enough. Worst of all, I am troubled by the fact that the HMO still does not provide the option for a doctor when delivering babies. This seems absolutely ludicrous to me."

- Linda Ross's mother died unattended at a Kaiser emergency room after a six-hour wait and not being administered an expensive blood thinner on hand. She says, "Under existing California law, I will never be able to do anything to hold these individuals accountable for my mother's death. They will hide behind the HMO's corporate veil, completely immune from any responsibility for their actions. Moreover, $250,000 is inconsequential to the giant HMO that let my mother die. I just have to keep telling myself that the justice the state laws deny me, I will have to count on God to provide."

Medical malpractice victims receive too little compensation, not too much. The Harvard School of Public Health's Medical Malpractice Study reports that only one out of every sixteen victims of medical malpractice ever receives *any* compensation for their injuries. The record of MICRA-type limits adds insult to injury.

The costs of these restrictions are born unequally by patients throughout society. Consider the following:

- **Arbitrary caps on "non-economic" compensation unfairly discriminate against the suffering of women.** Women are more frequently the victims of negligence because they undergo more surgery—sustaining injuries such as laceration of the uterus or loss of a newborn during childbirth. These injuries do not carry high "economic" price tags but involve significant loss. Caps not only deny women victimized by medical malpractice fair compensation and legal representation for their injuries, but subject women to the scalpels of incompetent but undeterred practitioners.

- **Arbitrary caps on "non-economic" compensation unfairly discriminate against the littlest victims, children.** Children cannot prove significant future wage loss. Their families cannot realistically estimate the expenses they are to incur over the course of a lifetime.

- **Caps on "non-economic" compensation devalue the lives and health of low income patients.** Caps on pain and suffering discriminate against the suffering of low-income people whose "economic" basis for the recovery of damages—wages—are limited. A strictly "economic" evaluation based on wages devalues what victims will create or produce in the future, their quality of life, as well as an injury's impact on their ability to nurture others. For instance, a laborer may lose his arms due to the exact same act of medical negligence as a corporate CEO, but the CEO would be able to collect millions (because of his high wage loss, which is reimbursable) and the laborer would be closely limited to the $250,000 cap. A housewife similarly would be limited to the cap no matter the physical or emotional depths of her injury. Caps assign greater value to the limbs and lives of some people than those of others.

- **Even taxpayers get it in the neck because caps make them foot the bill for dangerous doctors' mistakes.** Malpractice victims receive compensation only for medical bills and lost wages. But those who are not wage earners—such as seniors, women, and the poor—have no other resource from which to pay for unforeseen medical expenses and basic needs. A cap may force malpractice victims to seek public assistance from state or federal programs funded by taxpayers.

It's not just ERISA, which prevents suits, or damage caps that stack the deck against justice. Many awards are structured as annuities. As Kevin McCafferey alluded to above, the payment of the award for his son is not a lump sum but a periodic payment through an annuity. This arrangement creates problems for the victims, and further helps those committing the injustices.

- **Debts paid on a periodic basis are far from secure.** In particular, annuities purchased by defendants to satisfy periodic payment obligations can be risky ventures. For instance, Executive Life Insurance Co. of Los Angeles, one of California's major insurers and seller of annuities, failed in 1991 and was seized by government regulators. Many of the 350,000 policyholders received only dimes on the dollar. If the seller of the annuity falls into bankruptcy, it is the patient who is denied compensation, because the defendant is no longer responsible for the debt. This is a substantial shifting of risk onto innocent patients who, in states like California, already face other harsh restrictions.

- **If a patient dies, all payments stop and the victim's family receives nothing.** Wrongdoers are rewarded for causing the most severe, life threatening injuries. If a patient dies, periodic payments immediately cease and the guilty physician is allowed to keep the remainder of his money. Awards do not revert to the next of kin.

- **Periodic payments reduce the already limited compensation received by victims, as the value of the verdict diminishes over time due to inflation.** No adjustment is typically made in the payments to reflect the inflation rate or changes in the costs for medical care, which have risen sharply and well above the inflation rate for many years.

- **Periodic payment agreements put the burden on the victim to meet their basic needs.** The periodic payment arrangement, once approved, is extraordinarily difficult to modify. If costs of the victim's medical care increase beyond his means, or a special expensive medical technology is made available which the victim requires, the injured patient must retain a lawyer to have the schedule modified—and may very well not succeed.

The pernicious cumulative impact of these MICRA restrictions on patients can be seen in a recent Los Angeles case described in Chapter One. Dawnelle Barris, whose eighteen month old daughter Mychelle died from a treatable infection because her HMO would not authorize treatment at an out-of-network hospital, saw her $1.35 million award against the HMO and hospital slashed to $250,000 in March 1998. Even though the case involved violations of a federal patient-dumping statute, the California Supreme Court ruled that MICRA applied. The HMO and hospital will hardly learn their lesson. After costs and attorney fees, Dawnelle will receive less than $150,000 for her daughter's preventable death.[47]

The case shows that courts too often do not distinguish between an administrative decision based on financial consideration and an instance of medical negligence caused by incompetence. Medical malpractice compensation caps let HMOs and hospitals escape accountability by putting money ahead of good medicine.

There are more restrictions. Maybe the most frequent assault on a consumer's legal rights is capping a consumer attorney's contingency fees but not defense attorney fees. The legacy of MICRA, where a consumer's attorney's contingency fee is capped, demonstrates how patients are denied appropriate representation. Consider these implications:

- **Only the most seriously injured victims with clear-cut cases to prove can ever find legal representation.** In states with caps on attorney contingency fees for medical malpractice cases (and particularly in states such as California where a victim's pain and suffering compensation is also capped), injured patients simply cannot find legal representation. It is not cost-effective for attorneys to take the vast majority of cases. The President of Safe Medicine For Consumers, a California-based medical malpractice survivors group, notes, "The vast majority of individuals who contact us are women, parents of children or senior citizens. 90% of these individuals are unable to pursue meritorious medical malpractice cases because they can not find legal representation on a contingency basis and their savings have been wiped out."

- **Eroding the contingency fee mechanism contributes to a deteriorating quality of health care and passes costs onto taxpayers.** Left without legal representation, victims go uncompensated, and dangerous medicine goes undeterred. Taxpayers pay the cost of low-income victims' medical care and basic needs through public assistance programs if the physicians or HMOs responsible for the injuries are not held accountable.

- **Undermining the viability of the contingency fee mechanism discriminates against low-income patients who are most at risk of medical malpractice.** A contingency fee system is a poor patient's only hope of affording an attorney to challenge a negligent physician. Undermining such a system through caps on fees reduces incentives for attorneys to take malpractice cases and gives HMOs and hospitals a license to treat poor patients callously. Dr. Troyen Brennan of Harvard reported to Congress that: "Poor patients are one-fifth as likely to bring claims as are the wealthy. The aged are also unlikely to bring claims...the poor are more dependent on contingency fee mechanisms in order to bring claims,...[a proposal limiting contingency fees for plaintiffs] will likely worsen the inequity of the tort system.... [the proposal] will likely lead to less compensation for individuals injured by medical malpractice, will reduce the deterrence of practices that cause such injuries and overall will increase the costs of the medical-care system."[48]

- **Limiting plaintiff attorney contingency fees, but not defense attorney fees creates an uneven playing field for victims.** Defendants can typically afford very high-priced attorneys who fly special expert witnesses in from out of state. A contingency fee practice demands that a plaintiff's attorney must front the cost of expert witnesses to refute the testimony of experts flown in by the defendant. With caps on fees, such costs become prohibitive for the victim's legal counsel.

Perhaps the most important point lost in the thicket of these restrictions on patients' rights is this: HMOs and insurers would not have to limit their liability—through ERISA or MICRA-type restrictions—if they simply played fair and dealt with patients in good faith.

All other industries face the scrutiny of state common law liability. If HMOs and managed care insurers cannot withstand such scrutiny, why should they deserve to exist?

CHAPTER SIX

The Battle to Make
Health Care Work

D o HMOs serve only HMOs?

Will a system set up to maximize profit ever truly care for patients? One indication comes from looking at how HMOs organize their lists of approved drugs, or formularies, for their doctors to use. As one might expect, the drugs are often the cheapest and typically not the best. For instance, PacifiCare, now the nation's largest HMO for Medicare recipients, replaced an effective, high-cost schizophrenia drug called Risperdal with the low-cost, 36 year-old drug, Haldol. A thirty-day supply of Risperdal costs $240 compared to $2.50 for a similar supply of Haldol—nearly a 1,000% savings for PacifiCare. But the side effects of the inferior Haldol include severe, uncontrollable shaking.[1]

While such penuriousness at the expense of patients has come to be expected from HMOs, the example of how Foundation Health considered organizing its formulary shows that the hunt for profits never ends. Sabin Russell, a veteran health care writer at the *San Francisco Chronicle*, exposed a proposal by Bristol-Myers Squibb that would have given Foundation Health a million dollars a month as a fee for restricting its formulary exclusively to the products of the drug maker.[2]

"The draft agreement calls for Bristol-Myers to pay $1 million per month, for up to three years, to Sacramento-based Integrated Pharmaceutical Services," Russell reported, meaning a total fee of $36 million. "A Foundation Health subsidiary, IPS is a 'pharmacy benefits management' company that handles drug benefits of more than four million HMO members across the country. The deal appears to be the latest twist on a little-known practice called rebating, in which drug companies pay cash to insurers, hospitals and even doctor groups for high-volume sales of their products."

The rub with this kick-back was that the drugs in question were *neither* the most cost-effective nor medically effective in the class of drugs. Still, "preferred" status on the HMO drug list would go to Bristol-Myers' blood pressure drugs Monopril and Avapro; the antibiotic Cefzil; Plavix, a drug that inhibits blood clotting; and cholesterol-lowering drug Pravachol.

Patients who wanted or needed other drugs, which are more effective or less costly, would have to circumnavigate a time-consuming appeals process.

Foundation Health simply considered the deal for its $1 million per month kick-back at the expense of patients and the medical system.

According to Russell, "In fact, the Bristol-Myers draft agreement appears to rule out passing the payments to consumers. The drug company 'contribution' the memo states, 'is not an additional discount...and is not intended for benefit of payor organizations whose pharmacy benefits are managed by IPS.'"

Another troubling aspect of the arrangement, as the *Chronicle*'s Russell reports, is who makes the choices about which drugs Health Net would cover. Once the choices were in the hands of a committee of the HMO's participating doctors. Now, acting on the advice of a new committee of hired consultants, the choices are made by Health Net executives.

This kind of profit-at-all-costs orientation is having an impact, even on those in industry. "Along the hallways at Sprint headquarters here [in Kansas City, Missouri], the great expectations for managed care have dimmed," reported the *New York Times* in October 1998. "In a score of interviews with workers and managers, no one recounted the kind of HMO horror story that makes headlines: the wrong leg amputated, a child denied a transplant. Instead, they said they had found managed care to be exasperating, callous and sometimes just senseless."[3]

Health care executives and large employers both admit that quality has been a casualty of the managed care system. Amazingly, an academic survey of health care industry executives found that almost half—49%— believe the growth of managed care has *decreased* the quality of patient care. (At the same time, not surprisingly, 55% say there is no need for increased federal regulation of HMOs; 52% believe there is no need for more state regulation.)[4]

Employers concur. In 1998, 42% of employers polled believed cost pressures are hurting the quality of care, up from 33% in 1997 and 28% in 1996.[5]

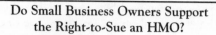

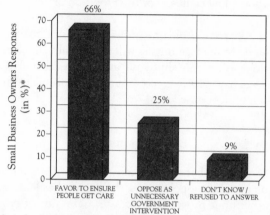

Do Small Business Owners Support
the Right-to-Sue an HMO?

The survey results in the chart are based on the responses of 401 out of 800 heads of companies and organizations with fewer than 100 full-time employees between March 18 and May 9, 1998.

Question asked: "How do you feel about a law requiring health plans to allow patients to sue a health plan for malpractice, like they can now sue a doctor? Do you favor it asked as a way to make sure people get the care they need, or oppose it as unnecessary government involvement in health care?"

Source: Kaiser Family Foundation/American Small Business Alliance Education Fund Survey, June 17, 1998.

Small employers are particularly disturbed, despite the pro-HMO leanings of the National Federation of Independent Business (NFIB). In a June 1998 Kaiser Family Foundation/Harvard survey of 800 executives of small businesses conducted for the American Small Business Alliance, 66% of the executives support enacting a new law to allow patients to sue their HMO as a way to make sure people get the care they need, rather than oppose it as unnecessary government intrusion.[6]

Managing costs does not mean the proper management of treatment. As we have seen in too many cases, those goals are often antagonistic.

Moreover, corporations managing their own money well does not translate to the health care system managing its costs effectively. Columbia's multi-billion dollar bilking of the taxpayer is one clear example. The recent HMO industry practice of dumping elders, because the companies are no longer permitted to cherry pick only the healthy seniors in Medicare, is another.

In mundane ways, too, HMO corporations have incentives and opportunities to make money for themselves at the expense of both cost-effectiveness and health-enhancement of the health care system.

"The price one pays to keep health care affordable is a degree of aggrava-tion," Health Net chief medical officer Dr. Alan Zwerner told Russell.[7] But affordable for whom? The company or the provision of a reasonable standard of health care?

Americans are learning from the growing exposure to HMO medicine that a system set up to manage money will never truly take care of patients. HMO corporations will simply shift costs away from themselves. The public and the patient will pay. HMO corporations will continue to charge.

But what alternatives do we have?

Big "R" Reforms

The HMO reform debate has taken place in state legislatures and Congress. In the province of politicians, the process has lent itself mostly to sound and fury without progress. Efforts to maintain a firewall between money managers and healers have fallen victim to the entrenched HMO lobby.

"They killed the health care Patients' Bill of Rights," Vice President Gore said at a White House press conference in October 1998. "I was in—I was in John Dingell's district in Dearborn—and this is a true story—an emergency room doctor told us of a man who came in to the emergency room in full cardiac arrest, his heart stopped, the doctor eventually brought him back to life. The HMO refused to pay the bill and said it was not an emergency. The man was dead! (Laughter.)"[8]

The *New York Times* reported in October 1998 that consumers' com-plaints about health insurers and HMOs are "surging," according to state health insurance commissioners. Interviews with twelve state insurance departments in the most densely populated states show that health care complaints have grown "50% over the last one to three years, far faster than the growth of enrollment in managed care plans."[9] Audiences across the nation cheered when the lead actress denounced HMOs in the 1997 movie, "As Good As It Gets."

During 1998, politicians in Congress and state legislatures, however, failed to enact many serious reforms, folding under pressure from the HMO lobby. The Patients' Bill of Rights was defeated in Congress. The Republicans offered fig-leaf reforms with no enforceable remedies. The insurance industry is similarly attempting to prevent states from regulating managed care plans.

In July 1999, the Republican-controlled United States Senate passed purported patient rights legislation that did not include significant reforms. The G.O.P. plan allegedly applied to 48 million Americans in federally regulated health plans, but in fact only 10% of that population are actually enrolled in HMOs. Vice President Al Gore said the minimal measure would be vetoed because, "it's a fraud." Senior G.O.P. Senator John Chaffee (Rhode Island) told the Associated Press, "What have we accomplished? It seems to me we've let down the American people."

In the debate over curbing HMO power, everyone—from patient advocates, to doctors, to the HMO industry—has his own definition of "reform."

The HMO industry favors greater disclosure and a so-called external review system, where patients' disputes with their HMO are appealed to a third party for review rather than heard before a court or jury.

Those on the side of the patient—consumer groups, nurses, doctors—have made the right-to-sue without ERISA's hurdles the litmus test for genuine HMO reform. In 1998, the American Medical Association, which for decades supported capping the damages of doctors and hospitals for medical negligence, shunned its sacred cow of national damage limits. GOP leaders offered this carrot to the AMA in an attempt to split the ERISA-reform coalition, but in a valiant act, the AMA refused to take it.

Real reform must stem from serious accountability measures. Can we get there? Can we create and regulate a system that puts public health first, so that the many tragedies told in this book never appear again in our wealthy country?

One vital step is the distinction between three types of reforms, each of which will be considered in turn. "First tier" reforms would even the playing field for patients, so that they have the necessary leverage over their HMOs to get the care they need and deserve. "Second tier" changes, discussed later, would fundamentally alter the health care system to provide coverage to more patients at less cost. Lastly, it is crucial to see through the third tier of phony reforms and political placebos the HMO industry has put forth in order to stave off genuine, systemic correctives.

Level-The-Playing-Field Reforms— Nailing Down Tier One

Restore the right to sue for damages at the federal level. The most "ripe" reform for those who know the system is to apply the same liability laws to HMOs now faced by every other industry in America. As discussed, federal ERISA law shields HMOs that administer private employer-paid insurance from damages for wrongdoing, so there is never a price to pay in court. (See Chapter Five). Congress can and should amend ERISA. Damages should be available under state common law when HMOs that administer employer-paid health care commit fraud, negligence, are responsible for a wrongful death, or breach the covenant of good faith and fair dealing that applies to every other type of business. From 1974 until 1987, patients with employer-paid benefits could receive damages against insurers. With the 1987 *Pilot Life v. Dedeaux* ruling, state common law was preempted in a way that the federal framers of ERISA did not intend. The easiest way to close the ERISA loophole is for Congress to specifically clarify the province of state courts and juries over HMOs that administer benefits. The Congressional Budget Office reported in July 1998 that giving patients the right to sue would add no more than 1.2% to health care premiums, including the costs of so-called defensive medicine.[10] At the time of this publication, in July 1999, a bipartisan "compromise" in Congress would give patients the right to recover only compensatory damages, such as lost wages, not punitive damages, which punish wrongdoing.

Unless HMOs face significant damages, they will continue to ignore patients' needs and doctors' recommendations. In most states patients cannot collect for their pain and suffering after their death, so HMOs could have an incentive to actually let them die without punitive damages.

States can enact new HMO liability laws to protect against profiteering HMOs that put money ahead of good medicine. States can pass legislation that specifically skirts the ERISA loophole and hold HMOs accountable for their decisions by creating a new "corporate negligence" cause of action for HMOs. HMOs do deny treatment, overturn doctors' decisions and dictate limits on medical treatments and care. New state laws could require that HMOs be held accountable for reckless health care decisions. As noted, Texas recently became the first state in the nation to offer its citizens a way around ERISA to protect themselves against poor quality medical care. The Texas law assures that the physician, not the HMO, is in charge of patient care. This begins to restore the doctor-patient relationship. HMOs are liable when they exercise "influence or control which result in the failure to exercise ordinary care," in other words accountable for medical negligence and quality-of-care issues.

In the fall of 1998, a federal district court judge upheld the Texas statute because, "In this case, the Act addresses the quality of benefits actually provided. ERISA 'simply says nothing about the quality of benefits received.' Dukes, 57 F.3d at 3576."[11] By contrast, the Court struck down the Texas independent review process as preempted by ERISA, because it deals with determinations of coverage disputes. The review process is the HMO industry's alternative to liability.

California legislators are also considering another way around ERISA. Pending legislation makes use of a clause in ERISA that "saves" for the states the right to regulate the business of insurance. The bill specifically makes damages available under the state's insurance law when HMOs breach their insurance contracts.[12] If the legislation passes, HMOs will no doubt sue to invalidate it.

Creation of an independent non-profit consumer watchdog association funded by voluntary contributions, and governed by a board with a majority elected by members. For years, utility consumers in three states have been able to unite in order to fight fraud and unnecessarily high rates because of Consumer Utility Boards or CUBs. These voluntary associations have been effective because they have been able to contact every utility ratepayer in the state and ask them to voluntarily join. The key to this reform—devised by consumer advocate Ralph Nader—is a voluntary "check off" on the utility bill, which allows consumers to join the association with a minimal contribution ($5–$12 per year).

Congress, the state legislature, or the people via ballot initiative in some states can establish a similar consumer association (a public corporation) for patients in HMOs.[13] It could be granted access to insurance company mailing lists and the power to advocate on behalf of individuals or groups of patients, and to publish reports on quality-of-service provided by HMOs, hospitals, nursing homes, and other health care businesses. The association would be a check on the health care industry's business practices, working to ensure that the profit motive does not diminish the standard of care and invade the doctor-patient relationship.

An effective consumer health care organization could save lives. Already CUBs have saved consumers billions of dollars. The Illinois Citizens Utility Board, with 200,000 members, has saved Illinois taxpayers more than $3 billion since 1983 by challenging utility rate hikes, and has successfully educated ratepayers on how to save money on services and on conservation issues.[14]

This vehicle is a model for HMO patients to join together to increase accountability and standards of care. It would be a democratic organization of HMO members interested solely in quality medical care.

Prohibit mandatory and secret arbitration of medical grievances as a condition for health coverage. As previously noted, most HMOs and managed care plans *require* the consumer to give up his rights to go to court in cases of malpractice or in disputes over quality of care—*as a condition of cov-*

erage. Instead of having access to the public forum of a court, patients are forced into a system of mandatory binding arbitration. Forced arbitration is costly, unfair, and conceals quality-of-care violations from public scrutiny.[15] Many states now prohibit mandatory binding arbitration agreements. Arizona's constitution, for instance, specifically bars any legislative limitation on the right to trial. However, in too many states, forced arbitration enables HMOs to hide from juries and judges in a secret and often biased justice system. Reforms to end binding arbitration as a condition of health coverage would force HMOs that delay and deny care to face the scrutiny of an open courtroom. This would publicly air quality-of-care violations so that they are not repeated.

Require prior approval from regulators before HMOs and insurers can raise their premiums or lower the rates they pay doctors via capitation. The property/casualty insurance industry has a system in most states in the nation requiring state approval before rates are raised or lowered, as opposed to the old "file and use" system, where the insurers simply filed the rate and used it. No such system is in place for health insurance, despite its life and death stakes. As mentioned earlier, many individual policyholders with Blue Cross of California saw their rates skyrocket by 58% in 1998. Elderly Kaiser individual members in Washington, D.C. saw a 49.4% increase in premiums.[16] Older Americans can become costly patients and the HMOs hope to discourage them from staying. HMOs say that the young should not subsidize the old, but this is precisely the definition of an insurance pool risk. You pay in when you are young and healthy, and utilize when you are older and sicker. Requiring prior approval for rate increases, and an opportunity for a public hearing and comment, will keep the HMO industry honest. Utilities face this scrutiny, and health care is certainly as vital a public commodity as water and power.

Health care businesses should be required to show the need for rate increases and where and how the money would be used. A fair rate of return must be set on health care companies and HMOs. If care is to be rationed, so should HMO profits.[17]

HMOs have used their leverage to squeeze down the capitated rates for doctors so low that it is virtually impossible for physicians to do all they can for their patients. Some primary care doctors receive rates as low as $6 dollars per month for all the care of a patient. A prior approval system could require that HMOs show that the capitated rates paid to their physicians and medical groups are actuarially sound and sufficient to take care of the patients' needs—particularly the sickest patients. If the rates paid to physicians who treat a disproportionate number of sick patients are not "risk adjusted" upward, doctors will simply compete for well patients. The public has a compelling interest in this type of rate regulation to make sure the insurance system serves the sick as well as the healthy.

Ban full-risk capitation. The idea of pitting doctors' financial interests against their patients' quality of care violates the fundamental doctor-patient relationship. Today some doctors accept nearly full risk for all of a patient's care, meaning almost *all* costs expended on the patient are paid by the doctors, not the HMO. This development happened without public debate, comment or approval. Large physician medical groups act essentially like insurers, without the solvency requirements to make sure they are fiscally secure or hold an insurance company license. Whatever doctors spend on patients comes out of their own pockets. "The less you do for patients, the more money you make" is an unacceptable public policy for most Americans. The federal government can outlaw the payment of capitated rates to physicians, or at least "full risk" capitated payments that turn physicians into insurers. If HMOs are prevented from passing full risk, or even any risk, on to physicians, then the fire wall between the doctor's focus on care and business concerns will be rebuilt.

Prohibiting HMO bureaucrats from second-guessing physicians who examine patients. HMOs claim that if they can no longer capitate doctors, they will have to increase the number and interference of company bureaucrats. An HMO should not be allowed to deny a patient a physician-recommended treatment unless another equally qualified doctor has examined the patient and made a medical determination that the care is not warranted. In addition, any HMO employee making treatment decisions should have a valid medical license in that state.

Would the HMO industry really oppose such basic reforms? Yes. In 1997 and 1998, California's HMO industry fought such legislation twice. The reform, aimed at curtailing the overriding of doctors' decisions, focused on extreme cases, where a patient's life and health was certified to be in jeopardy by the first doctor who examined them. The industry prevailed on Governor Pete Wilson to veto this eminently reasonable reform.[18] This common sense rule of law, however, must be applied to HMOs if bureaucrats are to be prevented from overruling qualified doctors and making life and death decisions. In particular, if capitation is prohibited, this reform will ensure that HMO bureaucrats do not interfere in the doctor-patient relationship when a doctor is seeking critical care for his patients. This vital legislation returns control over medicine to doctors, not accountants.

States must set safe staffing standards so that nurses and doctors are available to patients based on acuity of illness, regardless of whether the patient is in a nursing home or in a hospital. Typically, staffing protections exist only for the most severely ill patients in critical care units. Even in these areas, some businesses routinely violate the law. Stronger penalties are needed. Safe staffing requirements do not currently exist for hospital units outside of critical care, nursing homes, medical offices, and same-day surgery centers. This is why HMOs often seek to shunt patients who need to be in the hospital to so-called skilled nursing facilities or nursing homes, which are less costly because doctors and nurses do not have to be on the premises in any ratio to the patient population. Until safe nurse- and physician-staffing levels are set by regulators for all acute patients, HMOs and insurers will continue to cut corners and strand patients in inappropriate settings based solely on cost.

Mandate public disclosure of data on health care quality, financial information and complaints and arbitrations against the health care organization. One of the key components of our medical system should be informed consent by patients. HMOs may deal with questions of life or death, but they are under no obligation to tell you anything about their day-to-day operations. They do not disclose how they determine whether you receive needed care, how much money they make based on those decisions or about why any legal actions were taken against them. HMOs should be required to publicly disclose all information relating to quality of patient care. This includes all data and studies used to determine quality, staffing, and reduction of services; financial reports, including corporate affiliates or subsidiaries; and complaints and arbitrations. WARNING: Today HMOs claim they are trying to get more information into consumers' hands. But this information is often useless. For instance, patient-satisfaction surveys are often taken among people who are well and rarely use their HMO. And private report cards are maintained by industry-sponsored groups such as the Joint Commission on the Accreditation of Healthcare Organizations (JCAHO) and National Committee For Quality Assurance (NCQA).

NCQA was formed in 1979 by the trade associations for the managed care industry—the American Managed Care and Review Association and the Group Health Association of America. The group was founded, in fact, to counter the federal government's attempts to monitor HMOs.[19] The main funding source for NCQA continues to be HMOs, although the group is seeking to diversify its funding to appear more independent. In 1997, NCQA's board of directors was a "Who's Who" of HMO executives and corporate chieftains, including representatives from Aetna, Blue Cross, Henry Ford Health System, PacifiCare, Harvard Pilgrim Health Care. NCQA has created its own performance measurements, the Health Plan Employer Data & Information Set (HEDIS). "The critical point here is that 'value' as used by NCQA is to be measured strictly in terms of *cost* of health care delivery, as distinguished from the clinical needs of a patient as defined by the trained professional," said former U.S. Justice Department attorney Kenneth Anderson, an expert in anti-trust law who contends NCQA is a part of collusive behavior among the managed care industry. "Thus, the NCQA criteria by which performance is measured are initially framed by those entities—HMOs, managed care companies and employer payers—who have a strong incentive to define 'appropriate' levels of care in narrow economic (e.g. cost) terms."[20]

Anderson says "This NCQA effort is, in part, essentially a massive public relations program orchestrated by the managed care industry in hopes of averting the establishment of a truly independent and objective mechanism, whether private or governmental, to define what quality health care really is and then measure plan performance against such standards."[21]

As for JCAHO, a July 1996 audit by the national consumer group Public Citizen found JCAHO "views hospitals not as entities to be regulated, but as customers to be serviced and kept satisfied." Part of the basis for the finding is that twenty-one out of twenty-eight members of the JCAHO's Board of Commissioners were industry representatives who each paid $20,000 a year for a seat.

Prohibit health care businesses from selling medical records without the express written authorization of the patient. Here is a scary thought: It is easier for people to find out if you have cancer or AIDS than it is for them to get a list of the videos you have rented. Patient records are now a commodity for sale.

Hospitals, HMOs, and drug companies all maintain commercial data banks which collect and store individual medical records, containing sensitive personal information. Most states' civil codes have extensive provisions for maintaining medical confidentiality, but most were written before the computer explosion. The new technology changes everything and leaves patients extremely vulnerable. Dr. Beverly Woodward, an ethicist at Brandeis University, says employees at most Boston-area hospitals enter patient information directly on-line without consent from the patient. Any doctor at any affiliated hospital can access these records, including psychiatric records.[22] In Maryland, Medicaid clerks tapped into computers and accessed critical patient information—names, addresses, incomes, medical records—which they sold, sometimes for less than fifty cents per head, to HMO recruiters.[23] Breach of privacy can have serious consequences. Patients with AIDS or mental illnesses have a great deal to lose if their condition is made public—sometimes their jobs, even their families.

Prohibit HMOs, hospitals, nursing homes or other health care businesses from firing, delisting or retaliating against doctors and licensed caregivers who speak out on behalf of patients or who report patient care violations to authorities. "Gag" or "disparagement" clauses in contracts between physicians and HMOs or insurers pressure doctors to keep silent about practices or policies they believe may be injurious to patients.[24] Hospitals have fired, sanctioned, and threatened doctors, nurses and other licensed caregivers who advocate for their patients, challenge unsafe practices or cooperate with official investigations. These pernicious practices must be barred if doctors are to be trusted by their patients. HMOs say "gag" clauses do not exist today. If they do not, there is no reason not to ban them.

Fixing Long-term Care Insurance—Integrating Support Systems. The average life expectancy has lengthened more in the last 100 years than in the previous 2,000.[25] People are living longer, but their final years are not necessarily healthier. Half of all women and a third of all men 65 years of age and older will spend their last years in a nursing home, at a cost of about $40,000 a year.[26]

Long-term care is the assistance people need when they are not able to accomplish some of the basic "activities of daily living" like bathing, dressing, walking or moving from the bed to a chair. The National Center for Health Care Statistics reported in 1996 that half of those 85 and older require long-term care assistance. Unfortunately, traditional health insurance and Medicare will generally not cover home care or community-assisted nursing home living. One must be poor or become poor before becoming eligible for long-term care benefits through Medicaid. Standard health policies pay less than 1% of long term care costs. Medicare covers less than 4%. Private payments, which are costly to individuals and their families, account for 29%. Medicaid—which covers the poor and those who have "spent-down" their assets (a difficult process)—accounts for 68% of the payments.[27] Should it take becoming poor or disabled, or driving your family into poverty, in order to qualify for home-care coverage? Shut-ins who cannot afford home care develop bed sores or anorexia, then need to be hospitalized at a much higher cost.

Long-term care in California averages about $124 a day, or about $45,000 a year.[28] According to the Brookings Institute only 4 to 5% of the elderly nationwide have some kind of private long-term care coverage.

Marketing is not prompting consumers to buy policies at a younger age—the average purchaser of private long-term care insurance is 68 years-old. Plus, policies are sold almost exclusively on an individual, rather than group, basis, with concomitant high administrative costs for insurers. According to the National Association of Insurance Commissioners (NAIC), annual premiums for long-term care insurance can run as much as $2,000 for the average-aged purchaser. Premiums increase as one gets older and there are so many options in policies that even sophisticated consumers have difficulty understanding what they are buying and how it compares with other products.

Deceptive and fraudulent marketing is also increasingly a serious problem for long-term care insurance. federal legislation in 1996 created a national long-term care insurance policy to be sold by private insurers. Drafted at the behest of the insurance industry, the federal policy provides less generous benefit payments than many state-based policies, including California's—eliminating the most common form of disability, the inability to walk, as a trigger for paying benefits. The insurance lobby sold the less generous benefits policy to Congress, and then marketed it to seniors, under the pretense that because the policy's cost was tax deductible, older Americans would benefit. The problem is that the vast majority of seniors do not itemize their medical deductions and will not reap a tax benefit.

The affordability and availability of long-term care must be addressed in a coherent national health care policy, particularly as it relates to Medicare and Medicaid.

Can society afford to pay to keep all older Americans alive as long as they and their family want and technology allows? Critical to answering this question is a more reasonable long-term care public policy. One solution is for the federal government to issue long-term care insurance that includes the most common form of disability—the inability to walk—and for it to be jointly underwritten by private companies.

A second potential solution is to build long term care insurance into the federal Medicare package, so that families will not have to "spend-down" or "go-bankrupt" just to get nursing home care. Surveys show that the majority of the American public agree with expanding Medicare to include long term care.

Private companies like Columbia/HCA have milked and bilked the homecare market at the expense of the taxpayer, mostly through Medicaid. Meanwhile, those doing the job are underpaid and overworked. Integrating the continuum of home care into the medical care delivery system is vital to cost-effectiveness and health enhancement.

Systemic Changes:
The Second Tier Reforms

Important as they are, first-tier reforms will not fundamentally alter the drive to sacrifice care in the name of profit. More potent, systemic remedies like those enumerated below are likely needed.

End For-Profit, Investor Ownership of HMOs and Health Care Businesses. Medical care is not a commodity. It should not be bought and sold like automobiles. Health care does not fit the logic of the market. Many observers trace the reckless, profit-driven care-cutting at HMOs and managed care companies to the rise of for-profit, investor-owned HMOs and health care businesses. The easy money in managed care, though, is long gone. How do investor-owned HMOs respond to the current serious slide in their stock? They move to fewer facilities, reduced access to specialists, cheaper drugs, shorter hospital stays, fewer doctors and hospitals, less caution. In the current environment, the maintenance of the company's rate of return to attract investors demands that patients pay the price. The HMO network of doctors is made more restrictive, research and training programs are cut, doctors are fired.

Former United States Surgeon General C. Everett Koop and John Baldwin, the dean of the medical school at Dartmouth College, posed the question of control of health care this way: "Sustained profits require aggressive cost-cutting. This results, inevitably, in restriction of access and withholding of care. But do we really want to relegate such decisions to analysts within the health care industry, or should we assert the public interest in these crucial ethical, societal and medical issues?"[29]

When California-based PacifiCare bought failing FHP International in 1997, for instance, the executives and directors took home millions. FHP patients had already paid the price. Long before the sale, about one-third of FHP doctors were fired, training programs were dismantled and the drug list cut, according to FHP's founder, in order to dress the company up for sale by clearing FHP's books of expensive overhead. FHP shareholders, who took the HMO officers to court, claimed unscrupulous board members and execu-

Wall Street electronic ticker-tape machine constantly updating PacifiCare's
stock price above the elevator to the medical directors' office suite.

tives purposely destroyed a viable and healthy company just to sell off its
resources and make millions for themselves.

Without new controls to protect health resources, the current system is
clearly open to raids by profiteers. In the $9 billion U.S. Healthcare merger
with Aetna in 1996, for instance, U.S. Healthcare chief Leonard Abramson
walked away with over $900 million. PacifiCare medical directors, who are
responsible for approving or denying physician requests for expensive drugs
and treatment, view a constantly updated electronic ticker-tape of the company's stock price on the wall above the elevator to their offices. These medical directors decide physician requests that could affect that stock price. Do
business or medical decisions rule?

Patients deserve a moratorium on for-profit HMO takeovers of not-for-
profit HMOs, hospitals and clinics. This would discourage the quick buck
mentality by HMO executives while protecting the availability and accessi-
bility of health care. Medical resources are far too valuable a public commodity to evaporate the next time a Wall Street bubble bursts. A ban on
for-profit, investor ownership of HMOs would put HMOs back in the hands

of doctors and health care professionals who have been trained to run the system.

A study in the July 14, 1999 edition of the *Journal of the American Medical Association* found that not-for-profit HMOs deliver a better quality of care than investor-owned, for-profit HMOs in fourteen categories selected by the NCQA. For instance, investor-owned HMOs had lower rates of immunization, mammography and psychiatric hospitalization. One can only imagine how much better still the non-profits would perform if they did not have to compete in markets dominated by for-profit companies.

Some might say that doctors are for-profit enterprises themselves. This is correct. But, unlike HMOs, physicians also hold medical licenses that can be taken away and they can be held accountable in a court of law in every state. Effective checks on physician conflict of interest can be maintained. Doctors working within the framework of a non-profit medical system will have additional ethical constraints.

HMOs are starting to fail financially. Oxford in New York, for instance, fell apart after its stock tumbled. New Jersey officials were forced to take over HIP Health Plans of New Jersey in October of 1998 because it was bordering on insolvency. Governor Christine Whitman's administration announced that it wants to create a safety net for patients by exploring the possibility of a "guaranty fund" for HMOs—which, unlike traditional insurers, do not have reserve requirements. The stress on HMO finances will only continue.

For-profit HMOs operate in a climate of profiteering and investor demands for a strong rate of return on their capital. The non-profit HMOs compete in the same environment as the for-profits—trying to undercut their for-profit competitors' prices. This is what happened to Kaiser, a non-profit, competing in a for-profit environment. Kaiser reduced its once excellent service to maintain its price levels for employers. A disillusioned Paul Ellwood, the father of HMOs, who even coined the term managed care, relayed recently, "A Kaiser official told me the other day, 'Until better quality attracts more patients, I don't care about it any more. We've been talking about quality improvement for thirty or forty years without much to show for it.'"[30] The non-profits are subject to the same downsizing demands to lower costs in order to cut premiums so they can attract more customers. Take the investor-owned, for-profit company out of the managed care equation and the management of quality care within a budget will be the primary

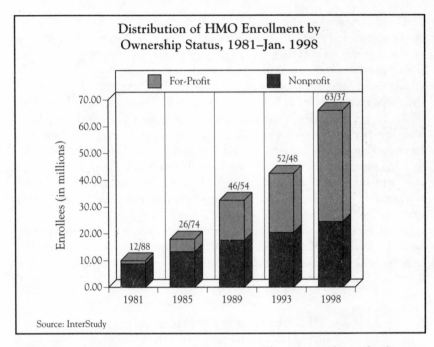

Distribution of HMO Enrollment by
Ownership Status, 1981–Jan. 1998

For-Profit   Nonprofit

Source: InterStudy

concern, rather than return on investment. The non-profit medical group can return to its primary goal of treating patients.

Boycott HMOs and Receive Health Care Direct From Employers. Motorola Corporation received so many complaints from its employees about their HMOs that it created a new system where the company itself contracts with a network of doctors and hospitals to take care of its employees' medical needs. Motorola cut out the unnecessary middle men—the HMOs and insurance companies. Employees report greater satisfaction with their health care and doctors say they now are the ones in control of managing care, knowing they must contain costs (or they will lose their contracts), but not at the expense of medically necessary treatment. Motorola's vice president for benefits, Rick Dorozil, told CBS News, "We will continue to do this as long as we can do it faster, better, cheaper, and at better quality." For $12.50 a week and 10% of bills, employees and their families can see any doctor in the network, including specialists, without preauthorization. Seventy percent of Motorola's 80,000 employees have enrolled in this new plan.[31] As more employers follow suit in this voluntary arrangement, at least patients with employer-paid health care will have more options.

There are two daunting problems with this model. First, employers have access to personal medical information about their employees. This creates a very real threat to patient privacy. AIDS patients, for instance, might find themselves out of work and filing discrimination lawsuits because of a bigoted employer. Most obviously, those without employer-paid health care would still have to deal with HMOs, and these patients would tend to be seniors on Medicare, the disabled and poor on Medicaid, and others without jobs or with low-paying jobs—people who tend to be sicker. HMOs would have to serve a sicker population without taking in the premiums from the healthier working population. This system would be destined to collapse. HMO medicine, which prefers to take in dollars from the healthy and limit care for the sick, would be destroyed by adverse selection—the "risk pool" being drained of the best risks and left with the worst.

A more comprehensive national strategy is warranted precisely because we must have one health care system that shares the risk equally for the healthy and the sick rather than many systems which compete for the healthiest and leave the sickest to the taxpayer's generosity.

The Fox Guarding the Henhouse:
Avoiding HMO Attempts to Control Reform

Privatization advocates have long tried to turn public control of our schools, courts, public assistance systems and municipal services over to private corporations in the name of greater efficiency. But Aetna, PacifiCare, Kaiser and others among the nation's largest HMOs have actually tried to privatize legislative reforms of their own industry by promising to implement private "independent" review systems, where the HMO voluntarily pays a third party to review patient problems, rather than submit to public mandates.[32]

State and federal legislators cannot trust the HMO industry's promise to reform itself. The HMOs' independent review systems purport to give patients facing delays and denials an appeal, but deliver infrequently.

First, reviewing companies are hardly 'independent' of the HMOs that contract and pay for their services. For instance, marketing communications from one such company, Medical Care Management Corporation of Bethesda Maryland, to HMO clients boast that the company "can save payers millions of dollars a year on just a few cases. Our expert physicians affirm the high cost, high risk procedures submitted for review in one-half to two-thirds of cases, depending on the type of disease and the patient's profile. If you are paying for 100 such cases now, inadvisable treatments may be costing you over $6 million." So the so-called independent reviewers market a "denial" rate of 33–50%.

California actually already enacted an "independent" review system in 1996 for patients in need of "experimental procedures" when standard therapies do not work. In theory, this "independent" review system was unassailable, but in practice no reviewing agency was accredited for six months to perform reviews under the law. Subsequently only two were accredited, one of which was Medical Care Management Corporation. Other companies have been unable or unwilling to prove their "independence" through detailed disclosure about their financial ties to HMOs, their protocols and their reviewers.

Appeals decided by such companies are the HMO industry's reform of choice because the private process permits bureaucratic maneuvers by HMOs against which the seriously ill patient has neither the time nor capacity to defend.

Folsom, California resident Barbara Brown, once a teacher of the year, ran up against this situation when she contracted advanced ovarian cancer and standard treatments would not do. On July 1, 1998 she appealed under California's new experimental treatment law. With no accredited reviewers, Kaiser picked an agency of its choice, Medical Care Management Corporation. Barbara says, "First, Kaiser made every effort to control all the information that went into the review process...Second, Kaiser biased the panel of experts against my proposed experimental therapy by steering the experts toward Kaiser's own leading set of questions...Third, in their reports, the experts all stated that their assigned role was to respond to Kaiser's questions."

Denied life-saving treatment by both Kaiser's internal grievance process and then its so-called external review, Barbara was forced to sell her house to pay for her treatment. Only a community bake sale and car wash that raised $25,000 provided the down payment for her care. Barbara is now recovering. Her "experimental" surgery, which her HMO said would kill her, resulted in the complete removal of all visible tumor from her abdomen. As of this writing in June 1999, she has had ten healthy months with her family. However, creditors are still pursuing her and she has had to move out of her home.

Private review systems are no substitute for civic scrutiny. Congress and state legislatures must not be deterred from enacting right-to-sue legislation and other public mandates. The wealthiest nation on earth must impose its civil values on private corporations rather than let the fate of mothers like Barbara Brown depend on the success of car washes and bake sales.

Third-party reviewing systems will only work well in conjunction with public laws for HMO accountability. Companies must know that if they do not play fair they will face large damage awards or other fines. Texas's independent review process, for instance, has been held out as successful, but the state is the only in the nation where a patient can take an HMO to state court for quality-of-care violations. The independent review and liability laws were passed simultaneously. While the review process was struck down by a federal judge as in violation of ERISA, the state and HMOs reached a voluntary agreement to continue using the system.

A private system of appeal without ultimate public accountability is destined to betray the HMO patient. Legislators who forget their public mandate to reform HMOs and favor a private solution do their constituents a grave disservice.

The Final Frontier:
The Uninsured

National Preventive Health Care.

One of HMO medicine's biggest promises was to reduce the number of uninsured Americans by making insurance more affordable. Unfortunately, HMO medicine has failed on this front too.

The Census Bureau reported in 1998 that the proportion of Americans without health insurance rose to its highest level in a decade: 16.1%. This is 43.2 million fellow citizens, a group in which most of the adults have jobs.

"In a healthy economy, you'd think you would have more people with jobs, and that would tend to increase coverage, so you'd see fewer people uninsured," Census Bureau statistician Robert L. Bennefield said.[33] In the largest states, like Texas and California, the proportion of the uninsured has soared to one in five people.

The HMO industry promised that by moderating premiums, health insurance would be in the reach of more Americans. Yet many employers, particularly small businesses, are now dropping workers and their families from coverage. As noted earlier, premiums are on the rise again. Paul Ellwood predicted in May 1999 that the double-digit increases in premiums will continue "with a vengeance."[34]

The *New York Times* reported in March 1999 that "the uninsured are not the poorest of the poor, who tend to be covered by Medicaid...Of the 43 million Americans without insurance, 75% work at least part time, but are not offered insurance through an employer or cannot afford their contribution. The rest tend to be students, children and early retirees…They are a diverse group, from the chronically ill woman in Harlem who borrows her mother's medicine because she cannot afford her own, to a roofer in Yonkers who is fending off bill collectors, to a young web site designer making about $65,000 a year who takes the calculated risk he will never have to see a doctor at all."[35]

A letter to the *New York Times* from Albany Medical Center President James Barba sums up the problem the uninsured pose not only to themselves and their families, but to the nation.

"Having no insurance does not mean that these patients do not get medical attention," wrote Barba. "Regrettably, many wait until they have a health crisis, then present themselves to emergency departments, with the tab picked up by all of us in the form of charity care. This process is highly expensive and inefficient. Prevention and wellness are less expensive. Getting the uninsured assigned to primary-care physicians so that ailments can be treated before they become full-blown crises is a better use of resources, with substantial savings to the country and taxpayers."[36]

Mr. Barba's point is not revolutionary. Well-educated policymakers in Washington have recognized this fundamental reality since the turn of the century. The question ever since has been *how* to insure, not *whether* to.

Government-run health insurance programs like Canada's have been opposed by the American insurance industry. Insurers have effectively used their deep pockets to turn the public against legislative and ballot attempts aimed at preventing private insurers and HMOs from running the system and mandating certain coverage levels. Some segments of the industry, particularly the smaller insurers, spent tens of millions of dollars to defeat President Clinton's proposed national health care system. Opponents of a government dominated system have asked whether Americans wanted the post office as a model for their medicine. Increasingly in the age of HMOs, however, Americans may respond that at least the post office lives up to its commitments and delivers the mail. Of course, it is the Medicare system, not the post office, which is the apt comparison. The Medicare program operates with a mere 2% for overhead costs. By contrast, private HMOs spend up to 30% for their overhead and profit.

Dr. Carl Weber of White Plains, New York summed up why recent exposés about HMO medicine make a compelling case for the ouster of corporate control of our medical system: "After years of interfering in doctor-patient relations, exacerbating the problem of the uninsured, denying responsibility for medical education and research and rationing health care, health maintenance organizations are refusing to cover the elderly while asking for rate increases. How much more evidence do we need before we realize that managed care is a failed system that should be abandoned?"[37]

Traditionally, there have been two fundamental approaches to "universal health care"—the premise that our society as a whole will insure everyone to protect us all.

First, employers could be required to pay for health care coverage, either through a pay-roll tax or simply by providing coverage for their employees. Such an employer mandate was first proposed by Richard Nixon, so it is hardly a radical idea. The business lobby has fought the employer mandate model on the national level. This model, which currently exists in Hawaii, does not cut private insurers out in favor of a government-run system. In Hawaii, workers and non-workers are covered by the state but given care by private HMOs and health insurers. The state is simply a financing mechanism. Hawaiians, as a whole, seem to feel more satisfied with their HMOs than the rest of Americans, probably because they have the choice of three major competitors and those companies have to compete with quality treatment to win business. President Clinton was working on a similar model for the nation in 1994, but his "managed competition" concept also turned the administration of the system over to HMOs and insurers, which would then tend to compete with each other for healthier customers from the start. Moreover, under "managed competition," too large a percentage of the health care dollar could still go to the companies' profit and overhead rather than to patient care.

A second, more straightforward (some might say radical) model is to make the federal government the payer for all health care services, the ultimate administrator and coordinator of a national health care system that is serviced by private health care service givers—doctors, nurses, hospitals, HMOs that "manage care" rather than simply manage money. This system could take many forms. Canada and most European nations have a "single payer" model, which guarantees universal health coverage to all citizens.[38] The problem for many American legislators, whose careers have been sustained by insurance company campaign contributions, is that the insurers are cut out of the deal. The government, not insurers, underwrites risk. More problematic, a single-payer system is typically financed by taxes on employers. Politically, the corporate lobby has teamed with the medical-insurance complex to stop implementation of a single payer health care system. The

Republican Congress, of course, needs little encouragement from corporations to oppose any government-run health care plan.

The conservative American Medical Association has opposed such a system in the past because of doctors' fears that a government-run system would cap their fees. But many doctors, having seen the horrors of corporate HMO controls, may yet be ready for a government system that is more reasonable to them. While the public once believed that for-profit companies were more capable of running the health care system, attitudes have changed after prolonged exposure to HMO medicine's vices. A February 1998 poll found that, for the first time, the public believes that not-for-profit companies would do better in running the nation's health care system. In HEDIS patient satisfaction data, not-for-profits also receive much higher ratings.[39]

Certainly, there is enough money in the system to insure everyone. A novel proposal by Boston University professor Alan Sager calls for simply freezing all national payments to the health care system from the previous year, and covering every American with a full benefit package from that pool of money.[40]

The trillion dollar health care economy could easily cover every American with comprehensive benefits. Canada, for example, spends 9% of its gross domestic product to insure everyone—while we spend 14% and leave 43 million without insurance. The new American health care system could be coordinated through regional administrations representing all the stakeholders—physicians, patients, payers, and others—that calculate reasonable fees for those providing treatment and monitor utilization of doctors, as well as watching for fraud. Such a government-run system could be far more efficient than the current one.

Sager's system would require no taxes, simply a freeze on payments currently made by employers and other payers. Alternatively the same program without the co-payments patients now are forced to make would include only a moderate increase in taxes, equal to 5% of health care spending. Such a tax would substitute for the co-pay, which Sager calls, "the tax on being sick." The question Americans and their representatives must ask themselves is which model ensures greater potential for the health of the nation—one run by corporations intent on profits or one run on a non-profit basis and regulated by the government.

Ellwood, whose change of heart about his own HMO concept was fostered by his personal experiences with bad medicine, now says, "Uneven health care in the United States is a national disgrace. Ultimately this thing is going to require government intervention. The question is what form government intervention will take. I think whatever it is, it's going to have to be a condition of doing business." Ellwood agrees reform "is not going to come from within" the industry.[41]

Two recent independent studies, commissioned by the Massachusetts Medical Society, indicate the waste and overhead in the current system. According to a report in the *Boston Globe*, a Canadian-style single-payer system would save between $170 million and $1 billion annually in the state. Additionally, hundreds of thousands of Massachusetts residents would have coverage; cutting back on the fiscal strain of emergency room medicine. Surely Massachusetts is not unique in this regard.[42]

It is, of course, significant that a state chapter of the AMA would sponsor such a study. The national organization has been steadfast in its opposition to a single-payer system. American doctors, however, have had both their incomes and freedom to exercise appropriate medicine eroded under for-profit managed care.

Any standardized system would reduce the needless paperwork that bogs down medical offices dealing with the vagaries of private insurers. Market enthusiasts should be interested in reducing the inefficiencies in the current system. Certainly American ingenuity can design a public/private partnership to restore the primacy of the doctor/patient relationship and insure more citizens. This will require the elimination of the for-profit insurers from any significant role in American medical care. It will be a bitter political struggle because of the billions of dollars involved. But it may become inevitable as the nation grows older, requires more medical care, and experiences the many flaws of managed care.

Never before in American history has there been such an intersection between the interests of the uninsured and of those who pay for insurance but lack peace of mind that they will receive coverage for their medical conditions.

In early 1998, an insured Massachusetts newspaper publisher killed himself, leaving behind a suicide note about his travails trying to get mental health care from his HMO. In the spring of 1998, a distraught man with health insurance parked his truck on a Los Angeles freeway and unfurled a banner that read, "HMOs are in it for the money." Observed by television viewers across the nation, he proceeded to set himself on fire, then discharge a gun in his mouth.

Such despair might once have been conceivable among the uninsured, but hardly from the insured in the wealthiest nation in the world. As extreme as the reactions were, too many Americans can identify with the intense frustrations of dealing with HMOs.

In June 1999, the *Los Angeles Times* reported that specialists on call with local emergency rooms are now refusing to respond to emergencies for HMO patients because their HMOs do not pay enough. In one case, a surgeon refused to come to the emergency room to operate on a seven month-old who fell and cut her upper lip down to the muscle.[43]

A system that manages treatment and costs is needed. But who will run it? The health care crisis that led to the national debate in 1994 over universal health coverage has only been deferred. The rising anger at the deficiencies of HMO medicine is merely a symptom of the same national malaise. Americans will ultimately have to weigh in, once and for all, about the future of their health care system.

If the people do not act, private entrepreneurs certainly will.

A high-profile group of investors are already raising venture capital to launch a for-profit HMO patient assistance service and 1-800 hotline, much like the pre-paid road service plan for motorists. For an annual premium or membership fee of about $80 per year, the corporation will provide information about HMOs and limited access to an advocate to help you navigate your HMO when you run into problems—more advanced advocacy packages would cost more. The program amounts to insurance for your health insurance. Should we need to buy more insurance just to collect on our HMO policy? Can the failure of HMOs to serve us be corrected by more market mechanisms? Will private solutions result in another proliferation of niche businesses that play on patients' fears and are just as exploitive as the HMOs? Unless civil society reasserts itself, the answers may be all too clear.

HMO Patient Self-Defense Kit

Corporate medicine is, by self-admission, intent on shackling health care expenses by doctors and other medical professionals against the interests of patients. For the patient denied treatment, this is an adversarial system.

Unfortunately, a seriously ill patient in need of a medical treatment is disabled—by definition, least able or unable to advocate for themselves.

The greatest mistake patients in need of critical care and their loved ones make is the assumption that the system is there to help them. Doctors and nurses may be there, but they do not control the corporate medical system. Often, it is a friend or family member who must lead the battle for a patient's care and they must remember that a likely response from the system will be delay and denial.

How can patients or their allies help themselves in a system that is set up not to help them get treatment?

Your tactics must be those of negotiation.

Everything is negotiable—with the HMO, the HMO doctor, the HMO hospital. In a negotiation, establishing what is reasonable is the goal.

- What should a reasonable person have to do in order to document his or her need for treatment?

- What should a reasonable corporation have to provide and how long should it take?

- Is the company living up to the letter and spirit of state law?

These are the types of standards someone negotiating with their HMO or HMO doctor must fight for.

The record has indicated that HMOs do not concede expensive treatment without constant and repeated demands.

HMOs have time on their side and they know it. They will delay as a tactic of denial. Enough delays will equal a denial for a patient in need of critical care. Because most patients cannot sue HMOs for a denial or delay of treatment and receive damages if they prevail, the company has an incentive to stonewall because there is no financial penalty. (See Chapter Five)

Reasonableness always includes a reasonable timetable. When will a decision be made to approve the care? Who is the decision-maker? How long will it take to schedule the procedure? What is the longest it will take before this doctor sees me?

The tactics of getting care from an HMO or HMO doctor may be no different than those involved in any other struggle against bureaucratic power. The major difference is that the patient is typically not in any condition to fight. That is why others close to them must take on that role. Patients themselves should make such contingency plans.

And even for the well, fighting for a just cause, such as with an HMO or HMO doctor for medically-appropriate treatment, is not an ordinary activity of daily living.

The fight begins with an understanding of the system and its foibles. (See Chapters One through Six).

There are also some general rules one can always follow in dealing with HMOs, but these are no panacea, simply precautionary measures.

- **Write everything down.** Bring a notepad and pencil to all medical facilities and take notes on what your doctor tells you. This may feel uncomfortable, but it will help to keep track of your care, catch any errors, and provide a record should there be a question of inappropriate treatment.

- **If you are denied care, ask for it in writing.** You will need a record of the denial if you want to dispute it. Memorialize in written correspondence all conversations if it becomes apparent that you are not receiving cooperation. Leaving a "paper trail" often helps to get results.

- **Find out the timelines.** Most states have regulations establishing the timeframe within which a treatment or coverage decision must be made. Contact the appropriate regulatory authority in your state and find out what those timelines are. Then make sure everyone you deal with at the medical group or the HMO know that you know what those timelines are and make sure they stick to them. Also, as part of their marketing, most HMOs are accredited by non-government groups such as National Committee for Quality Assurance [www.ncqa.org], American Accreditation HealthCare Commission/URAC [www.urac.org] and the Joint Commission on Accreditation of Health Care Organizations [www.jcaho.org]. These organizations often have timeline requirements even more stringent than the state requirements. Find out if your HMO is a member of any of these organizations and if it is, find out that organization's timeline requirements for the health plan's decision-making process. Again, make sure the HMO knows that you know those timelines and that you expect them to be followed.

- **Appeal a treatment denial to regulators.** HMOs are regulated by the state regulatory agencies, many of which have a consumer complaint hotline. The rules for each state differ. Find the appropriate state agency and their rules for filing a complaint. Medicare and Medicaid recipients can take a complaint to the federal Health Care Financing Administration. (WARNING: Don't rely on governmental agencies as your savior, however, because many are ineffective. Patients must be persistent if they hope to get a response from an HMO or government.) *HMOs do not like too many documented complaints, so including a carbon copy to state regulators and politicians of any contested correspondence is appropriate.*

- **Complain to the accrediting organization**. Because HMOs rely so strongly on their accreditation by the non-governmental organizations (NCQA, URAC and JCAHO) in their marketing to employers and unions, they dislike having complaints documented to those groups even less than they like having complaints on file with government regulators. In addition to copying your documentation to the state regulators, copy it to the accrediting organization or organizations that your HMO is a member of.

- **Find allies in the medical profession.** When medical experts advocate care, HMOs find it harder to deny treatment. Insist on a second or third opinion—from a qualified professional outside the HMO network, if necessary. If your HMO won't pay for a second opinion, pay out of your own pocket. It could save your life.

- **Ask how your doctor is paid**. Under new rules, Medicare recipients are entitled to see a summary of their physician's contract with their HMO, which details any financial incentives to withhold treatment.

Many states now also provide that such information must be given to plan members, if requested. Ask for it. Doctors should increasingly provide such information to all patients. File a complaint with your state's medical board if you believe your doctor is withholding treatment for his or her own pecuniary gain.

- **Never take "no" for an answer.** Always ask if there are treatment options available for you other than those the HMO recommends. If you have a problem, take it up the ladder—fast. Enlist the help of your employer's personnel department if you get your health care through your work.

- **Never stay in a hospital by yourself.** Have a spouse, loved one or friend present at all times when you are in the hospital, even if that means sleeping in a chair. Having an advocate present to monitor what is happening around you, to make sure you get the treatment you need, is essential. If something goes wrong, he or she can act quickly to secure assistance.

- **Do not be intimidated.** Do not permit yourself to be intimidated by someone else's uniform, occupation, credentials and stature. You're paying the bills, not only as a consumer, but also as a taxpayer who helps fund the medical system. Don't let the bureaucrats slow you down. Write and call everyone you can think of in the HMO—the CEO, the Medical Director, the President of Marketing, the Board of Directors. Contact your elected representatives for help. Write the newspapers. Enlist your doctor as an advocate for you whenever possible (good doctors will put aside any conflicts of interest to protect your health). Enlist your employer if you get your health care through your work.

But *always* maintain a reasonable, professional and calm demeanor, both in person and in writing—no matter how hard that is to do sometimes. If you lose control, make threats of violence or use foul language, you will simply be dismissed as a "crank," a "flake" or a "weirdo" and you will not accomplish your goal.

- **Get the medical care you need.** You must always remember that your health care is your most important priority. Do whatever you have to do to get the medical care you need—mortgage your house, get loans from friends and relatives, try to make deals with the doctors and hospitals, get the community to help with fundraisers, if necessary. But get the care and worry about the money later.

- **Get a lawyer if you need one.** Lawsuits are no fun. They can take years, involve endless and grueling maneuvering. Most who go through the process say they underestimated how hard it would be, especially to relive the medical trauma. And then, of course, there is the possibility that you have a legitimate case but will be unable to prove it in court, or laws won by the insurance industry may limit your right to even go to court. Nevertheless, legal options are often your only leverage against profit-driven managed care. A medical malpractice suit or a lawsuit for failing to pay claims properly can hit an HMO or insurer where it hurts it the most—the pocketbook.

- **If possible, never give up the right to go to court.** Avoid signing arbitration agreements that force you into HMO-controlled private justice systems. (Cross out the arbitration clause and initial it; if your employer has signed your right away, lobby to change that provision of the contract.) Also, some insurers require you to file complicated internal complaints before going to court. Follow these instructions exactly, but don't delay in consulting a lawyer in the meantime.

These are only tips. To be an effective advocate for yourself or someone else, there are a host of principles you can follow and many excellent books on the methods of advocacy, including two books by the pioneering insurance bad faith lawyer Bill Shernoff, *Fight Back & Win* (Bottom Line, 1998) and *Payment Refused* (Richard & Steinman, 1986). But here is a primer.

Effective Advocacy

The most effective advocate is the most persuasive. Persuasion is the goal of all advocacy.

Persuasion is the goal of the written word, the spoken word, unspoken messages. The right words or action from the right person or people to the key decision-makers at the appropriate time is the equation for success in advocating any position.

A series of small victories at being persuasive equals a successful campaign.

Get the right doctors on your side who will then write to the correct medical director with the appropriate language and you are more likely to get care.

Perhaps one doctor is a stumbling block to you getting appropriate treatment. This physician may have a financial incentive (capitation) not to refer you to a specialist or for a test, because the money for these procedures comes out of the doctor's own pocket. Ironically, in this case, the HMO could be one important ally. If the HMO is not paying for the treatment, since the risk is shouldered by the doctor, the HMO has no disincentive to helping you compel the doctor to provide appropriate care.

Being persuasive starts with forming a strategy.

Who is the right decision-maker? What words will most influence them and from whom? How much time should I give them to reply? These questions must be asked before mapping a strategy for action.

Forming A Strategy

Effective advocates do not make a first move without forming a strategy. The first formation of a strategy is a clear identification of your goal and your obstacles. The goal should be as specific as possible, but it may require many goals to achieve a large one.

For instance, receiving a specific course of high-cost treatment may be your goal.

1. To achieve this you will have to map out much smaller goals.

2. Each of these smaller goals should have a timeline attached to them, leading up to the large goal.

3. Identify potential allies as well as obstacles.

MAIN GOAL: Proton-beam therapy to start by January—referral from medical group for out-of-network treatment.

OBSTACLE: Primary Care Doctor X and His Medical Group Do Not Want To Make Referral Because They Are Responsible For Treatment's Costs But No Qualified Specialist Exists Within Medical Group

ALLIES: Government regulators; the HMO (it is not paying for the treatment because it passed full risk to the medical group, so it might as well help you get the care); the specialists out-of-network who will provide the care.

SUB-GOALS—MAP OF GOALS

First Goal: Letter From Specialist Physician To Medical Group Medical
  Director Asking For Treatment, Noting No Qualified Specialist Exists
  In Medical Group
Timeline: By Tuesday

Second Goal: Official Letter From Patient To Medical Group Asking
  For Treatment And Requesting A Response By Next Monday
Time Line: Today

Third Goal: File Preliminary Complaint with Regulatory Agency
Timeline: By Wednesday

Fourth Goal: Specialist Physician To Follow-up On Letter With Phone
  Call To Medical Group Medical Director
Timeline: By End Of Week

Fifth Goal: File Complaint with HMO's Customer Service Department
Timeline: By Wednesday

Sixth Goal: Have HMO Officer Call Medical Group About Treatment
Timeline: By End of Week

By creating a work plan and mapping your strategy, you can chart the
advancement or stalling of your strategy and react appropriately. Your strategy map is a formula for what is reasonable. When it runs astray, you should
react proportionately.

Achieving The Strategy

Passion is essential to any effective advocacy effort. When a loved one's
life and death is at stake, passion tends to enter the equation. But your goals
must always be to establish what is reasonable and not let your anger fog the
vision of what needs to be done or keep potential allies from helping you.

That is not to say that you should not communicate the urgency of the situation with every contact you make. You should. But you must be under control and maintain good human relationships. You should cultivate allies, rather than simply making enemies. Keep your dignity and composure even as you communicate a sense of urgency about the life and death stakes of the situation.

Consider the situation of Harry Christie, whose daughter Carley was stricken with a rare cancer called Wilms tumor and his HMO would not approve a surgeon who had performed the removal procedure before to do the job. (Chapter One) The Christies made a decision on the spot to have the care rendered and worry about payment later. Today, Carley is living a happy and healthy life as a result. Harry's strategy was then to go through every step of the process and get all the allies he could to force the HMO to pay for the care and be punished for their denial. While passionate, Harry's calm and deliberate demeanor, skills he had cultivated in the electronics industry, led to the state of California ultimately fining his HMO—Takecare, later FHP—$500,000 for its failure to approve the proper surgeon. Harry fought a three-year battle and only because he cultivated an employee in the state regulator's office who knew the system did he ultimately get justice for his daughter. Harry's strategy was to patiently do everything possible to reach his desire to hold the HMO accountable. His initial decision to make certain that his daughter received the care she needed without waiting for the HMO's approval was a wise strategic choice to put her health above the HMO's rules.

Harry's advice is "I thought I had approval the night before the surgery. Then they back-peddled and said we didn't seek pre-approval. That is a falsehood. Then it took eleven months to recover the medical bills. Next time I would have gone directly to the medical group. I thought I had to do all my dealings through the managed care plan. What I didn't know was that the medical group held its own set of cards. If you know in your heart of hearts what you are being told is not right, you have got to go with your instincts and do what needs to be done and fight it afterwards."

In dealing with a difficult medical situation, a balance of passion and reason is essential. It will also help keep key decision-makers to deadlines.

It is your job as a patient's advocate to set those deadlines for the key decision-makers.

Patient Advocate: We sent you the medical records Thursday, I am just following up to make sure you received them so you can issue the approval for my sister's treatment. As you probably know, she is in much pain and, as the letter attached to her medical records indicates, she must receive this treatment immediately.

Administrator: I have received the paperwork, but it is going to take a little while to process. The medical director has not yet reviewed it. I do not know that he has everything he needs to make a decision. But we will call you as soon as he reviews it.

Patient Advocate: What is the name of the medical director who is making this decision?

Administrator: It will either be Doctor Green or Doctor Yellow.

Patient Advocate: How soon will Doctor Green or Doctor Yellow be reviewing the file?

Administrator: I cannot say. We understand the urgency of the situation and will do this as soon as possible.

Patient Advocate: My sister is in so much pain. I need to give her a timeframe. What is your deadline for making this decision?

Administrator: I am certain they will look at the files this week, but they may need additional information, or to talk to the doctors involved. They will certainly begin the process this week. If they have everything they need, I am sure the decision will be made soon.

Patient Advocate: May I speak to Doctor Yellow or Doctor Green?

Administrator: They are not available. They are in a meeting. They will get to your sister's file as soon as they can ma'am. Please be patient.

Patient Advocate: I understand you are all very busy. I just would like a timeline for this decision so I can talk with my sister about her options. You understand, don't you?

Administrator: Of course.

Patient Advocate: Can you give me a timeline?

Administrator: I am sorry, ma'am. I can't.

Patient Advocate: I am sorry, your name was Debbie ____.

Administrator: Debbie Red.

Patient Advocate: And who is your Supervisor?

Administrator: Dr. Orange.

Patient Advocate: And who is Doctor Yellow and Doctor Green's Supervisor?

Administrator: Dr. Orange.

Patient Advocate: Is Dr. Orange available?

Administrator: Let me transfer you to his Secretary.

Patient Advocate: Before you do that, will you please leave a message for Doctor Green or Doctor Yellow, whichever will take care of this file, to call me.

Administrator: Yes, ma'am. I have your number. Let me transfer you to Doctor Orange's office.

"Pinning" is the art of getting a timeframe for a decision and working through the hierarchy in this or any other organization. To pin is to narrow a commitment, a timeframe, a decision. You pin someone down to either get a commitment or more information that will lead to a commitment from a decision-maker. It is especially helpful in this scenario to know what the timelines are that are established by the appropriate state regulations or the applicable accrediting organization. Communicate to the administrator that you know what those timelines are and that you expect them to be complied with.

The commitment is, of course, the goal of what you are pinning for but in some conversations it will be impossible to get a commitment because you are not speaking to a decision-maker.

Finding the chain of command and utilizing it is the modus operandi of pinning down a decision in the corporation. You must remember who you are talking to and what the purpose of your conversation is. The so-called administrator in the above example was not a decision-maker, but an "informer"—someone who could landscape how the company worked and what the chain of authority was. It would make no sense to argue with this employee about the details of the patient's condition, coverage or state law's requirements about covering the patient's condition. The purpose of this conversation was to find out who to write the letter detailing these facts to and putting the best case forward.

Know who you are talking to at an HMO. It makes no sense to argue your case before a bailiff, you must find the judge.

Sizing up an employee means a persistent but friendly conversation—pushing the limits of the conversation as far as they go, and gathering information. Persistence is the key to effective information gathering and pinning. Most people, however, are uncomfortable pushing the cusp of a conversation beyond what may be considered good manners. These are inhibitions which must be forgotten when an HMO acts unreasonably and jeopardizes a patient's health.

Chain of Command

"You never expected justice from a company, did you?" asked 19th century English writer and clergyman Sydney Smith. "They neither have a soul to lose, nor a body to kick."

But in every corporation there are people. People can be persuaded.

Every hierarchy has a chain of command. HMOs are nothing if not hierarchies. If a customer service representative cannot help you, talk to their supervisor immediately. If the supervisor cannot assist in the timeframe necessary, contact their boss, the division head, the medical director, the chief executive officer. Go as far up the chain of command as fast as possible. People make decisions most effectively when they feel that making the wrong decision will jeopardize their position. HMO values may not encourage compassion. But no HMO personnel wants a written record that they have blood on their hands.

Every fight with an HMO for receiving patient care today is a fight for whether civil society and medical ethics will succeed in reasserting itself against HMO and corporate values. The documentation, research and advocacy you contribute to this process can help change things for the better for others. When all else fails, or does not appear to be succeeding in time, enlist others who can help even the balance of power between the patient and the corporation, such as the media. The level of what is reasonable that you help to establish for yourself or loved one will help clear access to care for those in the future.

A list of all state HMO regulatory agencies follows.

For Medicare recipients, an internal appeal by an HMO must be reviewed and answered within thirty days. An expedited appeal should take seventy-two hours if the patient has a problem that could seriously jeopardize life or health or the ability to regain maximum function. If the HMO turns down the first appeal, an individual can ask for a reconsideration, and the health plan must answer within another thirty days, or seventy-two hours for an expedited appeal. If the appeal is rejected again, the HMO must send the case for independent review to the Center for Health Dispute Resolution, located at 1 Fishers Road (second floor), Pittsford, NY 14534. The center can be reached at (716) 586-1770.

State Regulators

Alabama

Department of Public Health
Division of Managed Care
  Compliance
Ray Scherer—Director
RSA Tower, Suite #750
P.O. Box 303017
Montgomery, AL 36130-3017

334-206-5366

Alaska

Division of Insurance
3601 C Street, Suite #1324
Anchorage, AK 99503-5948

907-269-7900

Consumer Services
800-467-8725

Arizona

Department of Insurance
2910 N 44th Street , Suite #210
Phoenix, AZ 85018

602-912-8444

Consumer Assistance Division
800-325-2548

Arkansas

Arkansas Insurance Department
Consumer Services Division
Third and Cross Streets
Little Rock, AR 72201

501-371-2640

Consumer Services Division
800-852-5494

California

Department of Corporations
980 9th Street, Suite #500
Sacramento, CA 95814-3860

916-445-7205

Consumer Services Unit
800-400-0815

Colorado

Division of Insurance
1560 Broadway, Suite #850

Denver, CO 80202

303-894-7499

Consumer Affairs Division
800-930-3745

Connecticut

Insurance Department
PO Box 816
Hartford, CT 06142-0816

860-297-3900

Consumer Affairs Division
800-203-3447

Delaware

Department of Insurance
841 Silver Lake Blvd.
Dover, DE 19904

302-739-4251

Consumer Services and Investigations
   Division
800-282-8611

Florida

Department of Insurance
200 East Gaines St.
Tallahassee, FL 32399-0300

850-922-3100

Insurance Consumer Helpline
800-342-2762

Georgia

Commissioner of Insurance
2 Martin Luther King, Jr. Drive
West Tower, Suite #704
Atlanta, GA 30334

404-656-2070

Consumer Services
800-656-2298

Hawaii

Insurance Division
250 S. King Street, 5th Floor
Honolulu, HI 96813

808-586-2790

Consumer Complaints
808-974-4000-ext. 62790
(from island of HI)
otherwise 808-586-2790

Idaho

Department of Insurance
700 W. State Street, 3rd Floor
PO Box 83720
Boise, ID 83720-0043

208-334-4320

Consumer Affairs Division
800-721-3272

Illinois

Department of Insurance
320 W. Washington, 4th Floor
Springfield, IL 62767-0001

217-782-4515

Consumer Services
217-782-4515 or 312-814-2427

Indiana

Department of Insurance
311 W. Washington Street
Suite #300
Indianapolis, IN 46204-2787

317-232-2395

Consumer Services Division
800-622-4461

Iowa

Insurance Division
330 Maple Street
Des Moines, IA 50319-0065

515-281-5705

Insurance Division
515-281-4241

Kansas

Insurance Department
420 SW 9th Street
Topeka, KS 66612

785-296-7850

Consumer Assistance Hotline
800-432-2484

Kentucky

Department of Insurance
Attn: Consumer Protection
PO Box 517
Frankfort, KY 40602-0517

502-564-6034

Consumer Protection and Education
  Division
800-595-6053

Louisiana

Department of Insurance
PO Box 94214
Baton Rouge, LA 70804-9214

225-342-5900

Consumer Complaints
800-259-5300

Maine

Bureau of Insurance
Life and Health Division
#34 State House of Maine
Augusta, ME 04333-0034

207-624-8475

Consumer Complaints
800-300-5000

Maryland

Insurance Administration
525 St. Paul Place
Baltimore, MD 21202-2272

410-468-2090

Consumer Complaints
Associate Commissioner Joy Hatchett
800-492-6116 ext. 2244

Massachusetts

Division of Insurance
Consumer Service Section
470 Atlantic Ave.
Boston, MA 02210-2223

617-521-7794

Consumer Services Section
617-521-7777

Michigan

Insurance Bureau
PO Box 30220
Lansing, MI 48909-7720

517-373-9273

Consumer Complaints
517-373-0240

Minnesota

Minnesota Department of Commerce
133 East 7th Street
St. Paul, MN 55101
Attention: Enforcement Division

651-296-2488

or

Department of Health
Health Policy & Systems
Compliance Division
Managed Care Section

651-282-5600

Department of Commerce
800-657-3602, or
Department of Health
Managed Care Systems Information
800-657-3916

Mississippi

Insurance Department
Consumer Services Division
PO Box 79
Jackson, MS 39205

601-359-3579

Consumer Services Division
800-562-2957

Missouri

Department of Insurance
PO Box 690
Jefferson City, MO 65102-0690

573-751-2640

or

Department of Insurance
State Office Building, Room 512
615 E. 13th Street

Kansas City, MO 64106-2829

816-889-2381

or

Department of Insurance
Wainwright Building, Suite #229
111 N. 7th Street

314-340-6830

MO DOI
Consumer Services
800-726-7390

Montana

State Auditor Mark O'Keefe
Consumer Complaints Division
PO Box 4009
Helena, MT 59604-4009

406-444-2040

Policy Holder Services
Consumer Complaints
800-332-6148

Nebraska

Department of Insurance
Terminal Building
941 "O" Street, Suite #400
Lincoln, NE 68508-3690

402-471-2201

Consumer Affairs Division
toll free: 877-564-7323

Nevada

Department of Business and Industry
Division of Insurance
1665 Hot Springs Road, Suite #152
Carson City, NV 89706-06

775-687-4270

Consumer Services
800-992-0900

or

NV DOI
888-872-3234

New Hampshire

Insurance Department
56 Old Suncook Road
Concord, NH 03301-5151

603-271-2261

Consumer Assistance
800-852-3416

New Jersey

Division of Insurance
Enforcement and Consumer
  Complaints
PO Box 329
Trenton, N.J. 08625-0329

609-292-5316

or

Department of Health and Senior
  Services
Office of Managed Care
PO Box 360
Trenton, NJ 08625-0360

609-588-2611

Division of Insurance
800-446-7467 (in New Jersey)

New Mexico

Public Regulations Commission
Consumer Division
PO Box 1269
Santa Fe, NM 87504-1269

505-827-4592

Consumer Division
800-947-4722

New York

Albany:
Consumer Services Bureau
NYS Insurance Department
Agency Bldg. 1-ESP
Albany, NY 12257

518 474-6600

or

New York City:

Consumer Services Bureau
NYS Insurance Deparment
25 Beaver Street
New York, NY 10004-2319

212-480-6400

or

Buffalo:
Consumer Services Bureau
NYS Insurance Department
65 Court Street #7
Buffalo, NY 14202

716-847-7618

Consumer Services Bureau
800-342-3736 (all of New York)

North Carolina

Department of Insurance
PO Box 26387
Raleigh, NC 27611

919-733-7343

Consumer Services
800-JIM-LONG (546-5664)

North Dakota

Department of Insurance
600 E. Boulevard, Dept. #401
Bismarck, ND 58505-0320

701-328-2440

ND DOI
800-247-0560

Oklahoma

Carroll Fisher
Insurance Department
PO Box 53408
3814 N. Santa Fe
Oklahoma City, OK 73152-3408

405-521-2828

Insurance Department—Consumer
 Assistance
800-522-0071

or

OK Dept. of Health
HMO Complaint Assistance Line
800-811-4552

Ohio

Department of Insurance
2100 Stella Ct.
Columbus, OH 43215-1067

614-644-2658

Consumer Service Division
800-686-1526

Oregon

Department of Consumer & Business
 Services
Insurance Division
Consumer Protection Section

350 Winter St. NE, Room #440-2
Salem, OR 97310-0765

503-947-7980

Consumer Protection Division
503-947-7984

Pennslyvania

Bureau of Managed Care
Department of Health
PO Box 90
Health and Welfare Building
Harrisburg, PA 17108

717-787-5193

Bureau of Managed Care Division
888-466-2787

Rhode Island

Department of Health
Division of Health Services Regulation
Office of Managed Care Regulation
3 Capitol Hill, Room #410
Providence, RI 02908

401-222-6015

South Carolina

Department of Insurance
1612 Marion St.
PO Box 100105
Columbia, SC 29202

803-737-6150

Consumer Services
800-768-3467

South Dakota

Patrick Powers—Health Investigator
Division of Insurance
118 West Capitol

Pierre, SD 57501

605-773-3563

Tennessee

Department of Commerce & Insurance
500 James Robertson Parkway
Nashville, TN 37243-0574

615-741-2218

Consumer Services
800-342-4029

Texas

Texas Department of Insurance
Consumer Protection Program (111-1A)
PO Box 149091
Austin, TX 78714-9091

512-305-7211

Consumer Complaints
800-599-7467

or

Consumer Help Line
800-252-3439

or

DOI IRO Information Line—for denials deemed not "medically necessary"

888-834-2476

512-322-3400 (in Austin)

Utah

Utah Insurance Department
Consumer Service Division
State Office Building Rm #3110

Salt Lake City, UT 84114

801-538-3805

Consumer Service Division
800-439-3805

Vermont

Department of Banking, Insurance, Securities & Health Care Administration
VHCA Office
89 Main St. Drawer 20
Montpelier, VT 05620-3601

802-828-2900

Division of Health Care Administration Consumer Assistance
800-631-7788

Virginia

Bureau of Insurance
PO Box 1157
Richmond, Virginia 23218

804-371-9206

Consumer Services
800-552-7945

Washington

Insurance Commissioner
Consumer Advocacy and Outreach
PO Box 40256
Olympia, WA 98504-0256

360-753-3613

Office of Ins. Commissioner
Consumer Advocacy division
800-562-6900

Statewide Health Insurance hotline
800-397-4422

West Virginia

Insurance Commission
Consumer Services Division
P.O. Box 50540
1124 Smith St.
Charleston, WV 25305-0540

304-558-3386

Consumer Services Division
800-642-9004

Wisconsin

Office of the Commissioner of
  Insurance
Information and Complaints Section
PO Box 7873
Madison, WI 53707-7873

608-266-3585

Consumer Complaints
800-236-8517

Wyoming

Insurance Department
122 W. 25th St.
Herschler Bldg., 3rd Floor East
Cheyenne, WY 82002

307-777-7401

Consumer Assistance
800-438-5768

Consumer Resources

American Medical Association (AMA)
515 North State Street
Chicago, IL 60610
Ph. 312-464-5000
Website: http://www.ama-assn.org

American Nurses Association (ANA)
600 Maryland Ave., SW
Suite #100 West
Washington, DC 20024
Ph. 800-274-4ANA
Website: http://www.nursingworld.org

Association of Trial Lawyers of America
1050 31ˢᵗ St. NW
Washington, DC 20007
Ph. 800-424-2725
Website: http://www.atlanet.org

California Nurses Association (CNA)
2000 Franklin St.
Oakland, CA 94612
Ph. 510-273-2200
Website: http://www.califnurses.org

Center for Health Dispute Resolution (CHDR)
1 Fishers Rd., 2ⁿᵈ Fl.
Pittsford, NY 14534-9597
Ph. 716-586-1770
Website: http://www.healthappeal.com

Center for Patient Advocacy
1350 Beverly Rd., Suite 108
McLean, VA 22101
Ph. 800-846-7444 or 703-748-0400
Website: http://www.patientadvocacy.org

Citizens Council on Health Care
1954 University Ave. West, Suite 8
St. Paul, MN 55104
Ph. 651-646-8935
Website: http://www.cchc-mn/.org

Consumer Coalition for Quality Health Care
1275 K St. NW, Suite 602
Washington, DC 20005
Ph. 202-789-3606
Webstite: http://www.consumers.org

Consumers for Quality Care
Jamie Court—Director
1750 Ocean Park Blvd., Ste. 200
Santa Monica, CA 90405
Ph. 310-392-0522
Website: http://www.consumerwatchdog.org

Empower! The Managed Care Patient Advocate
Co-Med Publications, Inc.
210 West Washington Square
Philadelphia, PA 19106
Ph. 215-592-1363
Website: http://www.comed.com/empower

Families USA
1334 G St. NW, 3rd Fl.
Washington, DC 20005
Ph. 202-628-3030
Website: http://www.familiesusa.org

The Health Administration Responsibility Project
552 12th St.
Santa Monica, CA 90402
Website: http://www.harp.org

Joint Commission on Accreditation of Healthcare Organizations
One Renaissance Blvd.
Oakbrook Terrace, IL 60181
Ph. 630-792-5000
Website: http://www.jcaho.org

National Association of Insurance Commission (NAIC)
Support & Services Office (SSO)
120 W. 12th St., Suite #1100
Kansas City, MO 64105-1925
Ph. 816-842-3600
Website: http://www.naic.org

National Center for Quality Assurance (NCQA)
2000 L St., NW, Suite #500
Washington, DC 20036
Ph. 202-955-3500
Website: http://www.ncqa.org

Pacific Business Group on Health
33 New Montgomery St., Suite 1450
San Francisco, CA 94105
Ph. 888-244-2124 or 415-281-8660
Website: http://www.healthscope.org

Patients Who Care
1215 Jones Maltsberger Rd., Suite #607
San Antonio, TX 78247
Ph. 210-656-7636
Patient Complaint Hotline: 800-800-5154
Website: http://www.patients.org

Physicians Who Care
1215 Jones Maltsberger Rd., Suite #607
San Antonio, TX 78247
Ph. 210-656-7636
Website: http://www.hmopage.org

Public Citizen
Health Research Group
1600 20th St. NW
Washington, DC 20009
Website: http://www.citizen.org/hrg/

US Department of Labor
Pension and Welfare Benefits Administration (PWBA)
Advice and Complaints about ERISA Plans
200 Constitution Ave. NW, Room #N-5656
Washington, DC 20210
Ph. 202-219-8921
Website: http://www.dol.gov

Notes

Foreword

1.   Michael Shadid, M.D., *Crusading Doctor*, University of Oklahoma Press, 1991.

Introduction

1.   Kaiser Family Foundation/Harvard Public Opinion Survey, September 17, 1998.
2.   Kaiser Family Foundation/Harvard National Survey of Americans' Views on Consumer Protection In Managed Care, January 21, 1998.
3.   "Sick People in Managed Care Have Difficulty Getting Services and Treatment," Robert Wood Johnson Foundation, June 28, 1995.
4.   Dr. John E. Ware, *Journal of the American Medical Association*, October 1,1996; Robert Pear, "Elderly and Poor Do Worse Under HMO Plans' Care," *New York Times*, Oct. 2, 1996.

Chapter One
The End of Health Care

1.   Linda Peeno, "Managed Care Ethics: The Close View," U.S. House of Representatives Committee On Commerce, Subcommittee On Health and Environment, May 30, 1996.
2.   Linda Peeno, Testimony to California Assembly Committee on Health, April 15, 1997.
3.   Linda Peeno, "Managed Care Ethics: The Close View," U.S. House of Representatives Committee on Commerce, Subcommittee on Health and Environment, May 30, 1996.
4.   Michael Fitzgerald, "Stockton MD Fed Up With HMOs," *Stockton Record*, May 29, 1998.
5.   Letter, Cheryl Tannigawa, Director of Utilization Management, Harriman Jones Medical Group, Memo To M.D., October 11, 1989.

6.   Peter Delevett, "Utilization Review Under The Scalpel," *San Jose Business Journal*, June 8, 1998.

7.   *Packevicz v. Mohawak Valley Medical Associates*, United States District Court Northern District of New York, Complaint and Request For Injunctive and Other Relief. 98-CV-0835(FJS)(DNH).

8.   The lawsuit argues that "community standards in the State of New York do not mandate slow, certain, miserable, hopeless, excruciating and inhumane death in plaintiff's case where there is a medically recommended reasonably feasible alternative a few dollars away." Is it really for an HMO or an individual to choose whether they live or die? The HMO, MVP, claimed the denial was based on a definition of community standard of medicine. When they violate that standard, isn't it medical negligence?

9.   *Renee Berman, Peter Berman v. Health Net*, Los Angeles Superior Court, Case No. BC 139 875 Second Amended Complaint.

10. Erik Larson, "The Soul of An HMO," *Time*, January 22, 1996 p.52.

11. George Anders, *Health Against Wealth*, Houghton Mifflin, 1996, p.115; Nina Martin, "As Shock of Cancer Verdict Spreads," *San Francisco Daily Journal*, January 7, 1994.

12. *Joyce Ramey v. Inter Valley Health Plan Inc.*, United States District Court Central District of California, Case No. CV 96-425 CBM (JGx) Binding Award of Arbitrator.

13. Anita Ostroff, Senior Counsel, Department of Corporations, Letter to Mr. Paul Brandes, Kaiser Foundation Health Plan, "Re Public Survey Report Kaiser Foundation Health Plan, Inc. Northern California Region," August 14, 1996, File No: 933-0055. pp. 6, 7.

14. *Ibid.*

15. Mark Silk, "$45 Million Malpractice Verdict; Fulton County Jury Award Against HMO Largest Ever In State," *Atlanta Constitution*, February 4, 1995, p. C10.

16. Julie Appleby, "$1 Million Fine Levied On Kaiser By Texas," *Contra Costa Times*, April 24, 1997.

17. *Dawnelle Barris, etc, et al. v. County of Los Angeles, et al.* Superior Court of the State of California for Los Angeles, Case No. TC 007062.

18. *Karen Johnson v. Humana Health Plan Inc.*, Jefferson Circuit Court, Kentucky, No 96-CI-00462.

19. Kim Wessel, "Woman Wins Humana Suit," *The Courier-Journal*, Louisville, Kentucky, October 21, 1998, p. A1.

20. *Estate of Glenn Nealy v. U.S. Healthcare*, United States District Court for the Southern District of New York, order by Judge Charles Haight, March 2, 1994. Unfortunately for the Nealys, Glenn received his health benefits through his private sector employer. Under federal ERISA law (see Chapter Five), the only legal remedy available to an injured patient is the cost of the benefit delayed or denied. Susan Nealy cannot recover economic losses—such as lost wages or salary—or non-economic losses. Because Glenn never incurred any medical expenses, the managed care company cannot be held responsible for any costs and Susan Nealy

has no remedy for the wrongful death of her husband. The District Court for the Southern District of New York had no choice but to dismiss Susan's claims for the breach of contract, misrepresentation and wrongful death.

21. *Betty Carol Hale v. California Physicians Service dba Blue Shield of California*, Superior Court of the State of California for the County of Los Angeles, Case No. BC 098790. Hale settled the complaint with Blue Shield and is limited by the agreement about what she can now say.

22. While the company employs doctors, Milliman's Internet site identifies the company as "Milliman & Robertson; Actuaries & Consultants" www.milliman-hmg.com/index.shtml.

23. Allen Myerson, "Helping Health Insurers Say No, Having a Caesarian? You Get 2 Days In the Hospital," *New York Times*, March 20, 1995, p. D1.

24. George Anders and Laurie McGinley, "Medical Cop: Actuarial Firm Helps Decide Just How Long You Spend In The Hospital," *Wall Street Journal*, June 15, 1998, p. A1.

25. *Ibid.*

26. Allen Myerson, "Helping Health Insurers Say No, Having a Caesarian? You Get 2 Days In the Hospital," *New York Times*, March 20, 1995.

27. John Vogt, MD, Director of Resource Management, "Inpatient Concurrent Management Systems, Kaiser Permanente Texas Region," December 3, 1995.

28. *Thomas Self v. Children's Associated Medical Group*, Superior Court of the State of California for the County of San Diego, Case No. 695870; Bill Callahan, "Doctor Wins Quality-of-care Lawsuit," *San Diego Union Tribune*, April 7, 1998; Julie Marquis, "Doctor Gets $2.5 Million Settlment," *Los Angeles Times*, April 28, 1998.

29. Linda Peeno, "Managed Care Ethics: The Close View," U.S. House of Representatives Committee on Commerce, Subcommittee on Health and Environment, May 30, 1996.

30. Milt Freudenheim, "Risky Business; A Set Fee For Each Patient Gives Doctors More Control and More of a Financial Stake," *New York Times*, May 30, 1998, p. D1.

31. Roni Rabin, "Blow To Managed Care? Ruling Backs LI Mom's Challenge Of Insurers Set Fees," *Newsday*, November 21, 1996.

32. Letter from Bruce Vladeck, The Administrator, United States Department of Health and Human Services Health Care Financing Administration, "To Dr. Gordon Schiff, Director of General Medicine Clinic, Department of Medicine, Cook County Hospital," October 31, 1994.

33. Milt Freudenheim, "Risky Business; A Set Fee For Each Patient Gives Doctors More Control and More of a Financial Stake," *New York Times*, May 30, 1998, p. D1.

34. Letter John M. Maggiano, MD, Orange County Retina Medical Group, To Jamie Court, "Re Dr. Self," April 8, 1998.

35. Internal Memo "From: Donald Drake, M.D., Medical Director, Greater Newport Physicians, Date: May 8, 1997, To: All GNP Physicians, Subject: Pharmacy Management."

36.   Jay Greene, "Prescribing Tighter Purse Strings," *Orange County Register*, October 16, 1997.

37.   "ABMG Physician Status Report October 1998."

38.   "Health Net Out-Patient Rx Physician Prescribing Profile For: July 1, 1996–September 30, 1996"

39.   Paul Elias, "Doctors Negligent In Woman's Cancer Death, Jury Finds," *Los Angeles Times*, November 16, 1995.

40.   David Olmos, "Cutting Medical Costs—Or Corners?" *Los Angeles Times*, May 5, 1995.

41.   John Hendren, "Sizable Health Care Cost Rise Seen," Associated Press, June 2, 1998.

42.   Testimony of Dr. Troyen Brennan, Harvard School of Public Health, on "Medical Malpractice and Health Care Reform," before the Subcommittee on Health and the Environment, Committee on Energy and Commerce, U.S. House Of Representatives, November 10, 1993, pp.6-7.

43.   "Sick People in Managed Care Have Difficulty Getting Services and Treatment," Robert Wood Johnson Foundation, June 28, 1995.

44.   Dr. John E. Ware, *Journal of the American Medical Association*, October 1,1996; Robert Pear, "Elderly and Poor Do Worse Under HMO Plans' Care," *New York Times*, October 2, 1996.

45.   Kaiser Family Foundation/Harvard National Survey of Americans' Views on Consumer Protection In Managed Care, January 21, 1998.

46.   Press Release, "Malpractice Reform Won't Have Much Effect On Defensive Medicine Costs," Office Of Technology Assessment, Congress of the United States, July 21, 1994.

47.   Sharp HealthCare Employee Handbook, "Employee Quality & Development," October 1, 1995, pp. 42–43.

48.   Rebecca Smith, "Doctors, nurses must take loyalty oaths, groups say," *San Jose Mercury News*, July 17, 1996.

49.   Health Net Provider Service Agreement, p. 9, p. 12 rev. 1/95.

50.   Alta Bates Employee Handbook, p. 23.

51.   U.S. Healthcare Primary Care Physician Agreement, 6/94.

52.   Foundation "VIP IPA" Participating Specialty Physician Agreement, p. 5.

53.   METLIFE Health Care Network IPA Service Agreement, Simi Valley Family Practice Group, p. 18.

Chapter Two
A Deadly Fraud

1.   Kaiser Permanente Southern California Region, Business Plan, 1995-1997, p. 18.

2.   This is but another form of fraud—price your product lower than it costs, then jack up the premium once you have the customers. The fact that a non-profit compa-

ny—considered one of the better ones in the market—has sunk to these lows is a barometer of the widespread deception perpetrated against the American public.

3. Julie Appleby, "$1 Million Fine Levied On Kaiser By Texas," April 24, 1997; David Olmos, "Texas Regulators Assail Kaiser On Physicians, Care," *Los Angeles Times*, April 24, 1997.

4. Julie Appleby, "Kaiser Warned It May Lose Federal Funding," *Contra Times*, April 18, 1997.

5. Anita Ostroff, Senior Counsel, Department of Corporations, Letter to Mr. Paul Brandes, Kaiser Foundation Health Plan, "Re Public Survey Report Kaiser Foundation Health Plan, Inc. Northern California Region," August 14, 1996, File No: 933-0055.

6. "HOPE: For S.C.P.M.G. Physicians—Catalyzing the Exchange of Ideas Within S.C.P.M.G." Volume 3, No.6, June–August 1997. P.O. Box 121 Cerritos, CA 90701; Consumers For Quality Care Press Release, "Kaiser Physicians Angry," September 25, 1997.

7. Videotape, "Kaiser Permanente On The Air Finally…The Personalized Advertising Campaign."

8. IRS records acquired by California Nurses Association.

9. "HOPE: For S.C.P.M.G. Physicians—Catalyzing the Exchange of Ideals Within S.C.P.M.G." Volume 3, No. 6, June–August 1997. PO Box 121 Cerritos, CA 90701—Consumers For Quality Care, "Kaiser Physicians Angry," September 25, 1997.

10. *Ibid.*

11. California Nurses Association, "Corporate Health Care: For-Profit, Not-for-Profit, or Not for Patients? Kaiser Permanente," December 1997.

12. Video tape, "Kaiser Permanente On The Air Finally…The Personalized Advertising Campaign."

13. David Olmos, "Early-Release Policy At HMOs Draws Fire: Kaiser Decision To Send Some Mothers And Newborns Home After Eight Hours Raises the Debate To A New Level," *Los Angeles Times*, June 16, 1995.

14. Associated Press, "Study Finds Big Savings In Early Discharge Following Childbirth," June 5, 1995.

15. Memo, Maternity Leave, "Positive Thoughts Regarding The Eight Hour Discharge," *Harper's*, February 1996.

16. *Orange County Register*, March 17, 1996.

17. Kaiser later claimed it stopped these bonuses tied to reduced hospital admissions in Southern California after the public outcry from the release of the business plan. Carl Hall, "Kaiser Dumps Bonus Plan," *San Francisco Chronicle*, December 20, 1995. The Northern California bonus system remained, according to the *Chronicle* article.

18. Video tape, "Kaiser Permanente On the Air Finally…The Personalized Advertising Campaign."

19. *Ibid.*

20. *Ibid.*

21.   *Ibid.*

22.   John Vogt, MD, Director of Resources Management, "Inpatient Concurrent Management Systems," Kaiser Permanente, Texas Region, December 3, 1995. The speech transcript was filed in a Texas lawsuit that Kaiser settled for $5.3 million. Ronald Henderson, of Irving Texas, died of a heart attack in 1995 after Kaiser allegedly provided inadequate care. Henderson's family claimed his death was due to Kaiser's cost-cutting. Charles Ornstein, "Kaiser Agrees To Pay $5.35 Million In Death," *Dallas Morning News*, December 17, 1997. p. A1.

23.   Sabin Russell and Carl Hall, "Discord in Kaiser Health Empire," *San Francisco Chronicle*, February 16, 1996; Email, "TO: GIL.ALL.PHYSICIANS, SUBJECT: NO ON DR. CAUFIELD," January 29, 1996.

24.   *Adrian Broughton vs. CIGNA Healthplans of California*, Court of Appeal No.2 Civ. B 093517 Los Angeles County Sup. Ct. No. BC 117680; K.Oanh Ha, "Lawsuit Seeks To Bypass HMO Arbitration Process," *Wall Street Journal*, California, Wednesday, September 10, 1997, p. CA2.

25.   Sabin Russell, "HMO's Sales Method Sharply Criticized in S.F.," *San Francisco Chronicle*, November 30, 1994; Nina Siegal, "Door to door health care," *San Francisco Bay Guardian*, January 18, 1995.

26.   *Rochin v. Foundation Health* Superior Court of the State of California for the County of Los Angeles, Case No. BC 125367, Complaints filed August 29, 1995 and April 6, 1995; "Medi-Cal Mom Charges Major HMO With Deceptive and Fraudulent Marketing Practices," April 6, 1995, Shernoff, Bidart, & Darras, Claremont, CA. The family settled its lawsuit.

27.   David Olmos, "HMO Accused of Deceptive Marketing," *Los Angeles Times*, February 2, 1995.

28.   Fred Shulte and Jenni Bergal, "Florida's Medicaid HMOs: Profits from Pain: A Reprint of a five part series published December 11–15, 1994," *The Sun Sentinel*, Fort Lauderdale, FL; Yvonne Chui, "Ex-workers file suit against Foundation," *Sacramento Bee*, March 3, 1995.

29.   Bettijane Levine, "Losing Patience," *Los Angeles Times*, July 9, 1997.

30.   Anne Peterson, "Doctors Say Anorexics and Bulimics Starving For Care Under HMO Plans," Associated Press, California, May 4, 1998.

31.   Vicky Que, National Public Radio's Morning Edition, September 1, 1998; The National Journal Group Inc., Health Line, September 1, 1998.

32.   Tom Abate, "Agency Tells Kaiser It Must Cover Viagra," *San Francisco Chronicle*, January 1, 1999.

33.   Foundation Health Marketing Manual; Claims in marketing materials. Title of Foundation Medi-Cal Marketing Manual: "Health Care At No Cost To You."

34.   Pam Slater, "Prescription for Profits," *Sacramento Bee*, June 26, 1994.

35.   Foundation VIP IPA Participating Specialty Physician Agreement.

36.   Bill Alpert, "Foundation Health Corp: Reserve Judgment," Dow Jones Wire Service, January 2, 1996.

37.   *Los Angeles Times* West Side, June 1, 1995; *Los Angeles Times* Insert February 8, 1999.

38. Jay Greene, "To Some, HMO Policies On Mental Illness Make Little Sense," *Orange County Register*, July 27, 1997. In the wake of the scandal, the company claims, however, that it has put an even more expensive drug, Zyprexia, on its formulary.

39. "Informed Health from Aetna Health Plans," advertisement on file with California Department of Corporations.

40. Letter From Dr. Thomas Reardon, MD, American Medical Association, To Richard Huber, CEO Aetna/U.S. Healthcare, February 24, 1998.

41. Charles Ornstein, "Morales Sues Six HMOs, Alleges Incentive Policies Threaten Care," *Dallas Morning News*, December 17, 1998.

42. American Medical Association Discussion Paper on Aetna/U.S. Healthcare Acquisition of Prudential Health Care, February 1999.

43. Advertisement on file with California Department of Corporations.

44. Letter from Bruce C. Vladeck, Administrator, Department of Health and Human Services, To Dr. Gordon Schiff, Department of Medicine, Cook County Hospital, October 31, 1994.

45. Source: California Medical Association, "Knox Keene Health Plan Expenditures Summary FY 1995–96," February 1997.

46. Advertisements on file with California Department of Corporations.

47. *Joyce Ramey v. Inter Valley Health Plan, Inc.* United States District Court Central District of California, Case No. CV 96-4245 CBM, Hon. John Trotter, Justice (Retired) Court Of Appeal, JAMS/ENDISPUTE, Orange, CA.

48. Joe Nicolson, "HMOs Sic Bad Ads On Elders—Report," *New York Daily News*, November 22, 1995, p. 55.

49. *Ibid.*

50. Milt Freudenheim, "Medicare HMOs To Trim Benefits For Elderly," *New York Times*, December 22, 1997, p. A1.

51. Robert Pear, "Government Says HMOs Misleading Medicare Recipients," *New York Times*, April 13, 1999.

52. Bob Rosenblatt, "US Overpaid HMOs $1 Billion, GAO Report Says," *Los Angeles Times*, February 26, 1997, p. D1.

53. U.S. General Accounting Office, "MEDICARE, Fewer and Lower Cost Beneficiaries With Chronic Conditions Enroll in HMOs," Report to the Chairman, Subcommittee on Health, Committee on Ways and Means, House of Representatives, August 1997. "While only 6% of all new enrollees returned to FFS within six months, the rates ranged from 4.5% for beneficiaries without a chronic condition to 10.2% for those with two or more chronic conditions. Also, disenrollees who returned to FFS had substantially higher costs prior to enrollment compared to those who remained in their HMO. These data indicated that favorable selection still exists in California Medicare HMOs because they attract and retain the least costly beneficiaries in each health status group."

54. Eric Weissman, "GAO: High Turnover at Medicare HMOs," *Modern Health Care Magazine*, March 11, 1998.

55. Sandra Sobieraj, "Clinton Shows Hint of Distraction," Associated Press, October 8, 1998.

56. Robert Pear, "Clinton Plans To Intervene As HMOs Exit Medicare," *New York Times*, October 8, 1998, p. A28.

57. Robert Pear, "Government Says HMOs Misleading Medicare Recipients," *New York Times*, April 13, 1999

58. Remarks by President Bill Clinton at Health Care Event, The Roosevelt Room, The White House, Washington, D.C., October 8, 1998, 12:30 Eastern Time, Federal Information Systems Corporation, Federal News Service.

59. While the case is public record, Sarver currently cannot talk about her son's condition because of a confidentiality clause. Blue Shield's PPO is regulated as a managed care entity under the California Department of Corporations. *Steven and Bradley Sarver v. Public Employees' Retirement System*, Superior Court of the State of California for the County of Los Angeles, BC 096228.

Chapter Three
The Death of Community Health Care and Hospitals

1. *Steven Andrew Olsen v. Sharp Rees-Stealy Medical Group*, Superior Court of California County of San Diego, Case No. 666808.

2. The Olsens recovered damages in a confidential settlement from the medical group and primary care physician. A jury awarded damages against the employer of the admitting physician. Unfortunately, the jury-awarded damages were reduced by nearly $7 million due to a state-imposed cap on the pain and suffering of injured patients in California. (See Chapter Six.)

3. Testimony of Dr. Troyen Brennan, Harvard School of Public Health, on "Medical Malpractice and Health Care Reform," before the Subcommittee on Health and the Environment, Committee on Energy and Commerce, U.S. House of Representatives, November 10, 1993, pp. 6–7.

4. James C. Robinson, PhD, MPH, "Decline in Hospital Utilization and Cost Inflation Under Managed Care In California," *Journal of the American Medical Association*, October 2, 1996, Vol 276, No 13, p. 1060.

5. Lucette Lagnado, "Patients Give Hospitals Poor Score Card," *Wall Street Journal*, January 28, 1997, p. B1.

6. *Ibid.*

7. *Ibid.*

8. Medical malpractice deaths based on projections by various commentators of data compiled by the Harvard School of Public Health as part of a comprehensive study of medical malpractice, Harvard Medical Practice Study Group, *Patients, Doctors, and Lawyers: Medical Injury, Malpractice Litigation and Patient Compensation In New York* (Cambridge, Mass.:Harvard University, 1990).

9. James C. Robinson, PhD, MPH, "Decline in Hospital Utilization and Cost Inflation Under Managed Care In California," *Journal of the American Medical Association*, October 2, 1996, Vol 276, No 13, p. 1060.

10. National Conference of State Legislators, National Institute For Health http://dccps.nci.nih.gov/DCCPS/http://www.ncsl.org/programs/health/cancer.htm.

11. Ellen Goodman, "Is This Any Way to Run a Health Care System?" *Boston Globe*, November 17, 1996.

12. California Nurses Association Patient Watch Program Report, October 20, 1997, Mildren Henderson, Napa, CA.

13. James C. Robinson, PhD, MPH, "Decline in Hospital Utilization and Cost Inflation Under Managed Care In California," *Journal of the American Medical Association*, October 2, 1996, Vol 276, No 13, p. 1060.

14. Sabin Russell, "Hospital Released Patient With Knife In Belly," *San Francisco Chronicle*, September 13, 1996.

15. CBS News 60 *Minutes*, "HMO," Produced by Patti Hassler, October 1, 1995, Volume XXVIII Number 3.

16. Julie Marquis, "Lifeline of Nurses Thinning; As Hospitals Turn To Lesser-Skilled Aides, RNs Are Working Double-Time To Compensate," *Los Angeles Times*, August 4, 1998 p. A1

17. *Ibid.*

18. "Work Week: A Special News Report About Life On The Job—and Trends Taking Shape There," *Wall Street Journal*, Tuesday June 25, 1996.

19. Letter Of Agreement, "Kaiser Permanente Medical Care Program Northern California Region and H.C.W.U., Local 250, Member Focused Care Initiative (Excluding the Fresno Medical Center)," 1996.

20. Julie Marquis, "Lifeline of Nurses Thinning; As Hospitals Turn To Lesser-Skilled Aides, RNs Are Working Double-Time To Compensate," *Los Angeles Times*, August 4, 1998, p. A1.

21. Steve Twedt, "Hospital Care; The cost of cutting," *Pittsburgh Post-Gazette*, February 11, 1996.

22. Dolores Kong, "Nurses Say Patients Feeling the Pain of Staffing Cutbacks," *Boston Globe*, October 31, 1994.

23. Craig Rose, "Medic! Area Nurses Warn of Problems in the System," *San Diego Union Tribune*, April 1, 1996.

24. *Ibid.*

25. Don Kazak, "Hospital Cited by the State Again," *Palo Alto Weekly*, January 10, 1996.

26. Kathy Robertson, "Sutter Roseville Is Cited For Understaffing ICUs," *Sacramento Business Journal*, April 29, 1996.

27. Carol Benfell, "Kaiser Cited For Use Of Unlicensed Help," *Santa Rosa Press Democrat*, August 18, 1998.

28. California Nurses Association Press Release, "Third Citation For Kaiser in Operating Room Abuses," August 19, 1998.

29. Carol Benfell, "Kaiser Cited For Use Of Unlicensed Help," *Santa Rosa Press Democrat*, August 18, 1998.

30. Kurt Laumann, "How Restructuring Affects Patient Care," *San Francisco Chronicle*, April 5, 1995, Op-Ed on editorial page.

31. *Ibid.*

32. Judith Shindul-Rothchild, "The 1996 AJN Patient Care Survey Final Results," Boston College, November 1996.

33. Patricia Prescott, "Nursing: An Important Component Of Hospital Survival Under A Reformed Health Care System," *Nursing Economics*, July–August 1993, Vol. 11, No. 4.

34. Editorial, "Paper Pushers Don't Improve Medical Care, A Philadelphia Daily News Editorial," *News & Record* (Greensboro, NC), February 23, 1996.

35. Mercy Healthcare Sacramento, 'To: Regional Leadership Council Date: July 8, 1998 Subject: Nursing Shortage/Recruitment Difficulties, From:Charlene Moore—Acting Emp Manager."

36. Barbara Gray, "What's Going On?" *NurseWeek*, February 12, 1998.

37. "Columbia/HCA Whistleblower Marc Gardner Predicts Company Will Be Hit With Three To Five Billion Dollar Fine, Then Will Be Folded Into Tenet," *Corporate Crime Reporter*, March 23, 1998.

38. Tom Philp, "Study: Doctor Hospital Use Falls Result of HMOs Tightening Strings," *Sacramento Bee*, June 5, 1997, p. B1.

39. Jeffrey Kaye, "Community Care—Part Two," *NewsHour* with Jim Lehrer, February 3, 1998.

40. *Modern Health Care*, May 20, 1996.

41. Jeffrey Kaye, "Community Care—Part One," *NewsHour* with Jim Lehrer, February 2, 1998.

42. CBS News, *60 Minutes*, "Not For Profit Hospitals," October 27, 1996, Vol. XXVIII, No. 7.

43. *Modern Health Care*, November 4, 1996.

44. Jeffrey Kaye, "Community Care—Part Two," *NewsHour* with Jim Lehrer, February 3, 1998.

45. *Ibid.*

46. Hugh Downs, Barbara Walters, "Former Columbia/HCA Executive Speaks Out," ABC *20/20*, September 26, 1997.

47. *Ibid.*

48. *Modern Health Care*, July 27, 1998, p. 26.

49. Kurt Eichenwald, "Health Care's Giant: Artful Accounting—A special report; Hospital Chain Cheated U.S. On Expenses, Documents Show," *New York Times*, December 18, 1997, p. A1.

50. Kurt Eichenwald, "Accounting Firm Is Named In Medicare Fraud Lawsuit," *New York Times*, May 29, 1999, p. B5.

51. Kurt Eichenwald, "Health Care's Giant: Artful Accounting—A special report; Hospital Chain Cheated U.S. On Expenses, Documents Show," *New York Times*, December 18, 1997, p. A1.

52. Marc Gardner, *Corporate Crime Reporter*, March 23, 1998.

53. Mike Wallace, CBS News 60 *Minutes* "Not For Profit Hospitals," October 27, 1996 Vol. XXVIII, No. 7.

54. *Ibid.*

55. Carl Ginsburg, "The Patient As Profit Center; Hospital Inc. Comes To Town," *The Nation*, November 18, 1996, p. 18.

56. *Ibid.*

57. Lucette Lagnado, "Ex-manager Describes The Profit-Driven Life Inside Columbia/HCA," *Wall Street Journal*, May 30, 1997, p. 1.

58. Bruce Japsen, "Columbia's Big Ad Bucks, Gain Chain Outspends Other Hospitals On Advertising," *Modern Health Care*, March 10, 1997, p. 2.

59. Carl Ginsburg, "The Patient As Profit Center; Hospital Inc. Comes To Town," *The Nation*, November 18, 1996, p. 20.

60. Lucette Lagnado, "Ex-manager Describes The Profit-Driven Life Inside Columbia/HCA," *Wall Street Journal*, May 30, 1997, p. 1.

61. Carl Ginsburg, "The Patient As Profit Center; Hospital Inc. Comes To Town," *The Nation*, November 18, 1996, p. 20.

62. Kurt Eichenwald, "Health Care's Giant: Artful Accounting—A special report; Hospital Chain Cheated U.S. On Expenses, Documents Show," *New York Times*, December 18, 1997, p. A1.

63. Sharon Bernstein, "Hospital Offers Apology for Denial of Epidural," *Los Angeles Times*, July 3, 1998.

64. Robert Pear, "Mothers on Medicaid Overcharged For Pain Relief," *New York Times*, March 8, 1999 p. A1.

65. Sharon Bernstein, "County C-Section Rule Took Heavy Toll," *Los Angeles Times*, January 25, 1998.

66. Abraham Verghese, "My Hospital, Dying a Slow Death," *New York Times*, November 30, 1996, p. 19.

67. Chuck Idelson, California Nurses Association study, 1996.

68. "Tenet To Buy Two HCA Hospitals," Associated Press, Monday June 22, 1998.

69. Lucette Lagnado, "Ex-manager Describes The Profit-Driven Life Inside Columbia/HCA," *Wall Street Journal*, May 30, 1997, p. 1.

70. Nancy McVicar and Ellen Forman "Tenet Hospitals Under Federal Investigation; Officials, Physicians at North Ridge Subpoenaed," Fort Lauderdale, *Sun Sentinel*, May 20, 1998.

71. Phil Galewitz, "Ontario Sues Tenet Healthcare, Two County Hospitals," *Palm Beach Post*, May 9, 1997.

72. Kurt Eichenwald, "$100 Million Settlement Seen In Tenet Suits," July 30, 1998, p. D1; David Olmos, "Tenet: To Settle Claims of 700 Former Patients," *Los Angeles Times*, July 31, 1997.

73. Paul Clegg, "Health Care Ties That Bind: Religious Control Often Ends Reproductive Services," *Sacramento Bee*, July 18, 1998.

74. *Ibid.*

75. *Ibid.*

76. Valeria Godines, "San Bernardino Hospital Accepts Merger Proposal: Independent Joins Catholic Healthcare West," *Riverside Press-Enterprise*, August 15, 1998.

77. *Ibid.*

78. Paul Clegg, "Health Care Ties That Bind: Religious Control Often Ends Reproductive Services," *Sacramento Bee*, July 18, 1998.

79. Rick Wartzman, "Hospitals Start To Look A Lot More Like HMOs," *Wall Street Journal*, California Edition, August 27, 1997.

80. *Modern Health Care* annual report on multi-unit hospital systems for 1997, May 25, 1998.

Chapter Four
The Financial Sting—Paying Less for More

1. Jennifer Steinhauer, "Sharpest Health Insurance Increases Hit Small Employees the Hardest," *New York Times*, January 9, 1999, p. A21; Sharon Bernstein, "CalPERS To Let Health Rates Rise 10%," *Los Angeles Times*, May 19, 1999, p. C1; David Hilzenrath, "Big HMO Rate Rise To Hit Older Americans," *Washington Post*, October 25, 1998.

2. Milt Freudenheim, "Humana Finds That The Going Gets Tougher," *New York Times*, April 9, 1999.

3. Sharon Bernstein, Alissa Rubin, Robert Rosenblatt, "An Rx For Disaster," *Los Angeles Times*, March 28, 1999, p. C1.

4. Cited in Opening Statement of Rep. Pete Stark, Medicare-Choice Ways and Means Health Subcommittee Hearing, March 18, 1999.

5. *Ibid.*

6. *Ibid.*

7. Summary, Dissenting Views of Senator Jay Rockefeller, Rep. John D. Dingell, Rep. Jim McDermott on the Bipartisan Commision on the Future of Medicare, March 16, 1999, p. 8.

8. *Ibid* at page 8, Citing National Academy of Social Insurance, *Medicare and the American Social Contract*, February 1999, p. 26.

9. California Medical Association, "Knox-Keene Health Plan Expenditure Summary FY 1995–1996" & "FY 1996–1997"; Corporate Research Group—Outlook for Managed Care 1997, Woolhandler and Himmelstein, *New England Journal of Medicine*, May 2, 1991; 324:1253.

10. Kathy Robertson, "Individual Health Plan Rates Leap," *Sacramento Business Journal*, August 24, 1998.

11. CIGNA Preferred Provider option; inter alia.

12. Frank McArdle PhD., Hewitt Associates, presentation "On Employer-Provided Retiree Health Benefits" to the Bipartisan Commission On The Future Of Medicare, July 14, 1998, Cited in Summary, Dissenting Views of Senator Jay Rockefeller, Rep. John D. Dingell, Rep. Jim McDermott on the Bipartisan Commision on the Future of Medicare, March 16, 1999, p. 9.

13. *USA Today*, July 15, 1998 citing Henry J. Kaiser Foundation charts. Peter T. Kilborn, "Reality of HMO System Does Not Live up to the Dream," *New York Times*, October 5, 1998, p. A2. Ronald Brownstein, "Budding Children's Health Program Could Seed Low-Income Adult Care," *Los Angeles Times*, February 22, 1999, p. A5.

14. Ron Winslow and Leslie Scism, "Aetna Agrees to Acquire U.S. Healthcare," *Wall Street Journal*, April 2, 1996, p. A2; Associated Press, "U.S. Healthcare Chief Will Get $1 Billion," June 15, 1996.

15. Managed Health Care Market Report 1/31/97, 7/15/97 cited in Center for National Health Program Studies, "For Our Patients, Not for Profit: A Call To Action," Chartbook and Slideshow, 1998 edition by Steffie Woolhandler and David Himmelstein.

16. Ron Pollack & Lorie Slass, "Premium Pay II: Corporate Compensation on America's HMOs," *Families USA*, September 1998.

17. *Forbes*, May 18, 1998.

18. George Anders, *Health Against Wealth*, Houghton-Mifflin, 1995, p. 73.

19. *Modern Health Care*, February 12, 1996, p. 126.

20. *New England Journal of Medicine*, 1997, 336:1828 cited in Center for National Health Studies, Chartbook 1998, p. 128.

21. The Crystal Report Online on Executive Compensation, "The Flap over HMO/Health Care CEO Pay Premiums," February 1999; *Bloomberg News*, "HMO Execs Among Highest Paid, Study Says," *Los Angeles Times*, December 10, 1998, p. C3.

22. Don DeMoro, "Abdicating Health Care Policy to the Market," *Institute for Health and Socio Economic Policy*, Oakland, CA, April 1996, p. 7.

23. *Ibid*, p. 8.

24. Dr. Eli Ginsburg, "The Uncertain Future Of Managed Care," *New England Journal of Medicine*, January 14, 1999.

25. Discussions with Dr. Robert Gumbiner, September 1997 at his home in Long Beach, California. See also Gumbiner's *FHP: The Evolution Of A Managed Care Health Maintenance Organization 1993–1997, Volume II, An Oral History*, University of California, Berkeley.

26. *FHP: The Evolution Of A Managed Care Health Maintenance Organization 1993–1997, Volume II, An Oral History*, University of California, Berkeley. p. 14, 21.

27. The case has been dismissed due to pleading deficiencies and is now on appeal.

28. George Anders, "HMOs Pile Up Billions In Cash," *Wall Street Journal*, December 21, 1994, p. A1.

29. Milt Freudenheim "Concerns Rising About Mergers," *New York Times*, January 13, 1999, p. 1.

30. "Industry News & Trends," *Health Care PR and Marketing News*, May 30, 1996, Vol. 5, No. 11.

31. California Medical Association, Testimony at PacifiCare/FHP merger hearing at Irvine Civic Center, June 29, 1997.

32.   Joseph Nocera, "The Tarnished Darlings of Wall Street," *New York Times*, January 4, 1998, sec. 4, p. 11.

33.   Bloomberg News, "Aetna Profit Up 15%," *Los Angeles Times*, April 29, 1999; "PacifiCare 1st Quarter Profits Up 79%" *Los Angeles Times*, May 6, 1999.

34.   Sharon Bernstein, "Much Of Ailing MedPartners Unregulated, State Says; Health Care: Company Takes Court Action To Overturn Department Of Corporations Takeover," *Los Angeles Times*, March 18, 1999.

35.   Michael Schrage "Are HMOs Too Big To Go Bust?" *Los Angeles Times*, February 11, 1996, p. D2.

36.   *Wall Street Journal* Texas Edition, March 31,1999—cited in Health Line, National Journal Group, March 31, 1999.

37.   David R. Olmos, "As Cutbacks Hit Limit, Health Costs Rise Anew," *Los Angeles Times*, April 16, 1997, p. A1.

38.   Milt Freudenheim, "Concern Rising About Mergers in Health Plans," *New York Times*, January 13, 1999, p. A1.

39.   U.S. News Online, September 23, 1998, www.usnes.com/usnews/nycu/health-/het-ophmo.htm.

40.   David R. Olmos, "Survey Ranks PacifiCare and Health Net Best HMOs in State," *Los Angeles Times*, June 24, 1998, p. D1.

41.   *St. Petersburg Times*, July 25, 1998; Healthline April 7, 1998, National Journal Group, reporting on *Albany Times Union* article that day.

42.   Milt Freudenheim, "Insurers Moving To Limit Doctors' Contract Choices," *New York Times*, February 8, 1999, p. A14.

43.   Charles Ornstein, "States target all-or-none health-care pacts," *The Dallas Morning News*, March 15, 1999, p. D1.

44.   Stuart Silverstein and Davan Maharaj, "Health Care Industry's Fiscal Crisis Creates Turmoil For Insured Patients; Medicine: Bankruptcies And Other Changes Shift Consumers Into New Programs. The Switch In Care Can Bring Disruptions And Discomfort," *Los Angeles Times*, March 28, 1999.

45.   Roni Rabin, "Blow to Managed Care?" *Newsday*, November 21, 1996, p. A26.

46.   Stuart Silverstein and Davan Maharaj, "Health Care Industry's Fiscal Crisis Creates Turmoil For Insured Patients; Medicine: Bankruptcies And Other Changes Shift Consumers Into New Programs. The Switch In Care Can Bring Disruptions And Discomfort," *Los Angeles Times*, March 28, 1999.

47.   *Ibid.*

48.   Milt Freudenheim, "Concern Rising About Mergers in Health Plans," *New York Times*, January 13, 1999, p. A1.

49.   Frank Browning, "Future of Managed Care in America," National Public Radio, March 1, 1999, interview.

50.   Allen Meyerson, "A Double Standard For Health Coverage," *New York Times*, March 17, 1996.

51.   *New York Times*, January 13, 1999, *Ibid.*

52. Sheryl Gay Stolberg "Managed Care Squeezes Research Funds and Charity Health Aid, Studies Find," *New York Times*, March 24, 1999, p. A20.

53. Harvey Shapiro, MD, *Managed Care Beware*, Dove Books, 1998, p. 184.

54. Commonwealth Fund Release 199, February 1999.

55. Bob Herbert, "Hospitals In Crisis," *New York Times*, April 15, 1999.

56. *Ibid.*

57. Amy Goldstein, "U.S. Will Pay To Reduce Doctor Glut; Teaching Hospitals That Shrink Programs To Receive Millions," *Washington Post*, August 24, 1997, p. A1. Is the medical market really free? "I don't know where the hell a Republican Congress gets off doing labor force planning for the medical profession," said Robert E. Moffit, deputy director for domestic policy studies at the conservative Heritage Foundation. "As an economic principle it is absurd."

58. *The Dallas Morning News*, November 28, 1998, p. 1.

59. *Journal of the American Medical Association*, December 23/30, 1998, Vol. 280, No. 24, p. 2060.

Chapter Five
Getting Away with Murder

1. *Corcoran v. United Healthcare Inc*, 965 F.2d 1321 (5th Cir 1992).

2. The Court held, "State common law causes of action arising from the improper processing of a claim are preempted." *Pilot Life Insurance v. Dedeaux*, 481 U.S. 44 (1987) ERISA's preemption clause supercedes state law relating to employer-employer benefits if that law is not specifically regulation of the business of insurance. The company lawyers argued that state common law was not technically the business of insurance and therefore not specifically "saved" from preemption by ERISA's savings clause which protects state regulation of insurance.

3. *Dishman v UNUM*, CV 96-0015 JSL Central Almanac, Vol. III, No. 4, 6/2/1997. pp. 3–6, 15–17.

4. *Andrews-Clark v Travelers Insurance Co.*, 1997 US Dist. LEXIS 17390,21 E.B.C.2137 (D Mass1997). Robert Pear, "Hands Tied, Judges Rue Law That Limits HMO Liability," *New York Times*, June 11, 1998.

5. The evidence was under a protective order, that has since been lifted, in *Richard Fisher v. Aetna Life Insurance Co.*, No. 3AN97-291, Alaska Super, Anchorage.

6. Laura Meckler, "Advocates Hope Video Will Jump Start Debate," Associated Press, October 13, 1998.

7. Fisher transcript, p. 16, court reporter corrected.

8. Fisher transcript, p. 16–17, court reporter corrected.

9. Fisher transcript at p. 58; Also see Dan Weintraub, "Tale of Aetna tape: fear of suit a factor in health claim reviews," *Orange County Register*, October 25, 1998, p. A4. Weintraub reports, "The tape captures a group of insurance company's lawyers sitting at a long table in what looks like a hotel conference room rustling papers and sipping from water glasses as they tell the workers who process disability insurance

claims to give extra attention to cases involving people who can take them to court and collect such damages. Here's the gist: The company won't deny a claim from someone who can sue for damages unless the firm first conducted a 'reasonable investigation' of the case. But other claimants can be denied benefits after only a cursory review."

10. Fisher transcript, p. 59—court reporter corrected.

11. Weintraub, p. A04.

12. Jane Bryant Quinn, "You Deserve the Right to Sue Greedy Insurers that Unreasonably Deny Health, Disability Claims," *Buffalo News*, November 22, 1998, Business section, p. 13B.

13. Fisher transcript, p. 52 court reporter corrected.

14. Trial testimony of Bryan Southall, *Ace v. Aetna Life Insurance Co.*, J94-018 Civil (JWS). Southall testified that Aetna's "Proper Claim Handling Guidelines" had been removed from its Methods and Procedures Manual.

15. Deposition excerpt from Judy Talley in *Fisher v. Aetna Life Insurance Co.*, 3AN 97-291 Civil (Superior Court, State of Alaska, Third Judicial District at Anchorage).

16. Fisher transcript, p. 43.

17. Fisher transcript, p. 56–57—court reporter corrected.

18. Much effort went into making it public. Congressman Lloyd Dogget—a former Justice on the Texas Supreme Court—wrote the judge in July 1998 to successfully break the seal on the evidence presented in this case. Dogget wrote, "The Congress is now grappling with the unintended consequences of ERISA, namely the legal immunity this federal law provides to insurers who wrongully delay or deny medical care to patients covered under ERISA plans…the Congess is in critical need of information relating to the manner in which insurers process and/or resolve claims filed by patients covered under both ERISA and non-ERISA plans…Specifically, Members of Congress are seeking information that helps to explain how, and why, insurers process ERISA and non-ERISA cases differently."

19. Kenneth Reich, "An Equal Chance/Wrestling With The Unmanageable Side Of Health Care," *Los Angeles Times*, September 24, 1998, p. B5.

20. *Cannon v. Group Health*, 77F.3d (10th circuit) 1996.

21. Robert Pear, "Move Under Way To Try To Slow Health Care Bills," November 4, 1997, p. A1.

22. Charlie Norwood, "Protection For Patients," *Washington Post* Op-Ed, February 18, 1998.

23. Coopers & Lybrand L.L.P., "Impact Of Potential Changes To ERISA," Kaiser Family Foundation, Menlo Park, CA, June 1998.

24. Congressional Budget Office Cost Estimate, "H.R. 3605/S. 1860," July 16, 1998.

25. Bush allowed the bill, SB 386, to become law without his signature.

26. *Corporate Health Insurance Inc., Aetna Health Plans of Texas Inc. v. Texas Department of Insurance*, United States Court for the Southern District of Texas, Houston Division, Civil Action No. H-97-2072 Order. By contrast, the Court struck down the HMO-backed independent review process as preempted by

ERISA—because it deals with determinations of coverage disputes. The review process is the HMO industry's suggested alternative to liability.

27. Letter from Texas State Senator David Sibley, The Texas Senate Economic Development Committee, to California Legislators, "RE: California Assembly Bill 2436 (Figueroa)—Support," June 24, 1998. Regarding imposing a medical malpractice compensation cap on liability, the Republican writes; "In Texas, civil liability for damages of a 'physician or health care provider' is limited...akin to California's Medical Injury Compensation Reform Act or MICRA. For the purposes of SB 386 [the Texas HMO liability law], however, we determined that managed care companies should not be treated any differently than other profit-making business enterprises that are subject to liability under traditional tort laws. Because HMOs and managed care companies (including doctor-run medical groups) often apply a financial filter to determine treatment denials, their liability must not be artificially limited by a compensation cap. Such restricted responsibility would mitigate against approval of the most expensive treatment, such as cancer care. Under the Texas law, physician-run medical groups are considered managed care entities and do not fall under the compensation cap applicable to sole practitioners."

28. Carol Marie Cropper, "In Texas, a Laboratory Test on the Effects of Suing HMOs," *New York Times*, September 13, 1998, Section 3, p. 1.

29. Source: Penn, Schoen & Berland For American Psychological Association "Support For Right to Sue," *USA Today*, June 23, 1998.

30. Michael A. Hiltzik and David R. Olmos, "Kaiser Justice System's Fairness Questioned," *Los Angeles Times*, August 30, 1995.

31. *Nida Engalla et al. v. The Permanente Medical Group, Inc.*, Petitioners' Opening Brief, No. SO48811 in the California Supreme Court, 1995.

32. Declaration of Michael Sullivan, *Nida Engalla et al. v. Kaiser Foundation Hospitals*, et al., Superior Court of the State of California, Alameda, No. H-15596-4.

33. Interoffice Memorandum "To Michael Hawkins From: Paul Fox Esq. Subject: December 5, 1995 Senate Insurance Committee Hearings," December 4, 1995; Exhibit in Engalla Case.

34. Bob Egelko, Associated Press, "Family May Sue Kaiser; High Court Says HMO Stalled Arbitration Over Dying Patient," *San Jose Mercury News*, July 1, 1997. p. 3B.

35. Linda Ross, Testimony before the California State Senate Judiciary Committee Interim Hearing, October 1995; see also Nancy Peverini, "ADR: A panacea for the civil justice system? Let's take a closer look," Docket, October 1995. Peverini is counsel for Consumer Attorneys of California.

36. American Arbitration Association Commercial Arbitration Rules pamphlet cited by Peverini, *Ibid.*

37. Michael A. Hiltzik and David Olmos, "Kaiser's Justice System's Fairness Is Questioned," *Los Angeles Times*, August 30, 1995.

38. *Ibid*, also Ken Sigelman, Testimony before California State Senate Judiciary Committee Interim Hearing, October, 1995.

39. Reynolds Holding, "Letting Patients Choose How to Air Their Beefs," *San Francisco Chronicle*, July 26, 1998; Margaret Jacobs, "Group Won't Arbitrate Patients' Disputes," *Wall Street Journal*, July 1, 1998.

40. *Olsen vs. Sharp Rees-Steely Medical Group et al.* (San Diego Superior Court, Case No. 666808).

41. Letters to the Editor, *San Diego Union Tribune*, May 20, 1995.

42. The following twenty states appear to have caps on non-economic damages as noted: Alaska ($500,000), Colorado ($250,000), Hawaii ($375,000), Idaho ($468,000 adjusted for inflation), Indiana ($750,000 total damages), Maryland ($454,000 adjusted for inflation), Massachusetts ($500,000), Michigan ($500,000), Missouri ($516,000), Montana ($250,000), New Mexico ($600,00 total damages), North Dakota ($500,000), Ohio ($500,000 total damages), Oregon ($500,000), South Dakota ($500,000), Texas ($1.321 million adjusted for inflation), Utah ($250,000), Virginia ($1,000,000), West Virginia ($1,000,000), and Wisconsin ($383,000 adjusted for inflation). Compiled by California Assembly Judiciary Committee, May 1999, in analysis of AB 1380.

43. Proposition 103 Enforcement Project, "MICRA: The Impact On Health Care Costs Of California's Experiment With Restrictions On Medical Malpractice Lawsuits," Santa Monica, CA, April, 1995.

44. *Ibid.*

45. Projections by study authors based on data compiled by the Harvard School of Public Health as part of a comprehensive study of medical malpractice, Harvard Medical Malpractice Study Group, *Patients Doctors, and Lawyers: Medical Injury, Malpractice Litigation, and Patient Compensation in New York*, (Cambridge, Mass.: Harvard University, 1990).

46. Letter from Texas State Senator David Sibley, The Texas Senate Economic Development Committee, to California Legislators, "RE: California Assembly Bill 2436 (Figueroa)—Support," June 24, 1998.

47. Maura Dolan, "Ruling Limits Damages In Girl's Death At Hospital," *Los Angeles Times*, March 26, 1999.

48. Testimony of Dr. Troyen Brennan, Harvard School of Public Health, on "Medical Malpractice and Health Care Reform" before the Subcommittee on Health and the Environment, Committee on Energy and Commerce, U.S. House of Representatives, November 10, 1993, p. 9.

Chapter Six
The Battle to Make Health Care Work

1. Susan Kelleher & Jay Greeene, "Man Calls Risperdal His Miracle Drug," *Orange County Register*, February 10, 1997. Following the fallout, PacifiCare now claims that that it has put Zyprexa on its formulary, which is more expensive than Risperdal.

2. Sabin Russell, "Drug Firm Plan Would Pay HMO To Favor 5 of Its Medications," *San Francisco Chronicle*, September 25, 1998, p. A1.

3. Peter Kilborn, "Reality of the H.M.O. System Doesn't Live Up to the Dream," *New York Times*, October 5, 1998, p. A1; The *Times* points out that in the newspaper's July 1998 poll "85% of respondents said the health care system needs fundamental change, barely below the 90% who said the same thing in a *Times*/CBS News poll in 1994 before the Clinton health plan died. Although 68% said they were satisfied with the quality of their family's health care, 30% said they were not, up from 19% in 1994. And the percentage dissatisfied with the cost of health care was practically unchanged, 46% now compared with 47% then."

4. News at Deadline, *Modern Health Care*, February 10, 1997, Late News, p. 4. The 165 executives were polled while attending the Health Care Forecast Conference at the University of California-Irvine Graduate School of Management in February 1997.

5. Late News, *Modern Health Care*, Crane Communications Inc., March 16, 1998, p. 4.

6. Kaiser Family Foundation/Harvard American Small Business Alliance, "National Survey of Small Business Executives on Health Care," June 17, 1998. Menlo Park, California.

7. Sabin Russell, "Drug Firm Plan Would Pay HMO To Favor 5 of Its Medications," *San Francisco Chronicle*, September 25, 1998, p. A1—Russell adds about the proportions of the problem "There are currently more than 100 Pharmacy Benefit Management companies, but an estimated 80% of the business is controlled by five companies that are either owned by or allied with pharmaceutical companies. Close ties between drug makers and formulary companies have attracted the attention of the Federal Trade Commission, which is concerned that such alliances could violate antitrust laws. Last month, pharmaceutical giant Merck & Co. signed an FTC consent agreement governing its relationship to Merck-Medco Managed Care, the nation's largest pharmacy benefits management company, which it bought in 1993 for $6.6 billion. The agreement requires that Merck-Medco set up an independent committee of doctor and academic experts to determine which drugs will be on its formulary."

8. "Remarks by Vice President Al Gore at Event in Recognition of the Budget Agreement, The Rose Garden, The White House, Washington, D.C." Federal News Service, October 16, 1998, Friday, 12:30 Eastern Time, White House Briefing Transcript By: Federal News Service, 620 National Press Building, Washington, D.C. 20045.

9. Peter Kilborn, "Complaints About HMOs Rise As Awareness Grows," *New York Times*, October 11, 1998.

10. Congressional Budget Office Cost Estimate, "H.R. 3605/S. 1890, Patients' Bill of Rights Act of 1998," July 15, 1998.

11. *Corporate Health Insurance Inc. et al v. Texas Department of Insurance*, U.S. District Court For the Southern District of Texas Houston Division, Civil Action No. H-97-2072 Order. The scope of the law, however, is limited—not addressing denials of coverage.

12. California State Senate Bill 21, authored by Senator Liz Figueroa and sponsored by the Foundation For Taxpayer and Consumer Rights, introduced in December 1998, www.sen.ca.gov.

13. Case law suggests it should be a public corporation, like a state bar association, rather than a private corporation, which some courts say state governments cannot create.

14. *Ottawa Citizen*, Dec. 12, 1995 and conversation with consumer advocate Ralph Nader.

15. See Chapter Four.

16. David Hilzenrath, "Big HMO Rate Rise To Hit Older Americans," *Washington Post*, October 25, 1998.

17. California Proposition 103, written by consumer advocate Harvey Rosenfield and approved by California voters in 1988 to reform the property-casualty insurance industry, instituted a "prior approval" system, which requires that any rate increases must first be approved by an elected insurance commissioner. Prior to the passage of Proposition 103, auto insurance rates in California had been rising 11% every year. Since 103's passage, auto rates have declined approximately 1% per year during the last five years, the only state to see such decreases.

18. California Assembly Bill 322 (Figueroa, D-Freemont) in 1998 and Assembly Bill 794 in 1997.

19. See *New England Journal of Medicine*, Vol. 335, No. 13, September 26, 1996, p. 9995 as cited by former United States Justice Department attorney Kenneth C. Anderson, "Collusive Behavior In the Managed Health Care Industry," September 10, 1997 on behalf of the National Coalition of Mental Health Professionals and Consumers and the Alliance for Universal Access to Psychotherapy, 1200 G. Street NW, Suite 200, Washington, D.C. 20005 p. 23.

20. Kenneth C. Anderson in his paper "Collusive Behavior In the Managed Health Care Industry," September 10, 1997 on behalf of the National Coalition of Mental Health Professionals and Consumers and the Alliance for Universal Access to Psychotherapy, 1200 G. Street NW, Suite 200, Washington, DC 20005, p. 25.

21. *Ibid.*

22. Gina Kolata, "When Patients' Records Are Commodities For Sale," *New York Times*, November 15, 1995.

23. Christine Gorman, "Who's Looking At Your Files?" *Time*, May 6, 1996.

24. David R. Olmos and Shari Roan, "HMO 'Gag Clauses' on Doctors Spur Protest," *Los Angeles Times*, April 14, 1996. On the "Donahue" show, David Himmelstein, MD, criticized U.S. Healthcare and other HMOs for rewarding doctors for denying needed care and forcing them to sign contracts pledging not to disparage the HMO. When he was dropped three days later by U.S. Healthcare, he wasn't surprised. "Every doctor who works with an HMO knows you are in trouble if you criticize," said Himmelstein.

25. Rick Weiss, "Aging: New Answers To Old Questions," *National Geographic*, November 1997, p. 12.

26. *Consumer Reports*, October 1998.

27. U.S. Department of Health & Human Services, 1988.

28. *California Consumer Guide to Long-term Care*, California Dept. of Aging, 1996.

29. John Baldwin, C. Everett Koop, "Search for the Cure," *Washington Post* Op-Ed, May 6, 1999.

30. Richard Knox, "HMOs' Creator Urges Reform In Quality Care," *Boston Globe*, May 2, 1999.

31. Wyatt Andrews, *CBS Evening News with Dan Rather*: Libertyville, Illinois Friday, October 30, 1998, 08:04 PM ET.

32. Nancy Ann Jeffrey, "Aetna To Set Reviews For HMO Coverage Disputes," *Wall Street Journal*, January 12, 1999.

33. Robert Pear, "Americans Lacking Health Insurance Put At 16%," *New York Times*, September 26, 1998, p. A1.

34. Richard Knox, "HMOs' Creator Urges Reform In Quality Care," *Boston Globe*, May 2, 1999.

35. Jennifer Steinhauer, "For the Medically Uninsured, Tough and Creative Choices," *New York Times*, "March 2, 1999, p. A1.

36. James Barba, "Medically Uninsured Still Cost Taxpayers," Letter to the Editor, *New York Times*, September 30, 1998.

37. Carl Weber, MD, "Managed Care Plans Shirk Their Duty," *New York Times*, Letters to the Editor, October 11, 1998.

38. The government is the single "payer."

39. Henry J. Kaiser Family Foundation, February 1998, Menlo Park, California; American Hospital Publishing Hospital and Health News, "Blue Skies or Black Eyes," April 20, 1998.

40. Alan Sager and Deborah Socolar, "If 'Single Payer' Is Our Best Slogan Should We Be Surprised That We Are Losing," American Public Health Association, November 18, 1996; Also see Alan Sager, Deborah Socolar, David Ford and Robert Brand, "More Care, At Less Cost," *Boston Globe*, April 25, 1999.

41. Richard Knox, "HMOs' Creator Urges Reform In Quality Care," *Boston Globe*, May 2, 1999.

42. Dolorus King, "State Medical Society Gives Boost To Single Payer Health Plan Backers," *Boston Globe*, May 8, 1999, p. B3.

43. Sharon Bernstein, "ER Patients Lose In Specialists' Rebellion," *Los Angeles Times*, June 1, 1999, p. A1.

Index

A

Abortions, 96–97
Abramson, Leonard, 104
Academic medical centers, 115–117
Access to care
  HMO fraud, 65
  HMOs vs FFS, 35
  and medical negligence, 18–19
  restriction of, 166
  and rewards to physicians, 63
  small business owners survey, 29
  specialist referrals, 4
Accountability
  and ERISA, 120–144
  and medical licenses, 168
  and reform, 157
Accreditation, of HMOs, 180
Acuity standards, 94
Acute myeloid leukemia, 138
Adams, Barry, 79
Adams, James, 16
Administration
  costs of, 113
  HMO costs, 30
  Kaiser increases in, 54
  Medicare costs, 30, 64
  overhead costs, 103
  physician satisfaction with, 46
  sample dialogue, 186–187
Admissions. see also
  Readmissions
  incentives to limit, 17–18
  protection of patients, 181
  rates of, 72
Advertising. see Marketing
Advocacy
  for the patient, 185
  and persuasion, 182–183
  sample dialogue, 186–187
Aetna. see also U.S. Healthcare
  anti-disparagement clause, 39
  executive compensation, 105
  growth of, 111
  handling of ERISA claims, 123–127
  marketing by, 62–63
  merger with U.S. Healthcare, 167

  on NCQA board, 163
  and Prudential, 110
Aetna U.S. Healthcare
  delayed cancer treatment, 1–5
  on gag clauses, 63
  slogans, 3
Aitken, Chad, 40–42
Aitken, Heather, 40–42, 54
Albert, Bill, 62
Allies, need for, 180
Alta Bates Medical Center, 38
Alta Bates Medical Group, 32
Alternative health care options, 102
Ambulance transport, 15–16
American Accreditation
  HealthCare
  Commission/URAC, 180
American Arbitration
  Association, 142
American Association of Health
  Plans, 118
American Bar Association, 142
American College of
  Obstetricians and
  Gynecologists, 47
American Managed Care and
  Review Association, 162
American Medical Association
  (AMA)
  on arbitration, 142
  on capitation, 29–30
  doctors' union, 114
  on gag clauses, 63
  and the GOP, 157
  on liability caps, 146
  on nationalization, 175
American Psychiatric
  Association, 62
American Psychological
  Association, 134–135
American Small Business
  Alliance, 155
Americans for Job Security, 118
Anderson, Kenneth, 163
Anderson Consulting, 47
Angina, 18–19
Angiograms, outpatient, 94
Anorexia, 60
Anti-disparagement clauses, 38–39, 63

Anti-trust laws, 108
Anxiety, of consumers, 51
Appeals
  of denials, 66
  procedure for, 188
  of treatment denials, 180
Apricio, Alfredo, 50
Arbitration
  costs of, 142
  delays by Kaiser, 140
  and HMO contracts, 59
  and malpractice, 26
  mandatory, 140, 147, 159–160
  public disclosure of, 162
Asquith, Edna, 77–78
Asquith, Nicole, 77–78
Associated Press, 125
Asthma, 51–52, 57
Atlantic Richfield, 115
Attorneys, 151
August Regional Hospital, 90
Autism, 60
Avapro, 154

B

Bad faith, and ERISA, 140
Bailouts, 109–112
Baldwin, John, 166
Barba, James, 173
Barris, Dawnelle, 16–17, 150
Barris, Mycelle, 150
Basic American Medical, 89
Bast, Rhonda Rae Flemming, 136
Beaver, Bill, 20–22
Beds. see Hospital beds
Bedsores, 84
Benchmarks, stay limits, 25
Bennefield, Robert L, 172
Berman, Renee, 11–12
Bernica, Greg, 111
Berstein, Sharon, 92
Bever, Bill, 138–139
Billing practices, fraudulent, 88
Blame, shifts of, 33–35
Blankersteen, Charles, 111
Blue Cross, 65, 102, 163
Blue Lines HMO, 128–129
Blue Shield, 23, 68–69
Blumenthal, David, 115
Blumenthal, Jeffrey, 123–124
Board of Registered Nursing, 80

Bond, Alan, 108
Bone infections, 25
Bone marrow transplants (BMTs)
  autologous (ABMTs), 23, 128
  denial of, 12–13, 14, 136, 138,
    139
Bonuses, for limiting care, 7,
  17–18, 29
Boston College School of
  Nursing, 80, 82
Boston Globe, 176
Bosworth, Janice, 13–14, 139
Bosworth, Steve, 13–14
Boycotts, of HMOs, 169
Bradley, Bruce, 115
Brain abscesses, 70–71
Brain tumors, 20–22, 130
Breast cancer, 23, 74, 139
Breast reconstruction, 60
Breast-feeding, 47
Brennan, Troyen, 35, 72, 83, 145,
  151
Bristol-Myers Squibb, 153–154
Brookings Institute, 165
Broughton, Adrian, 55, 56, 57,
  142
Brown, Barbara, 171
Burn units, 116
Bush, George, Jr., 133
Business Roundtable, 118

C

California Assembly Bill 332, 14
California Assembly Bill 794, 14
California Emergency Medical
  Services Authority, 94–95
California Insurance Code, 60
California Insurance
  Department, 60
California Medical Association,
  102
California Medical Board, 10
California Nurses Association
  (CNA)
  and census counts, 94
  on child-birth technique, 38
  handbook release, 37
  on Kaiser's marketing budget,
    47
  on outpatient mastectomies,
    74
  Patient Watch, 81, 84
Call bells, and understaffing, 81
Canada, 95–96, 175
Cancer. *see also* Specific Cancers
  delay of treatment for, 1–5,

10–11
  denial of treatment for, 11–12,
    17
Cannon, Jerry, 129
Cannon, Phyllis, 128–129
Capitation
  AMA survey of patients,
    29–30
  and catastrophic care, 30
  and delayed referrals, 32–33
  full-risk, 161
  functioning of, 8, 28
  inadequate compensation, 113
  medical group rates, 112
  physician motivation, 182–183
  rates of, 160
  and risk management, 35
Caps. *see also* Liability
  on awards, 143
  on damages, 33
  on liability, 156–152
  lifetime, 60
  on non-economic compensa-
    tion, 148–150
Cardiograms, availability of, 117
Care paths, 48
Career-ending moves (CEM), 25
Casenza, Stephanie, 38
Cataracts, 9, 24
Catastrophic care, 30, 114
Catholic Health Association,
  96–97
Catholic Healthcare West, 97
Cedar-Sinai, 97
Cefzil, 154
CEMs (career-ending moves), 25
Census, hospital beds, 94, 162
Center for Health Dispute
  Resolutions, 188
Ceronsky, David, 79
Chaffee, John, 157
Chain of command, 187–188
Chamber of Commerce, 119
Charity, at academic medical
  centers, 116
Charles Schwab, 115
Chemotherapy, 1, 94
Children's Associated Medical
  Group, 28
Ching, David, 32–33
Ching, Joyce, 32–33
Christie, Carrel, 20, 185
Christie, Harry, 20, 185
Chronic illnesses, 66
CIGNA
  arbitration agreements, 142

executive compensation, 105
  treatment denials, 69
CIGNA Health Care of
  California, 55–56
Claims
  finalization of, 127
  HMOs vs FFS, 35
  noncovered benefits, 60–68
Cleft palate, 60
Clerks overriding physicians,
  15–18. *see also* Utilization
  management
Clinical financial reviews. *see*
  Utilization management
Clinton, William, 67, 118, 174
Clinton administration, 109,
  117, 133
Cohen, Candis, 10
Colon cancer, 32–33
Columbia Good Samaritan
  Hospital, 87–88
Columbia Sunrise Hospital, 88
Columbia/HCA, 4, 86–95, 109,
  166
Columbia-Presbyterian Medical
  Center, 73
Columbia's Women's Hospital,
  90
Commerce Committee, 28
Commission on the Future of
  Health Care, 100
Commonwealth Fund, 116
Communications, responsibility
  for, 34–35
Communities
  effects of HMOs, 70–98, 115
  fundraising help, 181
Community Hospital, 97
Compensation, non-economic,
  148–150
Compensation agreements, 39,
  61
Complaints, 162, 180, 181
Complications, and under-
  staffing, 82
Composure, 185
Confidentiality
  of arbitrations, 140, 159–160
  of compensation agreements,
    39, 61
  of medical information, 170
  and medical malpractice, 37
  of medical records, 163–164
Conflict of interest, 9–10, 37
Congressional Budget Office, 158
Consumer resources, 197–200

Consumer Utility Boards, 159
Consumer watchdogs, 159
Consumers for Quality Care, 30, 37
Contingency fees, 151
Continuity of care, 40–42
Contraception, 96
Contracts
　with Aetna, 111
　cancellation threats, 13
　with patients, 58–60
　for physicians, 180–181
　physicians with HMOs, 37–39
Cooper, Charla, 22–23
Co-payments, 102
Corcoran, Florence, 120–122
"Corporate practice of medicine" laws, 135
Cosmetic surgery, 60
Costello, Kit, 37, 38, 78
Counseling, 22–23, 24, 74
Covered benefit limitation, 60–68
Covered lives, 28, 56
Cropper, Carol, 134
Crystal Report on Executive Compensation, 106
Cystic fibrosis, 138

D

Daly, John, 81
Dartmouth Medical School, 48
Daversa, Denise, 47, 51
Dearmas, Ariday, 138
deBlois, Sister Jean, 96
Deceptive business practices, 55
Deductibles, 102
Defensive medicine, 36–37
Dehydration, 47, 84
Delays, 131–132
　asthma, 51–52
　authorizations, 22–23
　and capitation, 32–33
　depression, 138
　of diagnostic tests, 137
　heart transplant, 137–138
　hospital transfers, 138
　of referrals, 18–19
　in treatment, 81–82
Delisting, 7, 164
Deloite & Touche, 46
deMeurers, Christine, 12–13, 139
DeMoro, Don, 106
Denials
　appeals, 180
　of biopsies, 15

for bone marrow transplant, 136
of care, 6
care for kidney cancer, 64
of diagnostic tests, 75–76, 137
effect of ERISA, 122
and exclusions, 58–60
HMO role in, 131
prostatic cancer, 137
of rehabilitation, 76
treatment for respiratory distress, 40–42
use of benchmarks, 25
Denmark, 117
Dental care, 65
Department of Health Services (DHS), 80
Depression, 138
DHS (Department of Health Services), 80
Diagnostic procedures
　delayed, 13–14
　denial of, 14–15, 70–71, 75–76, 137
　profiling of physicians, 31
Diets, specialized, 57
Dignity, 185
Dingell, John, 100, 156
Dingle, John, 118
Discharges
　premature, 24, 48–49, 53, 73, 75
　to SNFs, 77–78
Disenrollment, 66
Disparagement clauses, 164
Documentation. *see also* Paperwork
　by medical care workers, 83
　and patient self-defense, 179–180
Dorozil, Rick, 169
Dow Jones Wire Service, 62
Downsizing
　at academic medical centers, 117
　and acuity standards, 94
　effects of, 84
　HMO's responsibility in, 8–9
　hospital beds, 72
　at Kaiser, 54
　and level of care, 49–50
　and medication error rates, 85
　of nursing care, 78–81
　of services, 42–43
　of staff, 48
Drake, Donald, 31–32

Drug list. *see* Formulary
Drug utilization. *see* Pharmacy utilization
Dumping, of elderly patients, 67
Dwyer, Thomas, 10

E

Eating disorders, 60–61
Edelstine, Martin, 30
Education of patients
　about appeal procedures, 66
　anti-disparagement clauses, 63
　and medical malpractice, 37
　and medical necessity, 63
　and premature discharges, 47, 73
Edwards, John, 118
Elderplan Inc., 65
Ellwood, Paul, 119, 168, 172, 175–176
Emergency care
　delay in, 148
　denials of, 15–16
　HMOs vs FFS, 35
　triage, 26
　and the uninsured, 173
Emergency rooms
　and outpatient surgery patients, 74
　patient handling, 43
　returns to, 48
Empire Health, 110
Employee Handbook, 37
Employers
　and ERISA, 126, 157–158
　health care coverage by, 174
　and HMO benefits, 42
　provision of health care by, 169
　on regulation, 115
　role of, 114
Engalla, Patricia, 141
Engalla, Wilfredo, 140, 141
England, 117
Enrollments, 57–58
Enthoven, Alain, 31
Erb's palsy, 50
ERISA. *see* federal Employees Retirement Income Security Act
Exclusions, 58–60
Executive compensation, HMOs, 104–108
Executive Life Insurance Co., 149
Experimental treatments, 23,

128–129, 130, 171
Eyeglasses, 65

F

Federal Bureau of Investigation
  (FBI), 88
Federal Employees Health
  Benefits Plan, 99
Federal Employees Retirement
  Income Security Act
  (ERISA), 120–144
  effect on medical decision
    making, 121–122
  and remedy for loss, 129
  shield of HMOs, 157–158
Federal Securities and Exchange
  Act, 107
Fee-for-service (FFS) medicine
  disenrollment rates, 66
  Medicare, 100
  over-utilization, 35
  service compared to HMOs, 35
Fertility, 22–23
FFS. see Fee-for-service (FFS)
  medicine
FHP International
  delayed referrals, 185
  merger with PacifiCare,
    107–108, 109, 166
Fight Back & Win, 182
Filing fees, 142
Financial information disclosure,
  162
Fine print, 58–60
Fisher, Daniel, 8
Forbes, 105
Formulary, preferred status, 153
Fortune, 109
Foundation Health Systems
  confidentiality of agreements,
    39
  executive compensation, 105,
    106
  financial health of, 62
  formulary, 153
  losses, 109
  marketing abuses, 61–62
Fox, Nelene, 14, 33, 139
FPA, collapse of, 112
France, 117
Frank, Judith, 48
Fraud
  and access to care, 65
  by Columbia/HCA, 86–95
  investigation of Tenet, 95–96
Freidman Knowles Experimental

Treatment Act, 171
Fundraising
  community help, 181
  private, 12–13, 23, 104, 136

G

Gag clauses, 37, 62–63, 111, 164
Gannett, 115
Gardener, Marco, 4, 85, 88, 91
General Accounting Office
  (GAO), 66
General Motors, 115
Giles, Alex, 137
Gilmore, Vanessa, 133–134
Ginsburg, Eli, 107
Goals, achievement of, 183–184
Gold, Edward J., 113
Goodrich, David, 1–5
Goodrich, Teresa, 1–5
Gore, Al, 156
Government employers, 127
Greater Newport Physicians, 31
Grievance arbitration, 159–160
Group Health Association of
  America, 162
Guaranty funds, 168
Gumbiner, Robert, 107, 108

H

Haldol, 62, 153
Hale, Betty, 23, 104
Harriman Jones Medical Group,
  9
Hartford Courant, 1
*Harvard Medical Malpractice
  Study*, 72
Harvard Pilgrim Health Care, on
  NCQA board, 163
Hasan, Malik, 105, 106, 109
Health club memberships, 102
Health Net
  on affordability, 156
  agreement with doctors, 38
  denial of BMTs, 139
  denial of cancer treatment, 12
  denial of care by, 13–14
  marketing of, 58–59
  physician profiling, 32
  treatment denials, 69
Health Plan Employer Data &
  Information Set (HEDIS), 163
Health Systems International,
  108
Healthtrust, 89
Heart transplants, 137–138
HEDIS (Health Plan Employer

Data & Information Set), 163
Henry Ford Health System, 163
Hiepler, Mark, 14, 33
High-dose chemotherapy
  (HDCT), 23
HIP Health Plans, 110, 168
HIV/AIDS, 116
Ho, Sam, 13
Hoehn, 114
Hoops, Alan, 105
Hope, 43, 45–46
Hospital beds, 72, 93. *see also*
  Census
Hospital Corporation of
  America, 89
Hospitals, as HMOs, 97
House, Larry, 105
Hovey, Douglas, 138
Huber, Richard, 1, 63
Humana
  denial of care, 6, 17–18
  losses, 109
  premium increases, 99
  security of members, 69
Hurricane Opal, 90–91
Hysterectomies, 8, 17–18

I

Illinois Citizens Utility Board,
  159
Immunity, 122, 129–130
Impotence, 61
In vitro fertilization, 96
Incentives, 17–18, 122
Independent Medical Exams
  (IMEs), 125
Independent Practice
  Association (IPAs), 39
Indigent care
  at academic medical centers,
    116
  costs of, 93
  effects of HMOs, 115
  uninsured patients, 91
Information technology
  HEDIS data, 163
  Kaiser increases in, 54
  problems with, 104
Informed choice, and Aetna, 111
Ingram, Bob, 99
Injuries to patients, 82
Insurance
  licensing, 112
  long-term care, 164–165
  malpractice, 145
  Medigap, 65–66

patients without, 91
practiced by physicians, 112
reinsurance, 114
stop-loss, 30, 114
Insurance industry
California Insurance Code, 60
California Insurance
    Department, 60
Executive Life Insurance Co.,
    149
and the GOP, 132–133
liability of, 118
licensing, 161
lobbying by, 143–144
on long-term care, 165
National Academy of Social
    Insurance, 102
National Association of
    Insurance Companies
    (NIAC), 165
political muscle, 117–119
on regulation, 115
reserve requirements, 168
and return on investment, 35
Texas Department of
    Insurance, 134
Travelers Insurance, 123
Integrated Pharmaceutical
    Services, 153
Inter Valley Health Plan, 15, 64
Intimidation, 181
Investigational treatments, 23
IPAs (Independent Practice
    Association), 39
Irving Levin Associates, 97
Isreal, Sara, 58–59, 69
Izzo, Brian, 11

J

JACHO (Joint Commission on
    Accreditation of Healthcare
    Organizations), 162, 163, 180
JAMA. see Journal of the
    American Medical Association
Jaundice, 47
Jochum, George, 105
Johnson, Keya, 54–56
Johnson, Melody, 138
Joint Commission on
    Accreditation of Healthcare
    Organizations (JACHO), 162,
    163, 180
Jones, David, 105
Jordan, Harry, 145–146
Journal of Public Health, 83
Journal of the American Medical

Association
on bed capacity, 72
"Call to Action," 7
community effects of HMOs,
    115
on quality of care, 168
Juries, 2–3

K

Kaiser
arbitration loss, 26
authority of clinical financial
    review nurses, 15–16
business goals of, 48
competition, 42, 168
coverage of impotence, 61
delay of arbitration, 140–141
denial of care, 20–22
DHS citation, 80
downsizing of services, 42–43
elderly patients, 160
IT spending, 44
on large medical groups, 31
losses, 109
mandatory arbitration, 147
marketing message, 40
nursing recruitment, 83
premium increases, 99
service partners, 79
understaffing, 49–50
Kaiser Family Foundation, 133
Kaiser Family
    Foundation/Harvard survey,
    155
Kaiser Permanente. see Kaiser
Kaufman, Irving, 28
Kawamoto, Henry, 60
Kaye, Jeffrey, 87–88
Kearns, Thomas, 143–144
Kelly, Frank, 87, 90
Kennedy, Edward, 118
Kidneys, 14–15, 145–146
King, Carolyn Dineen, 120–121
Kinsey & Co., 47
Koop, C. Everett, 166
KPMG Peat Marwick, 89
Kresser, Stein, Robaire, 46
Kuhl, Bobby, 137–138

L

Lake, Cindie, 81–82
Lake, Dan, 81–82
Lange, Celeste, 88
Lawsuits
for deceptive business prac-
    tices, 55–56

ERISA loopholes, 120–144
to force treatment, 69
right to, 182
Leasure-Firesheets, Michelle, 136
Legg, Elaine, 87–88
Leifer, John, 86
Lengths of stay, 17–18, 72
Letts, J. Spencer, 123
Liability. see also Caps
caps on, 146–152
and ERISA claims, 123
of HMOs, 133, 158–159
Licensing
and decisions of medical
    necessity, 10
hospitals as HMOs, 97
insurance, 112
for insurance companies, 161
for medical practice, 161
Liver transplants, 10–11
Lobb, Dwight, 78–79
Lobb, Suzanne, 78–79, 147
Lobbying, by the insurance
    industry, 117–119, 132,
    143–144
Loma Linda University Medical
    Center, 130
Long-term care insurance,
    164–165
Los Angeles Times, 2, 92, 113,
    127, 142, 177
Lott, Trent, 132
Lucille Packard Children's
    Hospital, 80
Lung cancer, 140
Lupron, 137
Luvox, 34

M

Maharaj, Davan, 113
Malnutrition, 47, 84
Malpractice insurance, 145
Mammograms, 13–14, 117
Managed care organizations
    (MCOs), 3, 36
Marketing
by Aetna, 62–63
by CIGNA, 55–56
cost to patients, 118
deceptive, 54
by Foundation Health, 61–62
fraudulent to Medicare recipi-
    ents, 66
by Health Net, 58–59
by Inter Valley Health Plan,
    64

by Kaiser, 40, 43, 50–51
by MediFoundation Health, 56
by PacifiCare, 62
Markowitz, Melinda, 87–88
Massachusetts Medical Society, 176
Mastectomies, outpatient, 24, 42, 74
Maxicare, 105
McCafferey, Colin, 49
McCafferey, Kevin, 49, 147, 149
McDermott, Jim, 100
McGuire, William, 105
MCOs. see Managed care organizations
Medicaid
 at academic medical centers, 116
 anesthesia withheld, 92
 and the ERISA loopholes, 127
 fraudulent billing of, 88
 long-term care, 164
 medical information, 163
 Tenet investigation, 95–96
 vaccinations, 40
Medi-Cal, 55, 57
Medical Care Management Corporation, 170–171
Medical directors, 6, 9–10, 14, 28–29
Medical groups, 31, 161
Medical Injury Compensation Reform Act (MICRA), 145–146
Medical licenses, 168
Medical malpractice
 caps on compensation, 148–150
 and ERISA, 140
 insurance, 145
 and lawsuits, 182
 United Healthcare suit, 120
Medical Management Corporation, 110
Medical necessity
 and claim denial, 130
 decision of, 10
 definitions of, 68–69
 denial of treatment, 122
 and patient education, 63
Medical negligence
 and access to care, 18–19
 frequency of, 145
 by HMOs, 8
Medical records, 163–164
Medical research, 117

Medical savings accounts (MSAs), 106
Medical schools, 115–117
Medicare
 administrative costs, 30, 64
 appeals procedure, 188
 and the ERISA loopholes, 127
 fraud in marketing to, 66
 fraudulent billing of, 88, 92
 funding guidelines, 43
 HMO dropping of patients, 100
 HMOs dropout, 66–67
 Medigap insurance, 65–66
 overhead costs, 103
 overpayments to HMOs, 101
 patient rights, 180
 Tenet investigation, 95–96
Medicare Choice, 100
Medication errors, 82, 85
MediFoundation Health, 56, 57
Medigap insurance, 65–66
MedPartners, 110, 112
Megarian, Mike, 65
Melnick, Glenn, 111
Mental health, 33–34, 103
Mental illness, 60
Mercury News, 38
Mercy Healthcare, 83
Mergers and acquisitions, 96–98, 104–108, 108–112, 109–112, 167
MetLife, 39
Meyerson, Allen, 115
MICRA (Medical Injury Compensation Reform Act), 145–146
Midwifery, 49
Milliman & Robertson, 24, 134
Misdiagnoses, 20–22
Mohawk Valley Medical Plan (MVP), 10
Monopril, 154
Morale, of physicians, 45
Moran, Debra, 136
Morgan, Kyle, 137
"Morning after" pills, 96
Mortalities, and staffing, 82
Motorola Corporation, 169
MSAs (Medical savings accounts), 106
Mt. Sinai Hospital of New York City, 10–11

N
Nader, Ralph, 159

National Academy of Social Insurance, 102
National Association of Insurance Companies (NIAC), 165
National Center for Health Care Statistics, 164
National Committee for Quality Assurance (NCQA), 162–163, 180
National Federation of Independent Business (NFIB), 155
National Institute of Health, 117
National Medical Enterprises (NME). see Tenet
National preventive health care, 172–177
National Public Radio, 61
National Rehabilitation Hospital (NRH), 76
National Women's Health Network, 74
NCQA (National Committee for Quality Assurance), 162–163
Nealy, Glenn, 18–19, 128
New England Journal of Medicine, 102
New England Medical Center, 30
New York Life, 111
New York State Health Department, 65
New York Times, 67, 89, 92, 115, 134, 154, 156, 172, 173
Newborns, premature discharges, 47
NewsHour, 87
NIAC (National Association of Insurance Companies), 165
Nocera, Joseph, 109
Non-interference clauses, 39
North Shore Physicians Association, 30
Northern California Permanente Medical Group, 53
Northridge Hospital Medical Center, 92
Northrup, Anne, 118
Norwood, Charlie, 132–133
Nurses. see also California Nurses Association
 downsizing of, 78–81
 effects of downsizing, 84
 NewsHour interview, 87–88
 pressures on, 37
 satisfaction surveys, 46–47

threats to, 7
NurseWeek, 83
Nursing Economics, 83
Nursing homes, 48, 75

O

Office of Technological
　Assessment (OTA), 36
Olsen, Kathy, 70–71, 143–144
Olsen, Scott, 70–71
Olsen, Steven, 70–71, 143–144
Orange County Register, 31, 124
Orthopedic surgery, 102–103
Ostomy supplies, 136
Outcomes, 4, 82, 84
Out-of-network care, 12, 15–16,
　22–23, 38, 138. *see also*
　Referrals
Outpatient procedures, 48,
　73–74, 94
Outpatient therapy, 76–77
Overpayments, by Medicare to
　HMOs, 101
Over-utilization, 35
Ownership status, and enroll-
　ment, 169
Oxford Health Plans, 65, 105,
　109, 168

P

Pacific Business Group on Health
　Negotiating Alliance, 111
PacifiCare, 9
　delayed referrals, 33
　FHP merger, 109
　formulary, 153
　marketing by, 62
　merger, 166
　on NCQA board, 163
　profiling of physicians, 31
　purchase of FHP, 107
　stock prices, 167
Packevicz, Judith, 10–11, 128
Pallone, Frank, 118
Paperwork. *see also*
　Documentation
　burden on physicians, 116
　increase in, 83
Parrino, Stephen, 130–131
Patient assistance services, 177
Patient Protection Bill, 118
Patient Watch, 81, 84
Patients' Bill of Rights, 156–157
Payroll taxes, 174
Pearson, Cindy, 74
Pediatric emergency care, 16

Peeno, Linda, 6–7, 17, 28
Penalty clauses, 29
Persistence, the need for, 181
Persuasion, and advocacy,
　182–183
Pharmaceutical research, 117
Pharmacy utilization, 32
　cost of, 26
　high-cost drugs, 48
　at PacifiCare, 62
　physician profiling, 31, 103
Physical therapy, 102–103
Physician management groups
　(PMGs), 38
Physician profiles
　diagnostic procedures, 31
　pharmacy utilization, 31, 103
　referrals, 31, 38
Physician-patient relationships
　and HMO liability, 158–159
　in Kaiser marketing, 47
　and Kaiser's marketing, 52–53
　and medical decisions, 10
　overriding of, 10–18
Physicians. *see also* Physician pro-
　files
　bureaucratic control of, 14
　and capitation, 28
　compensation agreements,
　　180–181
　discontent of, 54
　HMO profiling of, 31
　indemnification of, 140
　negotiations with HMOs, 113
　overruled by HMOs, 1
　practicing insurance, 112
　professional protection, 164
　rewards for withholding care,
　　63
　second-guessing of, 161
　threats to, 7
Picker Institute, 73
*Pilot Life Insurance versus
　Dedeaux*, 122, 124, 125, 158
Plavix, 154
PMGs (Physician management
　groups), 38
Pon, Marilyn, 80
Porfilio, John, 129
Postoperative wound infections,
　74
PPOs (preferred provider organi-
　zations), 3
Pravachol, 154
Preferred provider organizations
　(PPOs), 3

Pregnancy, 49, 55, 58–59, 120
Premiums
　increases in, 99–119, 160–161,
　　165
　and overhead costs, 103
　and the right to sue, 134–135
Prescott, Patricia, 83
Prescription drugs, 65
Prescription drugs benefit, 67
Prescription habits, 8
Prescriptions, 103
Preventive care
　denial of, 26
　health club memberships, 102
　national, 172–177
　screening programs, 102
Procedure utilization profiling, 31
Profiling. *see* Physician profiles
Proprietary information, 62–63
Proton-beam therapy, 130–131
Prozac, 32, 34, 62
PruCare, 69, 127
Prudential, 99, 110, 127
Public assistance programs, 151
Public Citizen, 163
Pulmonary embolisms, 142

Q

Quality and quantity, 9
Quality control, and utilization
　review, 32
Quality of care
　decreases in, 154
　effect of arbitration, 140
　in not-for-profits, 168
　public disclosure of, 162
Quantity, focus on, 9
Quinn, Jane Bryant, 124

R

Rafferty, Hannah, 113
Rafferty, Paige, 113
Rainwater, Richard, 91
Rationing, 24, 48
R.E. Thomason General
　Hospital, 92, 93
Readmissions, 48, 82
Rebating, 154
Reconstructive surgery, 60
Referrals. *see also* Out-of-network
　care
　delayed, 18–19, 32–33
　denied, 137, 138
　HMOs vs FFS, 35
　and medical necessity, 136
　for new-onset seizures, 24

physician profiles, 31, 38
rates of, 25
Reforms, HMO, 156
Rehabilitation, 76, 102–103
Reich, Ken, 127
Reimbursements, 8, 111
Reinhardt, Uwe, 114
Reinsurance, 114
Reiter, Marvin, 97
Remedy for loss, 129
Republican party, 132–133, 157
Reputation, 43
Reputation Campaign, 47. see
   also Marketing
Reserve requirements, 168
Resources
   for consumers, 197–200
   state regulators, 189–196
Respiratory distress, 40–42
Responsibility, shifting of, 8–9,
   33–35
Restraints, 96
Retinopathy, 137
Review systems, 170–171
Richardson, Sally K., 92
Right to sue
   federal restoration of, 157–158
   small business owners support,
      155
   surrender of, 140
   in Texas, 134–135
Right to trial, 143
Risk management
   administration of, 113
   and defensive medicine, 36–37
   and HMOs, 35–39
   passed on to patients, 23
   and understaffing, 82
Risperdal, 62, 153
RJR Nabisco, 115
RN-to-patient ratios, 84
Roberts, Barbara, 25–26
Robinson, James, 72, 73–74, 75
Rochin, Albert, 57–58, 61
Rochin, Michael, 57–58, 61
Rochin, Monica, 57–58
Rockefeller, Jay, 100
Rodriquez, Richard, 16
Roe vs Wade, 96
Ross, Linda, 26, 142, 148
Rownd, Robert, 90
Rudensteine, Neil, 116
Russell, Sabin, 153, 154

S

Sacramento Bee, 61, 96

Safe Medicine for Consumers,
   151
Safety, 79, 87–88
Sage, William, 113
Sager, Alan, 175
Sakamoto, Milton, 50
San Diego Union Tribune, 143
San Francisco Chronicle, 153
Sarver, Bradley, 68–69
Sarver, Linda, 69
Sarver, Steven, 68–69
Satisfaction surveys
   of Kaiser physicians, 45
   of patients, 9, 29–30, 59–60
   Picker Institute, 73
   publication of, 162
Satzger, Bruce, 97
Savage, Joellyn, 43, 44
SBC Communications, 115
Schizophrenia, 62
Schrage, Michael, 110
Schriever, Bill, 33–34
Schriever, Mary, 33–34
Scott, Madison, 137
Scott, Richard, 89, 91
Screening, preventive health
   care, 102
Second opinions. see also
   Referrals
   and medical necessity,
      130–131
   referrals to specialists, 136
   on treatment options, 12
Secure Horizons, 62, 69
Sedative utilization, 32
Seizures, new-onset, 24
Self, Thomas W., 27–28, 30, 32
Self-defense kit, 178–188
Senior ambassadors, 65
Seniors
   covered lives, 65
   dumping of, 109–110, 155
   HMO dropping of, 100
   per capita spending, 102
Service Employees International
   Union (SEIU), 79
Service partners, 79–80
Sexual dysfunction, 138
Shaeffer, Leonard, 105
Shapiro, Harvey, 116
Sharp HealthCare, 37
Shernoff, Bill, 182
Shindul-Rothschild, Judith, 80,
   82
Sibley, David, 134, 146
Sierra Hospital, 92

Silen, Serenity, 138
Silverstein, Stuart, 113
Singer, Ben, 34
60 Minutes, 78–79, 90
Skilled nursing facilities (SNFs),
   48, 75, 77–78
Small business owners, 29, 135,
   155
Social workers, 74
Socialized medicine, 114
Specialists, 4, 18–19, 136. see also
   Referrals
Specialty Review Teams, 127
Speck, William, 73
Staffing, standards for, 162
Standards of care, 8, 38, 78–81
Stark, Pete, 100–101
State regulators, 189–196
Steiner, Hans, 61
Sterilization, 96
Stockholm Syndrome, 31
Stock-sharing, 9
Stop-loss insurance, 30, 114
Strategies, for self-protection,
   183, 184–185
Suicides, 33, 138
Sullivan, Michael, 140
Sung, Max, 11
Sutter Roseville Medical Center,
   80
Systemic lupus erythromatosus,
   136

T

"Take-all comers" law, 91
Takecare, 20. see also FHP
Tannigawa, Cheryl, 9
Teaching hospitals, 115–117
Tenet Healthcare, 92
Texas, right to sue, 134–135
Texas Department of Insurance,
   134
The Dallas Morning News, 63
Timelines, 179, 180
Timken Mercy Medical Center,
   90
Transfers, 138
Transports, 16, 43
Trauma units, 116
Travelers Insurance, 123
Traxona, Jon, 91
Treatment options, and patient
   education, 63
Triage, 26
Trotter, John, 15
Trust, 4, 52

Tumors, 138–139
23 hour stays, 74

U

UCSF Stanford Health Care, 116
Ulrich, Stephanie, 75–76, 128
Uninsured patients, 91
United Healthcare, 105, 109,
    120
United States House of
    Representatives, 28
U.S. Healthcare. *see also* Aetna
    anti-disparagement clause,
        38–39
    delays of referrals, 18–19
    executive compensation, 104
    merger with Aetna, 167
U.S. News and World Report, 111
USA Today, 135
USC Kenneth Norris, Jr. Cancer
    Hospital, 130
Utilization management
    authority at Kaiser, 15–16
    bonuses for limiting care,
        17–18
    cuts, 25
    denial of treatment for cancer,
        11–12
    and goals, 53
    outpatient procedures, 73–74
    qualifications of, 15
    system of, 6–7

V

Vaccination reactions, 40–42
Vaginal deliveries, 24, 72, 92
Van Etten, Peter, 116
Verghese, Abraham, 92
Viagra, 61
Vignola, Margo, 108
Vogt, John, 53–54

W

Wall Street Journal, 79
Wallace, Mike, 90
Ways and Means Committee,
    100
Weber, Carl, 173–174
Weiner, Howard, 112
Weintraub, Dan, 124
Whistleblowers, 87–89
Whitman, Christine, 168
Wiggins, Stephen, 104, 105
Williams, Mychelle, 16–17
Wilms tumor, 20

Wilson, Pete, 14, 161
Woods, Carol, 50, 51
Woodward, Beverly, 163
Wound care, 74
Wound infections, 82
Wurzbacher, Frank, 137

Y

Young, William, 123

Z

Zwerner, Alan, 156

About the Authors

JAMIE COURT is a nationally-recognized consumer advocate and Advocacy Director for the non-profit Foundation for Taxpayer and Consumer Rights in Santa Monica, California. In 1994, Court and consumer advocate Harvey Rosenfield established Consumers For Quality Care, the health care watchdog project of the Foundation, to protect the public interest in high quality health care. Court was named Consumer Educator of the Year by the Consumer Attorneys Association of Los Angeles in 1998; to the *Los Angeles Business Journal's* Top Fifty "Who's Who" of Health Care in 1997; and Patient Rights Advocate of the Year in 1996 by Consumer Attorneys of California. He is a frequent media commentator and contributor. Prior to his insurance reform efforts, Court was a homeless advocate and community organizer. He is a graduate of Pomona College in Claremont, California.

FRANCIS SMITH is president of Future Strategies, a Cambridge, Massachusetts, public policy consulting firm. He is also a Senior Fellow at the Institute for Civil Society, a Newton, Massachusetts, non-profit dedicated to strengthening our democratic civil society.

Smith, an attorney, is a graduate of Georgetown University and Boston College Law School.

*The aim of the Foundation is to provide an
effective voice for taxpayers and consumers
in an era when special interests dominate
public discourse, government and politics.
To this end, the Foundation has assembled
some of the nation's leading and most effective
public interest lawyers, advocates, strategists
and organizers under one roof, working on
the issues that affect people every day...*

- -

JOIN THE FIGHT FOR HMO REFORM

Yes, I want to stay informed about HMO reform efforts.

NAME

ADDRESS

CITY   STATE   ZIP CODE

PHONE

EMAIL

Foundation for Taxpayer and Consumer Rights

Return to: Attn: Advocacy Director Jamie Court
1750 Ocean Park Blvd., Suite #200
Santa Monica, CA 90405
Tel: (310) 392-0522
Fax: (310) 392-8874
Web: www.consumerwatchdog.org
Email: cqc@consumerwatchdog.org

DATE DUE			
DE 30 '03			